The ANONYMOUS PRESS MINI EDITION *of* ALCOHOLICS ANONYMOUS

v It Works
›age 58

The Promises
page 83

A Vision For You
page 164

Spiritual
Experience

The Original
Manuscript Ch. 5

Index

Translations

Intergroup
Phone List

STATEMENT OF PURPOSE

The Anonymous Press is made up of a bunch of A.A. members staying sober by carrying the message of A.A. Our primary purpose is to carry the message of A.A. by making our basic text affordable to all. Where we can, we also try to make the text easier to study and understand.

We realize that A.A., The Fellowship that saved our lives, is held together by The Traditions so The Traditions are what guide us. All of our books are sold at cost and we are certainly not organized.

Our efforts have resulted in the distribution of our fellowship's basic text to many hundreds of thousands of fellow alcoholics who otherwise may not have had a book of their own. Detoxes, rehabs, prisons and shelters can now afford to give away our text - offering countless alcoholics a chance to learn the unadulterated message of our program.

If you are a member of A.A. and would like to lend a hand to help in our work, volunteers and contributions are always welcome.

The Anonymous Press

Permission is granted to reproduce all or part of this book for use in the U.S.A. If it will help get the messsage to the still suffering alcoholic, please use whatever you want.

The Anonymous Press is not affiliated with Alcoholics Anonymous World Services, Inc. or with the General Service Office of Alcoholics Anonymous. The publication of this book has not been authorized or endorsed by, and does not imply affiliation with Alcoholics Anonymous World Services, Inc. or the General Service Office of Alcoholics Anonymous.

The Anonymous Press
1658 Milwaukee Ave #100-2883
Chicago IL 60647

http://anonpress.org ap@anonpress.org

First Printing 1992 Thirty-second Printing 2021

The bordered areas do not appear in the original text.

Printed in the United States of America

FOREWORD

WE, OF Alcoholics Anonymous, are more than one hundred men and women who have recovered from a seemingly hopeless state of mind and body. To show other alcoholics *precisely how we have recovered* is the main purpose of this book. For them, we hope these pages will prove so convincing that no further authentication will be necessary. We think this account of our experiences will help everyone to better understand the alcoholic. Many do not comprehend that the alcoholic is a very sick person. And besides, we are sure that our way of living has its advantages for all.

It is important that we remain anonymous because we are too few, at present to handle the overwhelming number of personal appeals which may result from this publication. Being mostly business or professional folk, we could not well carry on our occupations in such an event. We would like it understood that our alcoholic work is an avocation.

When writing or speaking publicly about alcoholism, we urge each of our Fellowship to omit his personal name, designating himself instead as "a member of Alcoholics Anonymous."

Very earnestly we ask the press also, to observe this request, for otherwise we shall be greatly handicapped.

We are not an organization in the conventional

sense of the word. There are no fees or dues whatsoever. The only requirement for membership is an honest desire to stop drinking. We are not allied with any particular faith, sect or denomination, nor do we oppose anyone. We simply wish to be helpful to those who are afflicted.

We shall be interested to hear from those who are getting results from this book, particularly from those who have commenced work with other alcoholics. We should like to be helpful to such cases.

Inquiry by scientific, medical, and religious societies will be welcomed.

Alcoholics Anonymous.

THE DOCTOR'S OPINION

WE OF Alcoholics Anonymous believe that the reader will be interested in the medical estimate of the plan of recovery described in this book. Convincing testimony must surely come from medical men who have had experience with the sufferings of our members and have witnessed our return to health. A well-known doctor, chief physician at a nationally prominent hospital specializing in alcoholic and drug addiction, gave Alcoholics Anonymous this letter:

To Whom It May Concern:

I have specialized in the treatment of alcoholism for many years.

In late 1934 I attended a patient who, though he had been a competent businessman of good earning capacity, was an alcoholic of a type I had come to regard as hopeless.

In the course of his third treatment he acquired certain ideas concerning a possible means of recovery. As part of his rehabilitation he commenced to present his conceptions to other alcoholics, impressing upon them that they must do likewise with still others. This has become the basis of a rapidly growing fellowship of these men and their families. This man and over one hundred others appear to have recovered.

I personally know scores of cases who were of the type with whom other methods had failed completely.

These facts appear to be of extreme medical importance; because of the extraordinary possibilities of rapid growth inherent in this group they may mark a new epoch in the annals of alcoholism. These men may well have a remedy for thousands of such situations.

You may rely absolutely on anything they say about themselves.

Very truly yours,
William D. Silkworth, M.D.

The physician who, at our request, gave us this letter, has been kind enough to enlarge upon his views in another statement which follows. In this statement he confirms what we who have suffered alcoholic torture must believe—that the body of the alcoholic is quite as abnormal as his mind. It did not satisfy us to be told that we could not control our drinking just because we were maladjusted to life, that we were in full flight from reality, or were outright mental defectives. These things were true to some extent, in fact, to a considerable extent with some of us. But we are sure that our bodies were sickened as well. In our belief, any picture of the alcoholic which leaves out this physical factor is incomplete.

The doctor's theory that we have an allergy to alcohol interests us. As laymen, our opinion as to its soundness may, of course, mean little. But as ex-problem drinkers, we can say that his explanation makes good sense. It explains many things for which we cannot otherwise account.

Though we work out our solution on the spiritual as well as an altruistic plane, we favor hospitalization for the alcoholic who is very jittery or befogged. More often than not, it is imperative that a man's brain be cleared before he is approached, as he has then a better chance of understanding and accepting what we have to offer.

The doctor writes:

> The subject presented in this book seems to me to be of paramount importance to those afflicted with alcoholic addiction.
>
> I say this after many years' experience as Medical Director of one of the oldest hospitals in the country treating alcoholic and drug addiction.
>
> There was, therefore, a sense of real satisfaction when I was asked to contribute a few words on a subject which is covered in such masterly detail in these pages.
>
> We doctors have realized for a long time that some form of moral psychology was of urgent importance to alcoholics, but its application presented difficulties beyond our conception. What with our ultra-modern standards, our scientific approach to everything, we are perhaps not well equipped to apply the powers of good that lie outside our synthetic knowledge.
>
> Many years ago one of the leading contributors to this book came under our care in this hospital and while here he acquired some ideas which he put into practical application at once.
>
> Later, he requested the privilege of being allowed to tell his story to other patients here and with some misgiving, we consented. The cases we have followed through have been most interesting; in fact, many of them are amazing. The unselfishness of these men as we have come to know them, the entire absence of profit motive, and their community spirit, is indeed inspiring to one who has labored long and wearily in this alcoholic field. They believe in themselves, and still more in the Power which pulls chronic alcoholics back from the gates of death.
>
> Of course an alcoholic ought to be freed from his physical

craving for liquor, and this often requires a definite hospital procedure, before psychological measures can be of maximum benefit.

We believe, and so suggested a few years ago, that the action of alcohol on these chronic alcoholics is a manifestation of an allergy; that the phenomenon of craving is limited to this class and never occurs in the average temperate drinker. These allergic types can never safely use alcohol in any form at all; and once having formed the habit and found they cannot break it, once having lost their self-confidence, their reliance upon things human, their problems pile up on them and become astonishingly difficult to solve.

Frothy emotional appeal seldom suffices. The message which can interest and hold these alcoholic people must have depth and weight. In nearly all cases, their ideals must be grounded in a power greater than themselves, if they are to re-create their lives.

If any feel that as psychiatrists directing a hospital for alcoholics we appear somewhat sentimental, let them stand with us a while on the firing line, see the tragedies, the despairing wives, the little children; let the solving of these problems become a part of their daily work, and even of their sleeping moments, and the most cynical will not wonder that we have accepted and encouraged this movement. We feel, after many years of experience, that we have found nothing which has contributed more to the rehabilitation of these men than the altruistic movement now growing up among them.

Men and women drink essentially because they like the effect produced by alcohol. The sensation is so elusive that, while they admit it is injurious, they cannot after a time differentiate the true from the false. To them, their alcoholic life seems the only normal one. They are restless, irritable and discontented, unless they can again experience the sense of ease and comfort which comes at once by taking a few drinks—drinks which they see others taking with impunity. After they have succumbed to the desire again, as so many do, and the phenomenon of craving develops, they pass through the well-known stages of a spree, emerging remorseful, with a firm resolution not to drink again. This is repeated over and over, and unless this person can experience an entire psychic change there is very little hope of his recovery.

On the other hand—and strange as this may seem to those who do not understand—once a psychic change has occurred, the very same person who seemed doomed, who had so many problems he despaired of ever solving them, suddenly finds himself easily able to control his desire for alcohol, the only effort necessary being that required to follow a few simple rules.

Men have cried out to me in sincere and despairing appeal: "Doctor, I cannot go on like this! I have everything to live for! I must stop, but I cannot! You must help me!"

Faced with this problem, if a doctor is honest with himself, he must sometimes feel his own inadequacy. Although he gives all that is in him, it often is not enough. One feels that something more than human power is needed to produce the essential psychic change. Though the aggregate of recoveries resulting from psychiatric effort is considerable, we physicians must admit we have made little impression upon the problem as a whole. Many types do not respond to the ordinary psychological approach.

I do not hold with those who believe that alcoholism is entirely a problem of mental control. I have had many men who had, for example, worked a period of months on some problem or business deal which was to be settled on a certain date, favorably to them. They took a drink a day or so prior to the date, and then the phenomenon of craving at once became paramount to all other interests so that the important appointment was not met. These men were not drinking to escape; they were drinking to overcome a craving beyond their mental control.

There are many situations which arise out of the phenomenon of craving which cause men to make the supreme sacrifice rather than continue to fight.

The classification of alcoholics seems most difficult, and in much detail is outside the scope of this book. There are, of course, the psychopaths who are emotionally unstable. We are all familiar with this type. They are always "going on the wagon for keeps." They are over-remorseful and make many resolutions, but never a decision.

There is the type of man who is unwilling to admit that he cannot take a drink. He plans various ways of drinking. He changes his brand or his environment. There is the type who always believes that after being entirely free from alcohol for a period of time he can take a drink without danger. There is the manic-depressive type, who is, perhaps, the least understood by his friends, and about whom a whole chapter could be written.

Then there are types entirely normal in every respect except in the effect alcohol has upon them. They are often able, intelligent, friendly people.

All these, and many others, have one symptom in common: they cannot start drinking without developing the phenomenon of craving. This phenomenon, as we have suggested, may be the manifestation of an allergy which differentiates these people, and sets them apart as a distinct entity. It has never been, by any treatment with which we are familiar, permanently eradicated. The only relief we have to suggest is entire abstinence.

This immediately precipitates us into a seething caldron of debate. Much has been written pro and con, but among physicians, the general opinion seems to be that most chronic alcoholics are doomed.

What is the solution? Perhaps I can best answer this by relating one of my experiences.

About one year prior to this experience a man was brought in to be treated for chronic alcoholism. He had but partially recovered from a gastric hemorrhage and seemed to be a case of pathological mental deterioration. He had lost everything worthwhile in life and was only living, one might say, to drink. He frankly admitted and believed that for him there was no hope. Following the elimination of alcohol, there was found to be no permanent brain injury. He accepted the plan outlined in this book. One year later he called to see me, and I experienced a very strange sensation. I knew the man by name, and partly recognized his features, but there all resemblance ended. From a trembling, despairing, nervous wreck, had emerged a man brimming over with self-reliance and contentment. I talked with him for some time, but was not able to bring myself to feel that I had known him before. To me he was a stranger, and so he left me. A long time has passed with no return to alcohol.

When I need a mental uplift, I often think of another case brought in by a physician prominent in New York. The patient had made his own diagnosis, and deciding his situation hopeless, had hidden in a deserted barn determined to die. He was rescued by a searching party, and, in desperate condition, brought to me. Following his physical rehabilitation, he had a talk with me in which he frankly stated he thought the treatment a waste of effort, unless I could assure him, which no one ever had, that in the future he would have the "will power" to resist the impulse to drink.

His alcoholic problem was so complex, and his depression so great, that we felt his only hope would be through what we then called "moral psychology," and we doubted if even that would have any effect.

However, he did become "sold" on the ideas contained in this book. He has not had a drink for a great many years. I see him now and then and he is as fine a specimen of manhood as one could wish to meet.

I earnestly advise every alcoholic to read this book through, and though perhaps he came to scoff, he may remain to pray.

William D. Silkworth, M.D.

Chapter 1

BILL'S STORY

WAR FEVER ran high in the New England town to which we new, young officers from Plattsburg were assigned, and we were flattered when the first citizens took us to their homes, making us feel heroic. Here was love, applause, war; moments sublime with intervals hilarious. I was part of life at last, and in the midst of the excitement I discovered liquor. I forgot the strong warnings and the prejudices of my people concerning drink. In time we sailed for "Over There." I was very lonely and again turned to alcohol.

We landed in England. I visited Winchester Cathedral. Much moved, I wandered outside. My attention was caught by a doggerel on an old tombstone:

"Here lies a Hampshire Grenadier
Who caught his death
Drinking cold small beer.
A good soldier is ne'er forgot
Whether he dieth by musket
Or by pot."

Ominous warning—which I failed to heed.

Twenty-two, and a veteran of foreign wars, I went home at last. I fancied myself a leader, for had not the men of my battery given me a special token of appreciation? My talent for leadership, I imagined, would place me at the head of vast enterprises which I would manage with the utmost assurance.

I took a night law course, and obtained employment as investigator for a surety company. The drive for success was on. I'd prove to the world I was important. My work took me about Wall Street and little by little I became interested in the market. Many people lost money—but some became very rich. Why not I? I studied economics and business as well as law. Potential alcoholic that I was, I nearly failed my law course. At one of the finals I was too drunk to think or write. Though my drinking was not yet continuous, it disturbed my wife. We had long talks when I would still her forebodings by telling her that men of genius conceived their best projects when drunk; that the most majestic constructions of philosophic thought were so derived.

By the time I had completed the course, I knew the law was not for me. The inviting maelstrom of Wall Street had me in its grip. Business and financial leaders were my heroes. Out of this alloy of drink and speculation, I commenced to forge the weapon that one day would turn in its flight like a boomerang and all but cut me to ribbons. Living modestly, my wife and I saved $1,000. It went into certain securities, then cheap and rather unpopular. I rightly imagined that they would some day have a great rise. I failed to persuade my broker friends to send me out looking over factories and managements, but my wife and I decided to go anyway. I had developed a theory that most people lost money in stocks through ignorance of markets. I discovered many more reasons later on.

We gave up our positions and off we roared on a motorcycle, the sidecar stuffed with tent, blankets, a change of clothes, and three huge volumes of a financial reference service. Our friends thought a lunacy commission should be appointed. Perhaps they were right. I had had some success at speculation, so we had a little money, but we once worked on a farm for a month to avoid drawing on our small capital. That was the last honest manual labor on my part for many a day. We covered the whole eastern United States in a year. At the end of it, my reports to Wall Street procured me a position there and the use of a large expense account. The exercise of an option brought in more money, leaving us with a profit of several thousand dollars for that year.

For the next few years fortune threw money and applause my way. I had arrived. My judgment and ideas were followed by many to the tune of paper millions. The great boom of the late twenties was seething and swelling. Drink was taking an important and exhilarating part in my life. There was loud talk in the jazz places uptown. Everyone spent in thousands and chattered in millions. Scoffers could scoff and be damned. I made a host of fair-weather friends.

My drinking assumed more serious proportions, continuing all day and almost every night. The remonstrances of my friends terminated in a row and I became a lone wolf. There were many unhappy scenes in our sumptuous apartment. There had been no real infidelity, for loyalty to my wife, helped at times by extreme drunkenness, kept me out of those scrapes.

In 1929 I contracted golf fever. We went at once to the country, my wife to applaud while I started out to overtake Walter Hagen.[1] Liquor caught up with me much faster than I came up behind Walter. I began to be jittery in the morning. Golf permitted drinking every day and every night. It was fun to carom around the exclusive course which had inspired such awe in me as a lad. I acquired the impeccable coat of tan one sees upon the well-to-do. The local banker watched me whirl fat checks in and out of his till with amused skepticism.

Abruptly in October 1929 hell broke loose on the New York stock exchange. After one of those days of inferno, I wobbled from a hotel bar to a brokerage office. It was eight o'clock—five hours after the market closed. The ticker still clattered. I was staring at an inch of the tape which bore the inscription XYZ-32. It had been 52 that morning. I was finished and so were many friends. The papers reported men jumping to death from the towers of High Finance. That disgusted me. I would not jump. I went back to the bar. My friends had dropped several million since ten o'clock—so what? Tomorrow was another day. As I drank, the old fierce determination to win came back.

Next morning I telephoned a friend in Montreal. He had plenty of money left and thought I had better go to Canada. By the following spring we were living in our accustomed style. I felt like Napoleon returning from Elba.[2,3] No St. Helena for me![4] But drinking caught up with me again and my generous friend had to let me go. This time we stayed broke.

We went to live with my wife's parents. I found a job; then lost it as the result of a brawl with a taxi driver. Mercifully, no one could guess that I was to have no real employment for five years, or hardly draw a sober breath. My wife began to work in a department store, coming home exhausted to find me drunk.

I became an unwelcome hanger-on at brokerage places.

Liquor ceased to be a luxury; it became a necessity. "Bathtub" gin, two bottles a day, and often three, got to be routine.[5] Sometimes a small deal would net a few hundred dollars, and I would pay my bills at the bars and delicatessens. This went on endlessly, and I began to waken very early in the morning shaking violently. A tumbler full of gin followed by half a dozen bottles of beer would be required if I were to eat any breakfast. Nevertheless, I still thought I could control the situation, and there were periods of sobriety which renewed my wife's hope.

Gradually things got worse. The house was taken over by the mortgage holder, my mother-in-law died, my wife and father-in-law became ill.

Then I got a promising business opportunity. Stocks were at the low point of 1932, and I had somehow formed a group to buy. I was to share generously in the profits. Then I went on a prodigious bender, and that chance vanished.

I woke up. This had to be stopped. I saw I could not take so much as one drink. I was through forever. Before then, I had written lots of sweet promises, but my wife happily observed that this time I meant business. And so I did.

Shortly afterward I came home drunk. There had been no fight. Where had been my high resolve? I simply didn't know. It hadn't even come to mind. Someone had pushed a drink my way, and I had taken it. Was I crazy? I began to wonder, for such an appalling lack of perspective seemed near being just that.

Renewing my resolve, I tried again. Some time

passed, and confidence began to be replaced by cock-sureness. I could laugh at the gin mills. Now I had what it takes! One day I walked into a cafe to telephone. In no time I was beating on the bar asking myself how it happened. As the whisky rose to my head I told myself I would manage better next time, but I might as well get good and drunk then. And I did.

The remorse, horror and hopelessness of the next morning are unforgettable. The courage to do battle was not there. My brain raced uncontrollably and there was a terrible sense of impending calamity. I hardly dared cross the street, lest I collapse and be run down by an early morning truck, for it was scarcely daylight. An all night place supplied me with a dozen glasses of ale. My writhing nerves were stilled at last. A morning paper told me the market had gone to hell again. Well, so had I. The market would recover, but I wouldn't. That was a hard thought. Should I kill myself? No—not now. Then a mental fog settled down. Gin would fix that. So two bottles, and—oblivion.

The mind and body are marvelous mechanisms, for mine endured this agony two more years. Sometimes I stole from my wife's slender purse when the morning terror and madness were on me. Again I swayed dizzily before an open window, or the medicine cabinet where there was poison, cursing myself for a weakling. There were flights from city to country and back, as my wife and I sought escape. Then came the night when the physical and mental torture was so hellish I feared I would burst through my window, sash and all. Somehow I managed to drag my mattress to a lower floor, lest I suddenly leap. A doctor came with a heavy sedative. Next day found me drinking both gin and sedative. This combination soon landed me on the rocks. People feared for my sanity. So did I. I could eat little or nothing when drinking, and I was forty pounds under weight.

My brother-in-law is a physician, and through his kindness and that of my mother I was placed in a nationally-known hospital for the mental and physical rehabilitation of alcoholics. Under the so-called belladonna treatment my brain cleared.[6] Hydrotherapy and mild exercise helped much. Best of all, I met a kind doctor who explained that though certainly selfish and foolish, I had been seriously ill, bodily and mentally.

It relieved me somewhat to learn that in alcoholics the will is amazingly weakened when it comes to combating liquor, though it often remains strong in other respects. My incredible behavior in the face of a desperate desire to stop was explained. Understanding myself now, I fared forth in high hope. For three for four months the goose hung high. I went to town regularly and even made a little money. Surely this was the answer—self-knowledge.

But it was not, for the frightful day came when I drank once more. The curve of my declining moral and bodily health fell off like a ski-jump. After a time I returned to the hospital. This was the finish, the curtain, it seemed to me. My weary and despairing wife was informed that it would all end with heart failure during delirium tremens, or I would develop a wet brain, perhaps within a year. She would soon have to give me over to the undertaker or the asylum.

They did not need to tell me. I knew, and almost welcomed the idea. It was a devastating blow to my pride. I, who had thought so well of myself and my abilities, of my capacity to surmount obstacles, was cornered at last. Now I was to plunge into the dark, joining that endless procession of sots who had gone on before. I thought of my poor wife. There had been much happiness after all. What would I not give to make amends. But that was over now.

No words can tell of the loneliness and despair I found in that bitter morass of self-pity. Quicksand stretched around me in all directions. I had met my match. I had been overwhelmed. Alcohol was my master.

Trembling, I stepped from the hospital a broken man. Fear sobered me for a bit. Then came the insidious insanity of that first drink, and on Armistice Day 1934, I was off again.[7] Everyone became resigned to the certainty that I would have to be shut up somewhere, or would stumble along to a miserable end. How dark it is before the dawn! In reality that was the beginning of my last debauch. I was soon to be catapulted into what I like to call the fourth dimension of existence. I was to know happiness, peace, and usefulness, in a way of life that is incredibly more wonderful as time passes.

Near the end of that bleak November, I sat drinking in my kitchen. With a certain satisfaction I reflected there was enough gin concealed about the house to carry me through that night and the next day. My wife was at work. I wondered whether I dared hide a full bottle of gin near the head of our bed. I would need it before daylight.

My musing was interrupted by the telephone. The cheery voice of an old school friend asked if he might come over. *He was sober.* It was years since I could remember his coming to New York in that condition. I was amazed. Rumor had it that he had been committed for alcoholic insanity. I wondered how he had escaped. Of course he would have dinner, and then I could drink openly with him. Unmindful of his welfare, I thought only of recapturing the spirit of other days. There was that time we had chartered an airplane to complete a jag! His coming was an oasis in this dreary desert of futility. The very thing—an oasis! Drinkers are like that.

The door opened and he stood there, fresh-skinned and glowing. There was something about his eyes. He was inexplicably different. What had happened?

I pushed a drink across the table. He refused it. Disappointed but curious, I wondered what had got into the fellow. He wasn't himself.

"Come, what's this all about?" I queried.

He looked straight at me. Simply, but smilingly, he said, "I've got religion."

I was aghast. So that was it—last summer an alcoholic crackpot; now, I suspected, a little cracked about religion. He had that starry-eyed look. Yes, the old boy was on fire all right. But bless his heart, let him rant! Besides, my gin would last longer than his preaching.

But he did no ranting. In a matter of fact way he told how two men had appeared in court, persuading the judge to suspend his commitment. They had told of a simple religious idea and a practical program of action. That was two months ago and the result was self-evident. It worked!

He had come to pass his experience along to me—if

I cared to have it. I was shocked, but interested. Certainly I was interested. I had to be, for I was hopeless.

He talked for hours. Childhood memories rose before me. I could almost hear the sound of the preacher's voice as I sat, on still Sundays, way over there on the hillside; there was that proffered temperance pledge I never signed; my grandfather's good natured contempt of some church folk and their doings; his insistence that the spheres really had their music; but his denial of the preacher's right to tell him how he must listen; his fearlessness as he spoke of these things just before he died; these recollections welled up from the past. They made me swallow hard.

That war-time day in old Winchester Cathedral came back again.

I had always believed in a Power greater than myself. I had often pondered these things. I was not an atheist. Few people really are, for that means blind faith in the strange proposition that this universe originated in a cipher and aimlessly rushes nowhere. My intellectual heroes, the chemists, the astronomers, even the evolutionists, suggested vast laws and forces at work. Despite contrary indications, I had little doubt that a mighty purpose and rhythm underlay all. How could there be so much of precise and immutable law, and no intelligence? I simply had to believe in a Spirit of the Universe, who knew neither time nor limitation. But that was as far as I had gone.

With ministers, and the world's religions, I parted right there. When they talked of a God personal to me, who was love, superhuman strength and direction, I became irritated and my mind snapped shut against such a theory.

To Christ I conceded the certainty of a great man, not too closely followed by those who claimed Him. His moral teaching—most excellent. For myself, I had adopted those parts which seemed convenient and not too difficult; the rest I disregarded.

The wars which had been fought, the burnings and chicanery that religious dispute had facilitated, made me sick. I honestly doubted whether, on balance, the religions of mankind had done any good. Judging from what I had seen in Europe and since, the power of God in human affairs was negligible, the Brotherhood of Man a grim jest. If there was a Devil, he seemed the Boss Universal, and he certainly had me.

But my friend sat before me, and he made the point-blank declaration that God had done for him what he could not do for himself. His human will had failed. Doctors had pronounced him incurable. Society was about to lock him up. Like myself, he had admitted complete defeat. Then he had, in effect, been raised from the dead, suddenly taken from the scrap heap to a level of life better than the best he had ever known!

Had this power originated in him? Obviously it had not. There had been no more power in him than there was in me at the minute; and this was none at all.

That floored me. It began to look as though religious people were right after all. Here was something at work in a human heart which had done the impossible. My ideas about miracles were drastically revised right then. Never mind the musty past; here sat a miracle directly across the kitchen table. He shouted great tidings.

I saw that my friend was much more than inwardly

reorganized. He was on a different footing. His roots grasped a new soil.

Despite the living example of my friend there remained in me the vestiges of my old prejudice. The word God still aroused a certain antipathy. When the thought was expressed that there might be a God personal to me this feeling was intensified. I didn't like the idea. I could go for such conceptions as Creative Intelligence, Universal Mind or Spirit of Nature but I resisted the thought of a Czar of the Heavens, however loving His sway might be.[8] I have since talked with scores of men who felt the same way.

My friend suggested what then seemed a novel idea. He said, *"Why don't you choose your own conception of God?"*

That statement hit me hard. It melted the icy intellectual mountain in whose shadow I had lived and shivered many years. I stood in the sunlight at last.

It was only a matter of being willing to believe in a Power greater than myself. Nothing more was required of me to make my beginning. I saw that growth could start from that point. Upon a foundation of complete willingness I might build what I saw in my friend. Would I have it? Of course I would!

Thus was I convinced that God is concerned with us humans when we want Him enough. At long last I saw, I felt, I believed. Scales of pride and prejudice fell from my eyes. A new world came into view.

The real significance of my experience in the Cathedral burst upon me. For a brief moment, I had needed and wanted God. There had been a humble willingness to have Him with me—and He came. But soon the sense of His presence had been blotted out by worldly clamors, mostly those within myself. And so it had been ever since. How blind I had been.

At the hospital I was separated from alcohol for the last time. Treatment seemed wise, for I showed signs of delirium tremens.

There I humbly offered myself to God, as I then understood Him, to do with me as He would. I placed myself unreservedly under His care and direction. I admitted for the first time that of myself I was nothing; that without Him I was lost. I ruthlessly faced my sins and became willing to have my new-found Friend take them away, root and branch. I have not had a drink since.

My schoolmate visited me, and I fully acquainted him with my problems and deficiencies. We made a list of people I had hurt or toward whom I felt resentment. I expressed my entire willingness to approach these individuals, admitting my wrong. Never was I to be critical of them. I was to right all such matters to the utmost of my ability.

I was to test my thinking by the new God-consciousness within. Common sense would thus become uncommon sense. I was to sit quietly when in doubt, asking only for direction and strength to meet my problems as He would have me. Never was I to pray for myself, except as my requests bore on my usefulness to others. Then only might I expect to receive. But that would be in great measure.

My friend promised when these things were done I would enter upon a new relationship with my Creator; that I would have the elements of a way of living which answered all my problems. Belief in the power of God, plus enough willingness, honesty and humility to establish and maintain the new order of things, were the essential requirements.

Simple, but not easy; a price had to be paid. It meant destruction of self-centeredness. I must turn in all things to the Father of Light who presides over us all.

These were revolutionary and drastic proposals, but the moment I fully accepted them, the effect was electric. There was a sense of victory, followed by such a peace and serenity as I had never known. There was utter confidence. I felt lifted up, as though the great clean wind of a mountain top blew through and through. God comes to most men gradually, but His impact on me was sudden and profound.

For a moment I was alarmed, and called my friend, the doctor, to ask if I were still sane. He listened in wonder as I talked.

Finally he shook his head saying, "Something has happened to you I don't understand. But you had better hang on to it. Anything is better than the way you were." The good doctor now sees many men who have such experiences. He knows that they are real.

While I lay in the hospital the thought came that there were thousands of hopeless alcoholics who might be glad to have what had been so freely given me. Perhaps I could help some of them. They in turn might work with others.

My friend had emphasized the absolute necessity of demonstrating these principles in all my affairs. Particularly was it imperative to work with others as he had worked with me. Faith without works was dead, he said. And how appallingly true for the alcoholic! For if an alcoholic failed to perfect and enlarge his spiritual life through work and self-sacrifice for others, he could not survive the certain trials and low spots ahead. If he did not work, he would surely drink again, and if he drank, he would surely die. Then faith would be dead indeed. With us it is just like that.

My wife and I abandoned ourselves with enthusiasm to the idea of helping other alcoholics to a solution of their problems. It was fortunate, for my old business associates remained skeptical for a year and a half, during which I found little work. I was not too well at the time, and was plagued by waves of self-pity and resentment. This sometimes nearly drove me back to drink, but I soon found that when all other measures failed, work with another alcoholic would save the day. Many times I have gone to my old hospital in despair. On talking to a man there, I would be amazingly lifted up and set on my feet. It is a design for living that works in rough going.

We commenced to make many fast friends and a fellowship has grown up among us of which it is a wonderful thing to feel a part. The joy of living we really have, even under pressure and difficulty. I have seen hundreds of families set their feet in the path that really goes somewhere; have seen the most impossible domestic situations righted; feuds and bitterness of all sorts wiped out. I have seen men come out of asylums and resume a vital place in the lives of their families and communities. Business and professional men have regained their standing. There is scarcely any form of trouble and misery which has not been overcome among us. In one western city and its environs there are one thousand of us and our families. We meet frequently so that newcomers may find the fellowship they seek. At these informal gatherings one may often see from 50 to 200 persons. We are growing in numbers and power.

An alcoholic in his cups is an unlovely creature. Our struggles with them are variously strenuous, comic, and tragic. One poor chap committed suicide in my home. He could not, or would not, see our way of life.

There is, however a vast amount of fun about it all. I suppose some would be shocked at our seeming worldliness and levity. But just underneath there is deadly earnestness. Faith has to work twenty-four hours a day in and through us, or we perish.

Most of us feel we need look no further for Utopia. We have it with us right here and now. Each day my friend's simple talk in our kitchen multiplies itself in a widening circle of peace on earth and good will to men.

Notes

1. Walter Hagen: a golf champion from 1914 to 1929.
2. Napoleon Bonaparte: The Emperor of France 1804 to 1814.
3. Elba: Italian island Napoleon was exiled to and escaped from in 1815.
4. St. Helena: British island where Napoleon was imprisoned after his brief reign as Emperor in 1815. He died from cancer there in 1821.
5. Bathtub Gin: slang term for homemade liquor.
6. Belladonna treatment: administration of the sedative and antispasmodic drug Belladonna; formerly used to relieve some of the effects of alcohol withdrawal.
7. Armistice Day: now known as Veterans Day.
8. Czar: a title historically used to signify the rank of emperor in Eastern Europe and Russia.

Chapter 2

THERE IS A SOLUTION

WE, OF ALCOHOLICS ANONYMOUS, know thousands of men and women who were once just as hopeless as Bill. Nearly all have recovered. They have solved the drink problem.

We are average Americans. All sections of this country and many of its occupations are represented, as well as many political, economic, social, and religious backgrounds. We are people who normally would not mix. But there exists among us a fellowship, a friendliness, and an understanding which is indescribably wonderful. We are like the passengers of a great liner the moment after rescue from shipwreck when camaraderie, joyousness and democracy pervade the vessel from steerage to Captain's table. Unlike the feelings of the ship's passengers, however, our joy in escape from disaster does not subside as we go our individual ways. The feeling of having shared in a common peril is one element in the powerful cement which binds us. But that in itself would never have held us together as we are now joined.

The tremendous fact for every one of us is that we have discovered a common solution. We have a way out on which we can absolutely agree, and upon which we can join in brotherly and harmonious action. This is the great news this book carries to those who suffer from alcoholism.

An illness of this sort—and we have come to believe it an illness—involves those about us in a way no other human sickness can. If a person has cancer all are sorry for him and no one is angry or hurt. But not so with the alcoholic illness, for with it there goes annihilation of all the things worth while in life. It engulfs all whose lives touch the sufferer's. It brings misunderstanding, fierce resentment, financial insecurity, disgusted friends and employers, warped lives of blameless children, sad wives and parents—anyone can increase the list.

We hope this volume will inform and comfort those who are, or who may be affected. There are many.

Highly competent psychiatrists who have dealt with us have found it sometimes impossible to persuade an alcoholic to discuss his situation without reserve. Strangely enough, wives, parents and intimate friends usually find us even more unapproachable than do the psychiatrist and the doctor.

But the ex-problem drinker who has found this solution, who is properly armed with facts about himself, can generally win the entire confidence of another alcoholic in a few hours. Until such an understanding is reached, little or nothing can be accomplished.

That the man who is making the approach has had the same difficulty, that he obviously knows what he is talking about, that his whole deportment shouts at the new prospect that he is a man with a real answer, that he has no attitude of Holier Than Thou, nothing whatever except the sincere desire to be helpful; that there are no fees to pay, no axes to grind, no people to please, no lectures to be endured—these are the conditions we have found most effective. After such an approach many take up their beds and walk again.

None of us makes a sole vocation of this work, nor do we think its effectiveness would be increased if we did. We feel that elimination of our drinking is but a beginning. A much more important demonstration of our principles lies before us in our respective homes, occupations and affairs. All of us spend much of our spare time in the sort of effort which we are going to describe. A few are fortunate enough to be so situated that they can give nearly all their time to the work.

If we keep on the way we are going there is little doubt that much good will result, but the surface of the problem would hardly be scratched. Those of us who live in large cities are overcome by the reflection that close by hundreds are dropping into oblivion every day. Many could recover if they had the opportunity we have enjoyed. How then shall we present that which has been so freely given us?

We have concluded to publish an anonymous volume setting forth the problem as we see it. We shall bring to the task our combined experience and knowledge. This should suggest a useful program for anyone concerned with a drinking problem.

Of necessity there will have to be discussion of matters medical, psychiatric, social, and religious. We are aware that these matters are, from their very nature, controversial. Nothing would please us so much as to write a book which would contain no basis for contention or argument. We shall do our utmost to achieve that ideal. Most of us sense that real tolerance of other people's shortcomings and viewpoints and a respect for their opinions are attitudes which make us more useful to others. Our very lives, as ex-problem drinkers, depend upon our constant thought of others and how we may help meet their needs.

You may already have asked yourself why it is that all of us became so very ill from drinking. Doubtless you are curious to discover how and why, in the face of expert opinion to the contrary, we have recovered from a hopeless condition of mind and body. If you are an alcoholic who wants to get over it, you may already be asking—"What do I have to do?"

It is the purpose of this book to answer such questions specifically. We shall tell you what we have done. Before going into a detailed discussion, it may be well to summarize some points as we see them.

How many times people have said to us:"I can take it or leave it alone. Why can't he?" "Why don't you drink like a gentleman or quit?" "That fellow can't handle his liquor." "Why don't you try beer and wine?" "Lay off the hard stuff." "His will power must be weak." "He could stop if he wanted to." "She's such a sweet girl, I should think he'd stop for her sake." "The doctor told him that if he ever drank again it would kill him, but there he is all lit up again."

Now these are commonplace observations on drinkers which we hear all the time. Back of them is a world of ignorance and misunderstanding. We see that these expressions refer to people whose reactions are very different from ours.

Moderate drinkers have little trouble in giving up liquor entirely if they have good reason for it. They can take it or leave it alone.

Then we have a certain type of hard drinker. He may have the habit badly enough to gradually impair him physically and mentally. It may cause him to die a few years before his time. If a sufficiently strong reason—ill health, falling in love, change of environment, or the warning of a doctor—becomes operative, this man can also stop or moderate, although he may find it difficult and troublesome and may even need medical attention.

But what about the real alcoholic? He may start off as a moderate drinker; he may or may not become a continous hard drinker; but at some stage of his drinking career he begins to lose all control of his liquor consumption, once he starts to drink.

Here is the fellow who has been puzzling you, especially in his lack of control. He does absurd, incredible, tragic things while drinking. He is a real Dr. Jekyll and Mr. Hyde.[1] He is seldom mildly intoxicated. He is always more or less insanely drunk. His disposition while drinking resembles his normal nature but little. He may be one of the finest fellows in the world. Yet let him drink for a day, and he frequently becomes disgustingly, and even dangerously antisocial. He has a positive genius for getting tight at exactly the wrong moment, particularly when some important decision must be made or engagement kept. He is often perfectly sensible and well balanced concerning everything except liquor, but in that respect he is incredibly dishonest and selfish. He often possesses special abilities, skills, and aptitudes, and has a promising career ahead of him. He uses his gifts to build up a bright outlook for his family and himself, and then pulls the structure down on his head by a senseless series of sprees. He is the fellow who goes to bed so intoxicated he ought to sleep the clock around. Yet early next morning he searches madly for the bottle he misplaced the night before. If he can afford it, he may have liquor concealed all over his house to be certain no one gets his entire supply away from him to throw down the wastepipe. As matters grow worse, he begins to use a combination of high-powered sedative and liquor to quiet his nerves so he can go to work. Then comes the day when he simply cannot make it and gets drunk all over again. Perhaps he goes to a doctor who gives him morphine or some sedative with which to taper off. Then he begins to appear at hospitals and sanitariums.

This is by no means a comprehensive picture of the true alcoholic, as our behavior patterns vary. But this description should identify him roughly.

Why does he behave like this? If hundreds of experiences have shown him that one drink means another debacle with all its attendant suffering and humiliation, why is it he takes that one drink? Why can't he stay on the water wagon? What has become of the common sense and will power that he still sometimes displays with respect to other matters?

Perhaps there never will be a full answer to these questions. Opinions vary considerably as to why the alcoholic reacts differently from normal people. We are not sure why, once a certain point is reached, little can be done for him. We cannot answer the riddle.

We know that while the alcoholic keeps away from drink, as he may do for months or years, he reacts much like other men. We are equally positive that once he takes any alcohol whatever into his system, something happens, both in the bodily and mental sense, which makes it virtually impossible for him to stop. The experience of any alcoholic will abundantly confirm this.

These observations would be academic and pointless if our friend never took the first drink, thereby setting the terrible cycle in motion. Therefore, the main problem of the alcoholic centers in his mind, rather than in his body. If you ask him why he started on that last bender, the chances are he will offer you any one of a hundred alibis. Sometimes these excuses have a certain plausibility, but none of them really makes sense in the light of the havoc an alcoholic's drinking bout creates. They sound like the philosophy of the man who, having a headache, beats himself on the head with a hammer so that he can't feel the ache. If you draw this fallacious reasoning to the attention of an alcoholic, he will laugh it off, or become irritated and refuse to talk.

Once in a while he may tell the truth. And the truth, strange to say, is usually that he has no more idea why he took that first drink than you have. Some drinkers have excuses with which they are satisfied part of the time. But in their hearts they really do not know why they do it. Once this malady has a real hold, they are a baffled lot. There is the obsession that somehow, someday, they will beat the game. But they often suspect they are down for the count.

How true this is, few realize. In a vague way their families and friends sense that these drinkers are abnormal, but everybody hopefully awaits the day when the sufferer will rouse himself from his lethargy and assert his power of will.

The tragic truth is that if the man be a real alcoholic, the happy day may not arrive. He has lost control. At a certain point in the drinking of every alcoholic, he passes into a state where the most powerful desire to stop drinking is of absolutely no avail. This tragic situation has already arrived in practically every case long before it is suspected.

The fact is that most alcoholics, for reasons yet obscure, have lost the power of choice in drink. Our so-called will power becomes practically nonexistent. We are unable, at certain times, to bring into our consciousness with sufficient force the memory of the suffering and humiliation of even a week or a month ago. We are without defense against the first drink.

The almost certain consequences that follow taking even a glass of beer do not crowd into the mind to deter us. If these thoughts occur, they are hazy and readily supplanted with the old threadbare idea that this time we shall handle ourselves like other people. There is a complete failure of the kind of defense that keeps one from putting his hand on a hot stove.

The alcoholic may say to himself in the most casual way, "It won't burn me this time, so here's how!" Or perhaps he doesn't think at all. How often have some of us begun to drink in this nonchalant way, and after the third or fourth, pounded on the bar and said to ourselves, "For God's sake, how did I ever get started again?" Only to have that thought supplanted by "Well, I'll stop with the sixth drink." Or "What's the use anyhow?"

When this sort of thinking is fully established in an individual with alcoholic tendencies, he has probably placed himself beyond human aid, and unless locked up, may die or go permanently insane. These stark and ugly facts have been confirmed by legions of alcoholics throughout history. But for the grace of God, there would have been thousands more convincing demonstrations. So many want to stop but cannot.

There is a solution. Almost none of us liked the self-searching, the leveling of our pride, the confession of shortcomings which the process requires for its successful consummation. But we saw that it really worked in others, and we had come to believe in the hopelessness and futility of life as we had been living it. When, therefore, we were approached by those in whom the problem had been solved, there was nothing left for us but to pick up the simple kit of spiritual tools laid at our feet. We have found much of heaven and we have been rocketed into a fourth dimension of existence of which we had not even dreamed.

The great fact is just this, and nothing less: That we have had deep and effective spiritual experiences* which have revolutionized our whole attitude toward life, toward our fellows and toward God's universe. The central fact of our lives today is the absolute certainty that our Creator has entered into our hearts and lives in a way which is indeed miraculous. He has commenced to accomplish those things for us which we could never do by ourselves.

If you are as seriously alcoholic as we were, we believe there is no middle-of-the-road solution. We were in a position where life was becoming impossible, and if we had passed into the region from which there is no return through human aid, we had but two alternatives: One was to go on to the bitter end, blotting out the consciousness of our intolerable situation as best we could; and the other, to accept spiritual help. This

*See "Spiritual Experience."

we did because we honestly wanted to, and were willing to make the effort.

A certain American business man had ability, good sense, and high character. For years he had floundered from one sanitarium to another. He had consulted the best known American psychiatrists. Then he had gone to Europe, placing himself in the care of a celebrated physician (the psychiatrist, Dr. Jung) who prescribed for him. Though experience had made him skeptical, he finished his treatment with unusual confidence. His physical and mental condition were unusually good. Above all, he believed he had acquired such a profound knowledge of the inner workings of his mind and its hidden springs that relapse was unthinkable. Nevertheless, he was drunk in a short time. More baffling still, he could give himself no satisfactory explanation for his fall.

So he returned to this doctor, whom he admired, and asked him point-blank why he could not recover. He wished above all things to regain self-control. He seemed quite rational and well-balanced with respect to other problems. Yet he had no control whatever over alcohol. Why was this?

He begged the doctor to tell him the whole truth, and he got it. In the doctor's judgment he was utterly hopeless; he could never regain his position in society and he would have to place himself under lock and key or hire a bodyguard if he expected to live long. That was a great physician's opinion.

But this man still lives, and is a free man. He does not need a bodyguard nor is he confined. He can go anywhere on this earth where other free men may go without disaster, provided he remains willing to maintain a certain simple attitude.

Some of our alcoholic readers may think they can do without spiritual help. Let us tell you the rest of the conversation our friend had with his doctor.

The doctor said: "You have the mind of a chronic alcoholic. I have never seen one single case recover, where that state of mind existed to the extent that it does in you." Our friend felt as though the gates of hell had closed on him with a clang.

He said to the doctor, "Is there no exception?"

"Yes," replied the doctor, "there is. Exceptions to cases such as yours have been occurring since early times. Here and there, once in a while, alcoholics have had what are called vital spiritual experiences. To me these occurrences are phenomena. They appear to be in the nature of huge emotional displacements and rearrangements. Ideas, emotions, and attitudes which were once the guiding forces of the lives of these men are suddenly cast to one side, and a completely new set of conceptions and motives begin to dominate them. In fact, I have been trying to produce some such emotional rearrangement within you. With many individuals the methods which I employed are successful, but I have never been successful with an alcoholic of your description."*

Upon hearing this, our friend was somewhat relieved, for he reflected that, after all, he was a good church member. This hope, however, was destroyed by the doctor's telling him that while his religious convictions were very good, in his case they did not spell the necessary vital spiritual experience.

*See "Spiritual Experience."

Here was the terrible dilemma in which our friend found himself when he had the extraordinary experience, which as we have already told you, made him a free man.

We, in our turn, sought the same escape with all the desperation of drowning men. What seemed at first a flimsy reed, has proved to be the loving and powerful hand of God. A new life has been given us or, if you prefer, "a design for living" that really works.

The distinguished American psychologist, William James, in his book "Varieties of Religious Experience," indicates a multitude of ways in which men have discovered God. We have no desire to convince anyone that there is only one way by which faith can be acquired. If what we have learned and felt and seen means anything at all, it means that all of us, whatever our race, creed, or color are the children of a living Creator with whom we may form a relationship upon simple and understandable terms as soon as we are willing and honest enough to try. Those having religious affiliations will find here nothing disturbing to their beliefs or ceremonies. There is no friction among us over such matters.

We think it no concern of ours what religious bodies our members identify themselves with as individuals. This should be an entirely personal affair which each one decides for himself in the light of past associations, or his present choice. Not all of us join religious bodies, but most of us favor such memberships.

In the following chapter, there appears an explanation of alcoholism, as we understand it, then a chapter addressed to the agnostic. Many who once were in this class are now among our members. Surprisingly enough, we find such convictions no great obstacle to a spiritual experience.

Further on, clear-cut directions are given showing how we recovered. These are followed by forty-three personal experiences.

Each individual, in the personal stories, describes in his own language and from his own point of view the way he established his relationship with God. These give a fair cross section of our membership and a clear-cut idea of what has actually happened in their lives.

We hope no one will consider these self-revealing accounts in bad taste. Our hope is that many alcoholic men and women, desperately in need, will see these pages, and we believe that it is only by fully disclosing ourselves and our problems that they will be persuaded to say, "Yes, I am one of them too; I must have this thing."

Note

1. Dr. Jekyll and Mr. Hyde: literary reference to describe a person with a split personality - one good and the other bad.

Chapter 3

MORE ABOUT ALCOHOLISM

MOST OF us have been unwilling to admit we were real alcoholics. No person likes to think he is bodily and mentally different from his fellows. Therefore, it is not surprising that our drinking careers have been characterized by countless vain attempts to prove we could drink like other people. The idea that somehow, someday he will control and enjoy his drinking is the great obsession of every abnormal drinker. The persistence of this illusion is astonishing. Many pursue it into the gates of insanity or death.

We learned that we had to fully concede to our innermost selves that we were alcoholics. This is the first step in recovery. The delusion that we are like other people, or presently may be, has to be smashed.

We alcoholics are men and women who have lost the ability to control our drinking. We know that no real alcoholic *ever* recovers control. All of us felt at times that we were regaining control, but such intervals—usually brief—were inevitably followed by still less control, which led in time to pitiful and incomprehensible demoralization. We are convinced to a man that alcoholics of our type are in the grip of a progressive illness. Over any considerable period we get worse, never better.

We are like men who have lost their legs; they never grow new ones. Neither does there appear to be any kind of treatment which will make alcoholics of our kind like other men. We have tried every imaginable remedy. In some instances there has been brief recovery, followed always by a still worse relapse. Physicians who are familiar with alcoholism agree there is no such thing as making a normal drinker out of an alcoholic. Science may one day accomplish this, but it hasn't done so yet.

Despite all we can say, many who are real alcoholics are not going to believe they are in that class. By every form of self-deception and experimentation, they will try to prove themselves exceptions to the rule, therefore nonalcoholic. If anyone who is showing inability to control his drinking can do the right- about-face and drink like a gentleman, our hats are off to him. Heaven knows, we have tried hard enough and long enough to drink like other people!

Here are some of the methods we have tried: Drinking beer only, limiting the number of drinks, never drinking alone, never drinking in the morning, drinking only at home, never having it in the house, never drinking during business hours, drinking only at parties, switching from scotch to brandy, drinking only natural wines, agreeing to resign if ever drunk on the job, taking a trip, not taking a trip, swearing off forever (with and without a solemn oath), taking more physical exercise, reading inspirational books, going to health farms and sanitariums, accepting voluntary commitment to asylums—we could increase the list ad infinitum.

We do not like to pronounce any individual as alcoholic, but you can quickly diagnose yourself. Step over to the nearest barroom and try some controlled drinking. Try to drink and stop abruptly. Try it more than once. It will not take long for you to decide, if you are honest with yourself about it. It may be worth a bad case of jitters if you get a full knowledge of your condition.

Though there is no way of proving it, we believe that early in our drinking careers most of us could have stopped drinking. But the difficulty is that few alcoholics have enough desire to stop while there is yet time. We have heard of a few instances where people, who showed definite signs of alcoholism, were able to stop for a long period because of an overpowering desire to do so. Here is one.

A man of thirty was doing a great deal of spree drinking. He was very nervous in the morning after these bouts and quieted himself with more liquor. He was ambitious to succeed in business, but saw that he would get nowhere if he drank at all. Once he started, he had no control whatever. He made up his mind that until he had been successful in business and had retired, he would not touch another drop. An exceptional man, he remained bone dry for twenty-five years and retired at the age of fifty-five, after a successful and happy business career. Then he fell victim to a belief which practically every alcoholic has—that his long period of sobriety and self-discipline had qualified him to drink as other men. Out came his carpet slippers and a bottle. In two months he was in a hospital, puzzled and humiliated. He tried to regulate his drinking for a while, making several trips to the hospital meantime. Then, gathering all his forces, he attempted to stop altogether and found he could not. Every means of solving his problem which money could buy was at his disposal. Every attempt failed. Though a robust man at retirement, he went to pieces quickly and was dead within four years.

This case contains a powerful lesson. Most of us have believed that if we remained sober for a long stretch, we could thereafter drink normally. But here is a man who at fifty-five years found he was just where he had left off at thirty. We have seen the truth demonstrated again and again: "Once an alcoholic, always an alcoholic." Commencing to drink after a period of sobriety, we are in a short time as bad as ever. If we are planning to stop drinking, there must be no reservation of any kind, nor any lurking notion that someday we will be immune to alcohol.

Young people may be encouraged by this man's experience to think that they can stop, as he did, on their own will power. We doubt if many of them can do it, because none will really want to stop, and hardly one of them, because of the peculiar mental twist already acquired, will find he can win out. Several of our crowd, men of thirty or less, had been drinking only a few years, but they found themselves as helpless as those who had been drinking twenty years.

To be gravely affected, one does not necessarily have to drink a long time nor take the quantities some of us have. This is particularly true of women. Potential female alcoholics often turn into the real thing and are gone beyond recall in a few years. Certain drinkers, who would be greatly insulted if called alcoholics, are astonished at their inability to stop. We, who are familiar with the symptoms, see large numbers of potential alcoholics among young people everywhere. But try and get them to see it!*

As we look back, we feel we had gone on drinking many years beyond the point where we could quit on our will power. If anyone questions whether he has entered this dangerous area, let him try leaving liquor alone for one year. If he is a real alcoholic and very far advanced, there is scant chance of success. In the early days of our drinking we occasionally remained sober for a year or more, becoming serious drinkers again later. Though you may be able to stop for a considerable period, you may yet be a potential alcoholic. We think few, to whom this book will appeal, can stay dry anything like a year. Some will be drunk the day after making their resolutions; most of them within a few weeks.

For those who are unable to drink moderately the question is how to stop altogether. We are assuming, of course, that the reader desires to stop. Whether such a person can quit upon a nonspiritual basis depends upon the extent to which he has already lost the power to choose whether he will drink or not. Many of us felt that we had plenty of character. There was a tremendous urge to cease forever. Yet we found it impossible. This is the baffling feature of alcoholism as we know it—this utter inability to leave it alone, no matter how great the necessity or the wish.

How then shall we help our readers determine, to their own satisfaction, whether they are one of us? The experiment of quitting for a period of time will be helpful, but we think we can render an even greater service to alcoholic sufferers and perhaps to the med-

*True when this book was first published. A 2001 U.S./Canada membership survey showed about one-tenth of AAs were thirty and under.

ical fraternity. So we shall describe some of the mental states that precede a relapse into drinking, for obviously this is the crux of the problem.

What sort of thinking dominates an alcoholic who repeats time after time the desperate experiment of the first drink? Friends who have reasoned with him after a spree which has brought him to the point of divorce or bankruptcy are mystified when he walks directly into a saloon. Why does he? Of what is he thinking?

Our first example is a friend we shall call Jim. This man has a charming wife and family. He inherited a lucrative automobile agency. He had a commendable World War record. He is a good salesman. Everybody likes him. He is an intelligent man, normal so far as we can see, except for a nervous disposition. He did no drinking until he was thirty-five. In a few years he became so violent when intoxicated that he had to be committed. On leaving the asylum he came into contact with us.

We told him what we knew of alcoholism and the answer we had found. He made a beginning. His family was re-assembled, and he began to work as a salesman for the business he had lost through drinking. All went well for a time, but he failed to enlarge his spiritual life. To his consternation, he found himself drunk half a dozen times in rapid succession. On each of these occasions we worked with him, reviewing carefully what had happened. He agreed he was a real alcoholic and in a serious condition. He knew he faced another trip to the asylum if he kept on. Moreover, he would lose his family for whom he had a deep affection.

Yet he got drunk again. We asked him to tell us exactly how it happened. This is his story: "I came to work on Tuesday morning. I remember I felt irritated that I had to be a salesman for a concern I once owned. I had a few words with the boss, but nothing serious. Then I decided to drive into the country and see one of my prospects for a car. On the way I felt hungry so I stopped at a roadside place where they have a bar. I had no intention of drinking. I just thought I would get a sandwich. I also had the notion that I might find a customer for a car at this place, which was familiar for I had been going to it for years. I had eaten there many times during the months I was sober. I sat down at a table and ordered a sandwich and a glass of milk. Still no thought of drinking. I ordered another sandwich and decided to have another glass of milk.

"Suddenly the thought crossed my mind that if I were to put an ounce of whiskey in my milk it couldn't hurt me on a full stomach. I ordered a whiskey and poured it into the milk. I vaguely sensed I was not being any too smart, but felt reassured as I was taking the whiskey on a full stomach. The experiment went so well that I ordered another whiskey and poured it into more milk. That didn't seem to bother me so I tried another."

Thus started one more journey to the asylum for Jim. Here was the threat of commitment, the loss of family and position, to say nothing of that intense mental and physical suffering which drinking always caused him. *He had much knowledge about himself as an alcoholic. Yet all reasons for not drinking were easily pushed aside in favor of the foolish idea that he could take whiskey if only he mixed it with milk!*

Whatever the precise definition of the word may be, we call this plain insanity. How can such a lack of proportion, of the ability to think straight, be called anything else?

You may think this an extreme case. To us it is not far-fetched, for this kind of thinking has been characteristic of every single one of us. We have sometimes reflected more than Jim did upon the consequences. But there was always the curious mental phenomenon that parallel with our sound reasoning there inevitably ran some insanely trivial excuse for taking the first drink. Our sound reasoning failed to hold us in check. The insane idea won out. Next day we would ask ourselves, in all earnestness and sincerity, how it could have happened.

In some circumstances we have gone out deliberately to get drunk, feeling ourselves justified by nervousness, anger, worry, depression, jealousy or the like. But even in this type of beginning we are obliged to admit that our justification for a spree was insanely insufficient in the light of what always happened. We now see that when we began to drink deliberately, instead of casually, there was little serious or effective thought during the period of premeditation of what the terrific consequences might be.

Our behavior is as absurd and incomprehensible with respect to the first drink as that of an individual with a passion, say, for jay-walking. He gets a thrill out of skipping in front of fast-moving vehicles. He enjoys himself for a few years in spite of friendly warnings. Up to this point you would label him as a foolish chap having queer ideas of fun. Luck then deserts him and he is slightly injured several times in succession. You would expect him, if he were normal, to cut it out. Presently he is hit again and this time has a fractured skull. Within a week after leaving the hospital a fast-moving trolley car breaks his arm. He tells you he has decided to stop jay-walking for good, but in a few weeks he breaks both legs.

On through the years this conduct continues, accompanied by his continual promises to be careful or to keep off the streets altogether. Finally, he can no longer work, his wife gets a divorce and he is held up to ridicule. He tries every known means to get the jay-walking idea out of his head. He shuts himself up in an asylum, hoping to mend his ways. But the day he comes out he races in front of a fire engine, which breaks his back. Such a man would be crazy, wouldn't he?

You may think our illustration is too ridiculous. But is it? We, who have been through the wringer, have to admit if we substituted alcoholism for jay-walking, the illustration would fit us exactly. However intelligent we may have been in other respects, where alcohol has been involved, we have been strangely insane. It's strong language—but isn't it true?

Some of you are thinking: "Yes, what you tell us is true, but it doesn't fully apply. We admit we have some of these symptoms, but we have not gone to the extremes you fellows did, nor are we likely to, for we understand ourselves so well after what you have told us that such things cannot happen again. We have not lost everything in life through drinking and we certainly do not intend to. Thanks for the information."

That may be true of certain nonalcoholic people who, though drinking foolishly and heavily at the present time, are able to stop or moderate, because their brains and bodies have not been damaged as ours were. But the actual or potential alcoholic, with hardly an exception, will be *absolutely unable to stop drinking on the basis of self-knowledge.* This is a point we wish to emphasize and re-emphasize, to smash home upon our alcoholic readers as it has been revealed to us out of bitter experience. Let us take another illustration.

Fred is partner in a well known accounting firm. His income is good, he has a fine home, is happily married and the father of promising children of college age. He has so attractive a personality that he makes friends with everyone. If ever there was a successful business man, it is Fred. To all appearance he is a stable, well balanced individual. Yet, he is alcoholic. We first saw Fred about a year ago in a hospital where he had gone to recover from a bad case of jitters. It was his first experience of this kind, and he was much ashamed of it. Far from admitting he was an alcoholic, he told himself he came to the hospital to rest his nerves. The doctor intimated strongly that he might be worse than he realized. For a few days he was depressed about his condition. He made up his mind to quit drinking altogether. It never occurred to him that perhaps he could not do so, in spite of his character and standing. Fred would not believe himself an alcoholic, much less accept a spiritual remedy for his problem. We told him what we knew about alcoholism. He was interested and conceded that he had some of the symptoms, but he was a long way from admitting that he could do nothing about it himself. He was positive that this humiliating experience, plus the knowledge he had acquired, would keep him sober the rest of his life. Self-knowledge would fix it.

We heard no more of Fred for a while. One day we were told that he was back in the hospital. This time he was quite shaky. He soon indicated he was anxious to see us. The story he told is most instructive, for here was a chap absolutely convinced he had to stop drinking, who had no excuse for drinking, who exhibited splendid judgment and determination in all his other concerns, yet was flat on his back nevertheless.

Let him tell you about it: "I was much impressed with what you fellows said about alcoholism, and I frankly did not believe it would be possible for me to drink again. I rather appreciated your ideas about the subtle insanity which precedes the first drink, but I was confident it could not happen to me after what I had learned. I reasoned I was not so far advanced as most of you fellows, that I had been usually successful in licking my other personal problems, and that I would therefore be successful where you men failed. I felt I had every right to be self-confident, that it would be only a matter of exercising my will power and keeping on guard.

"In this frame of mind, I went about my business and for a time all was well. I had no trouble refusing drinks, and began to wonder if I had not been making too hard work of a simple matter. One day I went to Washington to present some accounting evidence to a government bureau. I had been out of town before during this particular dry spell, so there was nothing new about that. Physically, I felt fine. Neither did I have any pressing problems or worries. My business came off well, I was pleased and knew my partners would be too. It was the end of a perfect day, not a cloud on the horizon.

"I went to my hotel and leisurely dressed for dinner. *As I crossed the threshold of the dining room, the thought came to mind that it would be nice to have a couple of cocktails with dinner. That was all. Nothing more.* I ordered a cocktail and my meal. Then I ordered another cocktail. After dinner I decided to take a walk. When I returned to the hotel it struck me a highball would be fine before going to bed, so I stepped into the bar and had one. I remember having several more that night and plenty next morning. I have a shadowy recollection of being in an airplane bound for New York and of finding a friendly taxicab driver at the landing field instead of my wife. The driver escorted me about for several days. I know little of where I went or what I said and did. Then came the hospital with unbearable mental and physical suffering.

"As soon as I regained my ability to think, I went carefully over that evening in Washington. *Not only had I been off guard, I had made no fight whatever against the first drink. This time I had not thought of the consequences at all.* I had commenced to drink as carelessly as though the cocktails were ginger ale. I now remembered what my alcoholic friends had told me, how they prophesied that if I had an alcoholic mind, the time and place would come—I would drink again. They had said that though I did raise a defense, it would one day give way before some trivial reason for having a drink. Well, just that did happen and more, for what I had learned of alcoholism did not occur to me at all. I knew from that moment that I had an alcoholic mind. I saw that will power and self-knowledge would not help in those strange mental blank spots. I had never been able to understand people who said that a problem had them hopelessly defeated. I knew then. It was a crushing blow.

"Two of the members of Alcoholics Anonymous came to see me. They grinned, which I didn't like so much, and then asked me if I thought myself alcoholic and if I were really licked this time. I had to concede both propositions. They piled on me heaps of evidence to the effect that an alcoholic mentality, such as I had exhibited in Washington, was a hopeless condition. They cited cases out of their own experience by the dozen. This process snuffed out the last flicker of conviction that I could do the job myself.

"Then they outlined the spiritual answer and program of action which a hundred of them had followed successfully. Though I had been only a nominal churchman, their proposals were not, intellectually, hard to swallow. But the program of action, though entirely sensible, was pretty drastic. It meant I would have to throw several lifelong conceptions out of the window. That was not easy. But the moment I made up my mind to go through with the process, I had the curious feeling that my alcoholic condition was relieved, as in fact it proved to be.

"Quite as important was the discovery that spiritual principles would solve all my problems. I have since been brought into a way of living infinitely more satisfying and, I hope, more useful than the life I lived before. My old manner of life was by no means a bad one, but I would not exchange its best moments for the worst I have now. I would not go back to it even if I could."

Fred's story speaks for itself. We hope it strikes home to thousands like him. He had felt only the first nip of the wringer. Most alcoholics have to be pretty badly mangled before they really commence to solve their problems.

Many doctors and psychiatrists agree with our conclusions. One of these men, staff member of a world-renowned hospital, recently made this statement to some of us: "What you say about the general hopelessness of the average alcoholic's plight is, in my opinion, correct. As to two of you men, whose stories I have heard, there is no doubt in my mind that you were 100% hopeless, apart from divine help. Had you offered yourselves as patients at this hospital, I would not have taken you, if I had been able to avoid it. People like you are too heartbreaking. Though not a religious person, I have profound respect for the spiritual approach in such cases as yours. For most cases, there is virtually no other solution."

Once more: The alcoholic at certain times has no effective mental defense against the first drink. Except in a few rare cases, neither he nor any other human being can provide such a defense. His defense must come from a Higher Power.

Chapter 4

WE AGNOSTICS

IN THE PRECEDING chapters you have learnedsomething of alcoholism. We hope we have made clear the distinction between the alcoholic and the nonalcoholic. If, when you honestly want to, you find you cannot quit entirely, or if when drinking, you have little control over the amount you take, you are probably alcoholic. If that be the case, you may be suffering from an illness which only a spiritual experience will conquer.

To one who feels he is an atheist or agnostic such an experience seems impossible, but to continue as he is means disaster, especially if he is an alcoholic of the hopeless variety. To be doomed to an alcoholic death or to live on a spiritual basis are not always easy alternatives to face.

But it isn't so difficult. About half our original fellowship were of exactly that type. At first some of us tried to avoid the issue, hoping against hope we were not true alcoholics. But after a while we had to face the fact that we must find a spiritual basis of life—or else. Perhaps it is going to be that way with you. But cheer up, something like half of us thought we were atheists or agnostics. Our experience shows that you need not be disconcerted.

If a mere code of morals or a better philosophy of life were sufficient to overcome alcoholism, many of us would have recovered long ago. But we found that such codes and philosophies did not save us, no matter how much we tried. We could wish to be moral, we could wish to be philosophically comforted, in fact, we could will these things with all our might, but the needed power wasn't there. Our human resources, as marshalled by the will, were not sufficient; they failed utterly.

Lack of power, that was our dilemma. We had to find a power by which we could live, and it had to be a *Power greater than ourselves.* Obviously. But where and how were we to find this Power?

Well, that's exactly what this book is about. Its main object is to enable you to find a Power greater than yourself which will solve your problem. That means we have written a book which we believe to be spiritual as well as moral. And it means, of course, that we are going to talk about God. Here difficulty arises with agnostics. Many times we talk to a new man and watch his hope rise as we discuss his alcoholic problems and explain our fellowship. But his face falls when we speak of spiritual matters, especially when we mention God, for we have re-opened a subject which our man thought he had neatly evaded or entirely ignored.

We know how he feels. We have shared his honest doubt and prejudice. Some of us have been violently anti-religious. To others, the word "God" brought up a particular idea of Him with which someone had tried to impress them during childhood. Perhaps we rejected this particular conception because it seemed inadequate. With that rejection we imagined we had abandoned the God idea entirely. We were bothered with the thought that faith and dependence upon a Power beyond ourselves was somewhat weak, even cowardly. We looked upon this world of warring individuals, warring theological systems, and inexplicable calamity, with deep skepticism. We looked askance at many individuals who claimed to be godly. How could a Supreme Being have anything to do with it all? And who could comprehend a Supreme Being anyhow? Yet, in other moments, we found ourselves thinking, when enchanted by a starlit night, "Who, then, made all this?" There was a feeling of awe and wonder, but it was fleeting and soon lost.

Yes, we of agnostic temperament have had these thoughts and experiences. Let us make haste to reassure you. We found that as soon as we were able to lay aside prejudice and express even a willingness to believe in a Power greater than ourselves, we commenced to get results, even though it was impossible for any of us to fully define or comprehend that Power, which is God.

Much to our relief, we discovered we did not need to consider another's conception of God. Our own conception, however inadequate, was sufficient to make the approach and to effect a contact with Him. As soon as we admitted the possible existence of a Creative Intelligence, a Spirit of the Universe underlying the totality of things, we began to be possessed of a new sense of power and direction, provided we took other simple steps. We found that God does not make too hard terms with those who seek Him. To us, the Realm of Spirit is broad, roomy, all inclusive; never exclusive or forbidding to those who earnestly seek. It is open, we believe, to all men.

When, therefore, we speak to you of God, we mean your own conception of God. This applies, too, to other spiritual expressions which you find in this book. Do not let any prejudice you may have against spiritual terms deter you from honestly asking yourself what they mean to you. At the start, this was all we needed to commence spiritual growth, to effect our first conscious relation with God as we understood Him. Afterward, we found ourselves accepting many things which then seemed entirely out of reach. That was growth, but if we wished to grow we had to begin somewhere. So we used our own conception, however limited it was.

We needed to ask ourselves but one short question. "Do I now believe, or am I even willing to believe, that there is a Power greater than myself ?" As soon as a man can say that he does believe, or is willing to believe, we emphatically assure him that he is on his way. It has been repeatedly proven among us that upon this simple cornerstone a wonderfully effective spiritual structure can be built.*

That was great news to us, for we had assumed we could not make use of spiritual principles unless we accepted many things on faith which seemed difficult to believe. When people presented us with spiritual approaches, how frequently did we all say, "I wish I had what that man has. I'm sure it would work if I could only believe as he believes. But I cannot accept as surely true the many articles of faith which are so plain to him." So it was comforting to learn that we could commence at a simpler level.

Besides a seeming inability to accept much on faith,

*Please be sure to read "Spiritual Experience."

we often found ourselves handicapped by obstinacy, sensitiveness, and unreasoning prejudice. Many of us have been so touchy that even casual reference to spiritual things made us bristle with antagonism. This sort of thinking had to be abandoned. Though some of us resisted, we found no great difficulty in casting aside such feelings. Faced with alcoholic destruction, we soon became as open minded on spiritual matters as we had tried to be on other questions. In this respect alcohol was a great persuader. It finally beat us into a state of reasonableness. Sometimes this was a tedious process; we hope no one else will be prejudiced for as long as some of us were.

The reader may still ask why he should believe in a Power greater than himself. We think there are good reasons. Let us have a look at some of them.

The practical individual of today is a stickler for facts and results. Nevertheless, the twentieth century readily accepts theories of all kinds, provided they are firmly grounded in fact. We have numerous theories, for example, about electricity. Everybody believes them without a murmur of doubt. Why this ready acceptance? Simply because it is impossible to explain what we see, feel, direct, and use, without a reasonable assumption as a starting point.

Everybody nowadays, believes in scores of assumptions for which there is good evidence, but no perfect visual proof. And does not science demonstrate that visual proof is the weakest proof? It is being constantly revealed, as mankind studies the material world, that outward appearances are not inward reality at all. To illustrate:

The prosaic steel girder is a mass of electrons whirling around each other at incredible speed. These tiny bodies are governed by precise laws, and these laws hold true throughout the material world. Science tells us so. We have no reason to doubt it. When, however, the perfectly logical assumption is suggested that underneath the material world and life as we see it, there is an All Powerful, Guiding, Creative Intelligence, right there our perverse streak comes to the surface and we laboriously set out to convince ourselves it isn't so. We read wordy books and indulge in windy arguments, thinking we believe this universe needs no God to explain it. Were our contentions true, it would follow that life originated out of nothing, means nothing, and proceeds nowhere.

Instead of regarding ourselves as intelligent agents, spearheads of God's ever advancing Creation, we agnostics and atheists chose to believe that our human intelligence was the last word, the alpha and the omega, the beginning and end of all. Rather vain of us, wasn't it?

We, who have traveled this dubious path, beg you to lay aside prejudice, even against organized religion. We have learned that whatever the human frailties of various faiths may be, those faiths have given purpose and direction to millions. People of faith have a logical idea of what life is all about. Actually, we used to have no reasonable conception whatever. We used to amuse ourselves by cynically dissecting spiritual beliefs and practices when we might have observed that many spiritually-minded persons of all races, colors, and creeds were demonstrating a degree of stability, happiness and usefulness which we should have sought ourselves.

Instead, we looked at the human defects of these people, and sometimes used their shortcomings as a basis of wholesale condemnation. We talked of intolerance, while we were intolerant ourselves. We missed the reality and the beauty of the forest because we were diverted by the ugliness of some of its trees. We never gave the spiritual side of life a fair hearing.

In our personal stories you will find a wide variation in the way each teller approaches and conceives of the Power which is greater than himself. Whether we agree with a particular approach or conception seems to make little difference. Experience has taught us that these are matters about which, for our purpose, we need not be worried. They are questions for each individual to settle for himself.

On one proposition, however, these men and women are strikingly agreed. Every one of them has gained access to, and believes in, a Power greater than himself. This Power has in each case accomplished the miraculous, the humanly impossible. As a celebrated American statesman put it, "Let's look at the record."

Here are thousands of men and women, worldly indeed. They flatly declare that since they have come to believe in a Power greater than themselves, to take a certain attitude toward that Power, and to do certain simple things, there has been a revolutionary change in their way of living and thinking. In the face of collapse and despair, in the face of the total failure of their human resources, they found that a new power, peace, happiness, and sense of direction flowed into them. This happened soon after they wholeheartedly met a few simple requirements. Once confused and baffled by the seeming futility of existence, they show the underlying reasons why they were making heavy going of life. Leaving aside the drink question, they tell why living was so unsatisfactory. They show how the change came over them. When many hundreds of people are able to say that the consciousness of the Presence of God is today the most important fact of their lives, they present a powerful reason why one should have faith.

This world of ours has made more material progress in the last century than in all the millenniums which went before. Almost everyone knows the reason. Students of ancient history tell us that the intellect of men in those days was equal to the best of today. Yet in ancient times material progress was painfully slow. The spirit of modern scientific inquiry, research and invention was almost unknown. In the realm of the material, men's minds were fettered by superstition, tradition, and all sorts of fixed ideas. Some of the contemporaries of Columbus thought a round earth preposterous.[1] Others came near putting Galileo to death for his astronomical heresies.[2]

We asked ourselves this: Are not some of us just as biased and unreasonable about the realm of the spirit as were the ancients about the realm of the material? Even in the present century, American newspapers were afraid to print an account of the Wright brothers' first successful flight at Kitty Hawk.[3] Had not all efforts at flight failed before? Did not Professor Langley's flying machine go to the bottom of the Potomac River? Was it not true that the best mathematical minds had proved man could never fly? Had not people said God had reserved this privilege to the birds? Only thirty years later the conquest of the air was almost an old story and airplane travel was in full swing.

But in most fields our generation has witnessed complete liberation of our thinking. Show any longshoreman a Sunday supplement describing a proposal to explore the moon by means of a rocket and he will say "I bet they do it — maybe not so long either." Is not our age characterized by the ease with which we discard old ideas for new, by the complete readiness with which we throw away the theory or gadget which does not work for something new which does?

We had to ask ourselves why we shouldn't apply to our human problems this same readiness to change our point of view. We were having trouble with personal relationships, we couldn't control our emotional natures, we were a prey to misery and depression, we couldn't make a living, we had a feeling of uselessness, we were full of fear, we were unhappy, we couldn't seem to be of real help to other people — was not a basic solution of these bedevilments more important than whether we should see newsreels of lunar flight? Of course it was.

When we saw others solve their problems by a simple reliance upon the Spirit of the Universe, we had to stop doubting the power of God. Our ideas did not work. But the God idea did.

The Wright brothers' almost childish faith that they could build a machine which would fly was the mainspring of their accomplishment. Without that, nothing could have happened. We agnostics and atheists were sticking to the idea that self-sufficiency would solve our problems. When others showed us that "God-sufficiency" worked with them, we began to feel like those who had insisted the Wrights would never fly.

Logic is great stuff. We liked it. We still like it. It is not by chance we were given the power to reason, to examine the evidence of our senses, and to draw conclusions. That is one of man's magnificent attributes. We agnostically inclined would not feel satisfied with a proposal which does not lend itself to reasonable approach and interpretation. Hence we are at pains to tell why we think our present faith is reasonable, why we think it more sane and logical to believe than not to believe, why we say our former thinking was soft and mushy when we threw up our hands in doubt and said, "We don't know."

When we became alcoholics, crushed by a self-imposed crisis we could not postpone or evade, we had to fearlessly face the proposition that either God is everything or else He is nothing. God either is, or He isn't. What was our choice to be?

Arrived at this point, we were squarely confronted with the question of faith. We couldn't duck the issue. Some of us had already walked far over the Bridge of Reason toward the desired shore of faith. The outlines and the promise of the New Land had brought lustre to tired eyes and fresh courage to flagging spirits. Friendly hands had stretched out in welcome. We were grateful that Reason had brought us so far. But somehow, we couldn't quite step ashore. Perhaps we had been leaning too heavily on Reason that last mile and we did not like to lose our support.

That was natural, but let us think a little more closely. Without knowing it, had we not been brought to where we stood by a certain kind of faith? For did we not believe in our own reasoning? Did we not have confidence in our ability to think? What was that but a sort of faith? Yes, we had been faithful, abjectly faithful to the God of Reason. So, in one way or another, we discovered that faith had been involved all the time!

We found, too, that we had been worshippers. What a state of mental goose-flesh that used to bring on! Had we not variously worshipped people, sentiment, things, money, and ourselves? And then, with a better motive, had we not worshipfully beheld the sunset, the sea, or a flower? Who of us had not loved something or somebody? How much did these feelings, these loves, these worships, have to do with pure reason? Little or nothing, we saw at last. Were not these things the tissue out of which our lives were constructed? Did not these feelings, after all, determine the course of our existence? It was impossible to say we had no capacity for faith, or love, or worship. In one form or another we had been living by faith and little else.

Imagine life without faith! Were nothing left but pure reason, it wouldn't be life. But we believed in life — of course we did. We could not prove life in the sense that you can prove a straight line is the shortest distance between two points, yet, there it was. Could we still say the whole thing was nothing but a mass of electrons, created out of nothing, meaning nothing, whirling on to a destiny of nothingness? Of course we couldn't. The electrons themselves seemed more intelligent than that. At least, so the chemist said.

Hence, we saw that reason isn't everything. Neither is reason, as most of us use it, entirely dependable, though it emanate from our best minds. What about people who proved that man could never fly?

Yet we had been seeing another kind of flight, a spiritual liberation from this world, people who rose above their problems. They said God made these things possible, and we only smiled. We had seen spiritual release, but liked to tell ourselves it wasn't true.

Actually we were fooling ourselves, for deep down in every man, woman, and child, is the fundamental idea of God. It may be obscured by calamity, by pomp, by worship of other things, but in some form or other it is there. For faith in a Power greater than ourselves, and miraculous demonstrations of that power in human lives, are facts as old as man himself.

We finally saw that faith in some kind of God was a part of our make-up, just as much as the feeling we have for a friend. Sometimes we had to search fearlessly, but He was there. He was as much a fact as we were. We found the Great Reality deep down within us. In the last analysis it is only there that He may be found. It was so with us.

We can only clear the ground a bit. If our testimony helps sweep away prejudice, enables you to think honestly, encourages you to search diligently within yourself, then, if you wish, you can join us on the Broad Highway. With this attitude you cannot fail. The consciousness of your belief is sure to come to you.

In this book you will read the experience of a man who thought he was an atheist. His story is so interesting that some of it should be told now. His change of heart was dramatic, convincing, and moving.

Our friend was a minister's son. He attended church school, where he became rebellious at what he thought an overdose of religious education. For years thereafter he was dogged by trouble and frustration. Business failure, insanity, fatal illness, suicide — these calamities in his immediate family embittered and depressed him. Post-war disillusionment, ever more serious alcoholism, impending mental and physical collapse, brought him to the point of self-destruction.

One night, when confined in a hospital, he was approached by an alcoholic who had known a spiritual experience. Our friend's gorge rose as he bitterly cried out: "If there is a God, He certainly hasn't done anything for me!" But later, alone in his room, he asked himself this question: "Is it possible that all the religious people I have known are wrong?" While pondering the answer he felt as though he lived in hell. Then, like a thunderbolt, a great thought came. It crowded out all else:

"Who are you to say there is no God?"

This man recounts that he tumbled out of bed to his knees. In a few seconds he was overwhelmed by a conviction of the Presence of God. It poured over and through him with the certainty and majesty of a great tide at flood. The barriers he had built through the years were swept away. He stood in the Presence of Infinite Power and Love. He had stepped from bridge to shore. For the first time, he lived in conscious companionship with his Creator.

Thus was our friend's cornerstone fixed in place. No later vicissitude has shaken it. His alcoholic problem was taken away. That very night, years ago, it disappeared. Save for a few brief moments of temptation the thought of drink has never returned; and at such times a great revulsion has risen up in him. Seemingly he could not drink even if he would. God had restored his sanity.

What is this but a miracle of healing? Yet its elements are simple. Circumstances made him willing to believe. He humbly offered himself to his Maker — then he knew.

Even so has God restored us all to our right minds. To this man, the revelation was sudden. Some of us grow into it more slowly. But He has come to all who have honestly sought Him.

When we drew near to Him He disclosed Himself to us!

Notes

1. Columbus: Christopher Columbus, Italian explorer often credited with the discovery of North America in 1492.

2. Galileo: Galileo Galilei, Italian physicist and astronomer persecuted for his belief that the Earth rotated around the sun. He died under house arrest in 1642.

3. Wright Brothers: Wilbur and Orville Wright flew the first piloted and powered airplane at Kitty Hawk, North Carolina in 1903.

Chapter 5

HOW IT WORKS

RARELY HAVE we seen a person fail who has thoroughly followed our path. Those who do not recover are people who cannot or will not completely give themselves to this simple program, usually men and women who are constitutionally incapable of being honest with themselves. There are such unfortunates. They are not at fault; they seem to have been born that way. They are naturally incapable of grasping and developing a manner of living which demands rigorous honesty. Their chances are less than average. There are those, too, who suffer from grave emotional and mental disorders, but many of them do recover if they have the capacity to be honest.

Our stories disclose in a general way what we used to be like, what happened, and what we are like now. If you have decided you want what we have and are willing to go to any length to get it-then you are ready to take certain steps.

At some of these we balked. We thought we could find an easier, softer way. But we could not. With all the earnestness at our command, we beg of you to be fearless and thorough from the very start. Some of us have tried to hold on to our old ideas and the result was nil until we let go absolutely.

Remember that we deal with alcohol-cunning, baffling, powerful! Without help it is too much for us. But there is One who has all power-that One is God. May you find Him now!

Half measures availed us nothing. We stood at the turning point. We asked His protection and care with complete abandon.

Here are the steps we took, which are suggested as a program of recovery:

1. We admitted we were powerless over alcohol- that our lives had become unmanageable.
2. Came to believe that a Power greater than ourselves could restore us to sanity.
3. Made a decision to turn our will and our lives over to the care of God *as we understood Him.*
4. Made a searching and fearless moral inventory of ourselves.
5. Admitted to God, to ourselves, and to another human being the exact nature of our wrongs.
6. Were entirely ready to have God remove all these defects of character.
7. Humbly asked Him to remove our shortcomings.
8. Made a list of all persons we had harmed, and became willing to make amends to them all.
9. Made direct amends to such people wherever possible, except when to do so would injure them or others.
10. Continued to take personal inventory and when we were wrong promptly admitted it.
11. Sought through prayer and meditation to improve our conscious contact with God *as we understood Him,* praying only for knowledge of His will for us and the power to carry that out.

12. Having had a spiritual awakening as the result of these steps, we tried to carry this message to alcoholics, and to practice these principles in all our affairs.

Many of us exclaimed, "What an order! I can't go through with it." Do not be discouraged. No one among us has been able to maintain anything like perfect adherence to these principles. We are not saints. The point is, that we are willing to grow along spiritual lines. The principles we have set down are guides to progress. We claim spiritual progress rather than spiritual perfection.

Our description of the alcoholic, the chapter to the agnostic, and our personal adventures before and after make clear three pertinent ideas:

(a) That we were alcoholic and could not manage our own lives.

(b) That probably no human power could have relieved our alcoholism.

(c) That God could and would if He were sought.

Being convinced, *we were at Step Three*, which is that we decided to turn our will and our life over to God as we understood Him. Just what do we mean by that, and just what do we do?

The first requirement is that we be convinced that any life run on self-will can hardly be a success. On that basis we are almost always in collision with something or somebody, even though our motives are good. Most people try to live by self-propulsion. Each person is like an actor who wants to run the whole show; is forever trying to arrange the lights, the ballet, the scenery and the rest of the players in his own way. If his arrangements would only stay put, if only people would do as he wished, the show would be great. Everybody, including himself, would be pleased. Life would be wonderful. In trying to make these arrangements our actor may sometimes be quite virtuous. He may be kind, considerate, patient, generous; even modest and self-sacrificing. On the other hand, he may be mean, egotistical, selfish and dishonest. But, as with most humans, he is more likely to have varied traits.

What usually happens? The show doesn't come off very well. He begins to think life doesn't treat him right. He decides to exert himself more. He becomes, on the next occasion, still more demanding or gracious, as the case may be. Still the play does not suit him. Admitting he may be somewhat at fault, he is sure that other people are more to blame. He becomes angry, indignant, self-pitying. What is his basic trouble? Is he not really a self-seeker even when trying to be kind? Is he not a victim of the delusion that he can wrest satisfaction and happiness out of this world if he only manages well? Is it not evident to all the rest of the players that these are the things he wants? And do not his actions make each of them wish to retaliate, snatching all they can get out of the show? Is he not, even in his best moments, a producer of confusion rather than harmony?

Our actor is self-centered—ego-centric, as people like to call it nowadays. He is like the retired business man who lolls in the Florida sunshine in the winter complaining of the sad state of the nation; the minister who sighs over the sins of the twentieth century; politicians and reformers who are sure all would be Utopia if the rest of the world would only behave; the outlaw safe cracker who thinks society has wronged him; and the alcoholic who has lost all and is locked up. Whatever our protestations, are not most of us concerned with ourselves, our resentments, or our self-pity?

Selfishness—self-centeredness! That, we think, is the root of our troubles. Driven by a hundred forms of fear, self-delusion, self-seeking, and self-pity, we step on the toes of our fellows and they retaliate. Sometimes they hurt us, seemingly without provocation, but we invariably find that at some time in the past we have made decisions based on self which later placed us in a position to be hurt.

So our troubles, we think, are basically of our own making. They arise out of ourselves, and the alcoholic is an extreme example of self-will run riot, though he usually doesn't think so. Above everything, we alcoholics must be rid of this selfishness. We must, or it kills us! God makes that possible. And there often seems no way of entirely getting rid of self without His aid. Many of us had moral and philosophical convictions galore, but we could not live up to them even though we would have liked to. Neither could we reduce our self-centeredness much by wishing or trying on our own power. We had to have God's help.

This is the how and why of it. First of all, we had to quit playing God. It didn't work. Next, we decided that hereafter in this drama of life, God was going to be our Director. He is the Principal; we are His agents. He is the Father, and we are His children. Most good ideas are simple, and this concept was the keystone of the new and triumphant arch through which we passed to freedom.

When we sincerely took such a position, all sorts of remarkable things followed. We had a new Employer. Being all powerful, He provided what we needed, if we kept close to Him and performed His work well. Established on such a footing we became less and less interested in ourselves, our little plans and designs. More and more we became interested in seeing what we could contribute to life. As we felt new power flow in, as we enjoyed peace of mind, as we discovered we could face life successfully, as we became conscious of His presence, we began to lose our fear of today, tomorrow or the hereafter. We were reborn.

We were now at Step Three. Many of us said to our Maker, *as we understood Him:* "God, I offer myself to Thee-to build with me and to do with me as Thou wilt. Relieve me of the bondage of self, that I may better do Thy will. Take away my difficulties, that victory over them may bear witness to those I would help of Thy Power, Thy Love, and Thy Way of life. May I do Thy will always!" We thought well before taking this step making sure we were ready; that we could at last abandon ourselves utterly to Him.

We found it very desirable to take this spiritual step with an understanding person, such as our wife, best friend or spiritual adviser. But it is better to meet God alone than with one who might misunderstand. The wording was, of course, quite optional so long as we expressed the idea, voicing it without reservation. This was only a beginning, though if honestly and humbly made, an effect, sometimes a very great one, was felt at once.

Next we launched out on a course of vigorous action, the first step of which is a personal housecleaning, which many of us had never attempted. Though our decision was a vital and crucial step, it could have little permanent effect unless at once followed by a strenuous effort to face, and to be rid of, the things in ourselves which had been blocking us. Our liquor was but a symptom. So we had to get down to causes and conditions.

Therefore, we started upon a personal inventory. *This was Step Four.* A business which takes no regular inventory usually goes broke. Taking a commercial inventory is a fact-finding and a fact-facing process. It is an effort to discover the truth about the stock-in-trade. One object is to disclose damaged or unsalable goods, to get rid of them promptly and without regret. If the owner of the business is to be successful, he cannot fool himself about values.

We did exactly the same thing with our lives. We took stock honestly. First, we searched out the flaws in our make-up which caused our failure. Being convinced that self, manifested in various ways, was what had defeated us, we considered its common manifestations.

Resentment is the "number one" offender. It destroys more alcoholics than anything else. From it stem all forms of spiritual disease, for we have been not only mentally and physically ill, we have been spiritually sick. When the spiritual malady is overcome, we straighten out mentally and physically. In dealing with resentments, we set them on paper. We listed people, institutions or principles with whom we were angry. We asked ourselves why we were angry. In most cases it was found that our self-esteem, our pocketbooks, our ambitions, our personal relationships (including sex) were hurt or threatened. So we were sore. We were "burned up."

On our grudge list we set opposite each name our injuries. Was it our self-esteem, our security, our ambitions, our personal, or sex relations, which had been interfered with?

We were usually as definite as this example:

I'm resentful at:	*The Cause*	*Affects my:*
Mr. Brown	His attention to my wife.	Sex relations. Self-esteem (fear)
	Told my wife of my mistress.	Sex relations. Self-esteem (fear)
	Brown may get my job at the office.	Security. Self-esteem (fear)
Mrs. Jones	She's a nut - she snubbed me. She committed her husband for drinking. He's my friend She's a gossip.	Personal relationship. Self-esteem (fear)
My employer	Unreasonable-Unjust -Overbearing- Threatens to fire me for drinking and padding my expense account.	Self-esteem(fear) Security.
My wife	Misunderstands and nags. Likes Brown. Wants house put in her name.	Pride - Personal sex relations - Security (fear)

We went back through our lives. Nothing counted but thoroughness and honesty. When we were finished we considered it carefully. The first thing apparent was that this world and its people were often quite wrong. To conclude that others were wrong was as far as most of us ever got. The usual outcome was that people continued to wrong us and we stayed sore. Sometimes it was remorse and then we were sore at ourselves. But the more we fought and tried to have our own way, the worse matters got. As in war, the victor only *seemed* to win. Our moments of triumph were short-lived.

It is plain that a life which includes deep resentment leads only to futility and unhappiness. To the precise extent that we permit these, do we squander the hours that might have been worth while. But with the alcoholic, whose hope is the maintenance and growth of a spiritual experience, this business of resentment is infinitely grave. We found that it is fatal. For when harboring such feelings we shut ourselves off from the sunlight of the Spirit. The insanity of alcohol returns and we drink again. And with us, to drink is to die.

If we were to live, we had to be free of anger. The grouch and the brainstorm were not for us. They may be the dubious luxury of normal men, but for alcoholics these things are poison.

We turned back to the list, for it held the key to the future. We were prepared to look at it from an entirely different angle. We began to see that the world and its people really dominated us. In that state, the wrong-doing of others, fancied or real, had power to actually kill. How could we escape? We saw that these resentments must be mastered, but how? We could not wish them away any more than alcohol.

This was our course: We realized that the people who wronged us were perhaps spiritually sick.

Though we did not like their symptoms and the way these disturbed us, they, like ourselves, were sick too. We asked God to help us show them the same tolerance, pity, and patience that we would cheerfully grant a sick friend. When a person offended we said to ourselves, "This is a sick man. How can I be helpful to him? God save me from being angry. Thy will be done."

We avoid retaliation or argument. We wouldn't treat sick people that way. If we do, we destroy our chance of being helpful. We cannot be helpful to all people, but at least God will show us how to take a kindly and tolerant view of each and every one.

Referring to our list again. Putting out of our minds the wrongs others had done, we resolutely looked for our own mistakes. Where had we been selfish, dishonest, self-seeking and frightened? Though a situation had not been entirely our fault, we tried to disregard the other person involved entirely. Where were we to blame? The inventory was ours, not the other man's. When we saw our faults we listed them. We placed them before us in black and white. We admitted our wrongs honestly and were willing to set these matters straight.

Notice that the word "fear" is bracketed alongside the difficulties with Mr. Brown, Mrs. Jones, the employer, and the wife. This short word somehow touches about every aspect of our lives. It was an evil and corroding thread; the fabric of our existence was shot through with it. It set in motion trains of circumstances which brought us misfortune we felt we didn't deserve. But did not we, ourselves, set the ball rolling? Sometimes we think fear ought to be classed with stealing. It seems to cause more trouble.

We reviewed our fears thoroughly. We put them on paper, even though we had no resentment in connection with them. We asked ourselves why we had them. Wasn't it because self-reliance failed us? Self-reliance was good as far as it went, but it didn't go far enough. Some of us once had great self-confidence, but it didn't fully solve the fear problem, or any other. When it made us cocky, it was worse.

Perhaps there is a better way—we think so. For we are now on a different basis; the basis of trusting and relying upon God. We trust infinite God rather than our finite selves. We are in the world to play the role He assigns. Just to the extent that we do as we think He would have us, and humbly rely on Him, does He enable us to match calamity with serenity.

We never apologize to anyone for depending upon our Creator. We can laugh at those who think spirituality the way of weakness. Paradoxically, it is the way of strength. The verdict of the ages is that faith means courage. All men of faith have courage. They trust their God. We never apologize for God. Instead we let Him demonstrate, through us, what He can do. We ask Him to remove our fear and direct our attention to what He would have us be. At once, we commence to outgrow fear.

Now about sex. Many of us needed an overhauling there. But above all, we tried to be sensible on this question. It's so easy to get way off the track. Here we find human opinions running to extremes—absurd extremes, perhaps. One set of voices cry that sex is a lust of our lower nature, a base necessity of procreation. Then we have the voices who cry for sex and more sex; who bewail the institution of marriage; who think that most of the troubles of the race are traceable to sex causes. They think we do not have enough of it, or that it isn't the right kind. They see its significance everywhere. One school would allow man no flavor for his fare and the other would have us all on a straight pepper diet. We want to stay out of this controversy. We do not want to be the arbiter of anyone's sex conduct. We all have sex problems. We'd hardly be human if we didn't. What can we do about them?

We reviewed our own conduct over the years past. Where had we been selfish, dishonest, or inconsiderate? Whom had we hurt? Did we unjustifiably arouse jealousy, suspicion or bitterness? Where were we at fault, what should we have done instead? We got this all down on paper and looked at it.

In this way we tried to shape a sane and sound ideal for our future sex life. We subjected each relation to this test—was it selfish or not? We asked God to mold our ideals and help us to live up to them. We remembered always that our sex powers were God-given and therefore good, neither to be used lightly or selfishly nor to be despised and loathed.

Whatever our ideal turns out to be, we must be willing to grow toward it. We must be willing to make amends where we have done harm, provided that we do not bring about still more harm in so doing. In other words, we treat sex as we would any other problem. In meditation, we ask God what we should do about each specific matter. The right answer will come, if we want it.

God alone can judge our sex situation. Counsel with

persons is often desirable, but we let God be the final judge. We realize that some people are as fanatical about sex as others are loose. We avoid hysterical thinking or advice.

Suppose we fall short of the chosen ideal and stumble? Does this mean we are going to get drunk? Some people tell us so. But this is only a half-truth. It depends on us and on our motives. If we are sorry for what we have done, and have the honest desire to let God take us to better things, we believe we will be forgiven and will have learned our lesson. If we are not sorry, and our conduct continues to harm others, we are quite sure to drink. We are not theorizing. These are facts out of our experience.

To sum up about sex: We earnestly pray for the right ideal, for guidance in each questionable situation, for sanity, and for the strength to do the right thing. If sex is very troublesome, we throw ourselves the harder into helping others. We think of their needs and work for them. This takes us out of ourselves. It quiets the imperious urge, when to yield would mean heartache.

If we have been thorough about our personal inventory, we have written down a lot. We have listed and analyzed our resentments. We have begun to comprehend their futility and their fatality. We have commenced to see their terrible destructiveness. We have begun to learn tolerance, patience and good will toward all men, even our enemies, for we look on them as sick people. We have listed the people we have hurt by our conduct, and are willing to straighten out the past if we can.

In this book you read again and again that faith did

for us what we could not do for ourselves. We hope you are convinced now that God can remove whatever self-will has blocked you off from Him. If you have already made a decision, and an inventory of your grosser handicaps, you have made a good beginning. That being so you have swallowed and digested some big chunks of truth about yourself.

Chapter 6

INTO ACTION

HAVING MADE our personal inventory, what shall we do about it? We have been trying to get a new attitude, a new relationship with our Creator, and to discover the obstacles in our path. We have admitted certain defects; we have ascertained in a rough way what the trouble is; we have put our finger on the weak items in our personal inventory. Now these are about to be cast out. This requires action on our part, which, when completed, will mean that we have admitted to God, to ourselves, and to another human being, the exact nature of our defects. This brings us to *the Fifth Step* in the program of recovery mentioned in the preceding chapter.

This is perhaps difficult—especially discussing our defects with another person. We think we have done well enough in admitting these things to ourselves. There is doubt about that. In actual practice, we usually find a solitary self-appraisal insufficient. Many of us thought it necessary to go much further. We will be more reconciled to discussing ourselves with another person when we see good reasons why we should do so. The best reason first: If we skip this vital step, we may not overcome drinking. Time after time newcomers have tried to keep to themselves certain facts about their lives. Trying to avoid this humbling experience, they have turned to easier methods. Almost invariably they got drunk. Having persevered with the rest of the program, they wondered why they fell. We think the reason is that they never completed their housecleaning. They took inventory all right, but hung on to some of the worst items in stock. They only *thought* they had lost their egoism and fear; they only *thought* they had humbled themselves. But they had not learned enough of humility, fearlessness and honesty, in the sense we find it necessary, until they told someone else *all* their life story.

More than most people, the alcoholic leads a double life. He is very much the actor. To the outer world he presents his stage character. This is the one he likes his fellows to see. He wants to enjoy a certain reputation, but knows in his heart he doesn't deserve it.

The inconsistency is made worse by the things he does on his sprees. Coming to his senses, he is revolted at certain episodes he vaguely remembers. These memories are a nightmare. He trembles to think someone might have observed him. As fast as he can, he pushes these memories far inside himself. He hopes they will never see the light of day. He is under constant fear and tension—that makes for more drinking.

Psychologists are inclined to agree with us. We have spent thousands of dollars for examinations. We know but few instances where we have given these doctors a fair break. We have seldom told them the whole truth nor have we followed their advice. Unwilling to be honest with these sympathetic men, we were honest with no one else. Small wonder many in the medical profession have a low opinion of alcoholics and their chance for recovery!

We must be entirely honest with somebody if we

expect to live long or happily in this world. Rightly and naturally, we think well before we choose the person or persons with whom to take this intimate and confidential step. Those of us belonging to a religious denomination which requires confession must, and of course, will want to go to the properly appointed authority whose duty it is to receive it. Though we have no religious connection, we may still do well to talk with someone ordained by an established religion. We often find such a person quick to see and understand our problem. Of course, we sometimes encounter people who do not understand alcoholics.

If we cannot or would rather not do this, we search our acquaintance for a close-mouthed, understanding friend. Perhaps our doctor or psychologist will be the person. It may be one of our own family, but we cannot disclose anything to our wives or our parents which will hurt them and make them unhappy. We have no right to save our own skin at another person's expense. Such parts of our story we tell to someone who will understand, yet be unaffected. The rule is we must be hard on ourself, but always considerate of others.

Notwithstanding the great necessity for discussing ourselves with someone, it may be one is so situated that there is no suitable person available. If that is so, this step may be postponed, only, however, if we hold ourselves in complete readiness to go through with it at the first opportunity. We say this because we are very anxious that we talk to the right person. It is important that he be able to keep a confidence; that he fully understand and approve what we are driving at;

that he will not try to change our plan. But we must not use this as a mere excuse to postpone.

When we decide who is to hear our story, we waste no time. We have a written inventory and we are prepared for a long talk. We explain to our partner what we are about to do and why we have to do it. He should realize that we are engaged upon a life-and-death errand. Most people approached in this way will be glad to help; they will be honored by our confidence.

We pocket our pride and go to it, illuminating every twist of character, every dark cranny of the past. Once we have taken this step, withholding nothing, we are delighted. We can look the world in the eye. We can be alone at perfect peace and ease. Our fears fall from us. We begin to feel the nearness of our Creator. We may have had certain spiritual beliefs, but now we begin to have a spiritual experience. The feeling that the drink problem has disappeared will often come strongly. We feel we are on the Broad Highway, walking hand in hand with the Spirit of the Universe.

Returning home we find a place where we can be quiet for an hour, carefully reviewing what we have done. We thank God from the bottom of our heart that we know Him better. Taking this book down from our shelf we turn to the page which contains the twelve steps. Carefully reading the first five proposals we ask if we have omitted anything, for we are building an arch through which we shall walk a free man at last. Is our work solid so far? Are the stones properly in place? Have we skimped on the cement put into the foundation? Have we tried to make mortar without sand?

If we can answer to our satisfaction, we then look at *Step Six.* We have emphasized willingness as being indispensable. Are we now ready to let God remove from us all the things which we have admitted are objectionable? Can He now take them all—every one? If we still cling to something we will not let go, we ask God to help us be willing.

When ready, we say something like this: "My Creator, I am now willing that you should have all of me, good and bad. I pray that you now remove from me every single defect of character which stands in the way of my usefulness to you and my fellows. Grant me strength, as I go out from here, to do your bidding. Amen." We have then completed *Step Seven.*

Now we need more action, without which we find that "Faith without works is dead." Let's look at *Steps Eight and Nine.* We have a list of all persons we have harmed and to whom we are willing to make amends. We made it when we took inventory. We subjected ourselves to a drastic self-appraisal. Now we go out to our fellows and repair the damage done in the past. We attempt to sweep away the debris which has accumulated out of our effort to live on self-will and run the show ourselves. If we haven't the will to do this, we ask until it comes. Remember it was agreed at the beginning *we would go to any lengths for victory over alcohol.*

Probably there are still some misgivings. As we look over the list of business acquaintances and friends we have hurt, we may feel diffident about going to some of them on a spiritual basis. Let us be reassured. To some people we need not, and probably should not emphasize the spiritual feature on our first approach.

We might prejudice them. At the moment we are trying to put our lives in order. But this is not an end in itself. Our real purpose is to fit ourselves to be of maximum service to God and the people about us. It is seldom wise to approach an individual, who still smarts from our injustice to him, and announce that we have gone religious. In the prize ring, this would be called leading with the chin. Why lay ourselves open to being branded fanatics or religious bores? We may kill a future opportunity to carry a beneficial message. But our man is sure to be impressed with a sincere desire to set right the wrong. He is going to be more interested in a demonstration of good will than in our talk of spiritual discoveries.

We don't use this as an excuse for shying away from the subject of God. When it will serve any good purpose, we are willing to announce our convictions with tact and common sense. The question of how to approach the man we hated will arise. It may be he has done us more harm than we have done him and, though we may have acquired a better attitude toward him, we are still not too keen about admitting our faults. Nevertheless, with a person we dislike, we take the bit in our teeth. It is harder to go to an enemy than to a friend, but we find it much more beneficial to us. We go to him in a helpful and forgiving spirit, confessing our former ill feeling and expressing our regret.

Under no condition do we criticize such a person or argue. Simply we tell him that we will never get over drinking until we have done our utmost to straighten out the past. We are there to sweep off our side of the street, realizing that nothing worth while can be accomplished until we do so, never trying to tell him what he should do. His faults are not discussed. We stick to our own. If our manner is calm, frank, and open, we will be gratified with the result.

In nine cases out of ten the unexpected happens. Sometimes the man we are calling upon admits his own fault, so feuds of years' standing melt away in an hour. Rarely do we fail to make satisfactory progress. Our former enemies sometimes praise what we are doing and wish us well. Occasionally, they will offer assistance. It should not matter, however, if someone does throw us out of his office. We have made our demonstration, done our part. It's water over the dam.

Most alcoholics owe money. We do not dodge our creditors. Telling them what we are trying to do, we make no bones about our drinking; they usually know it anyway, whether we think so or not. Nor are we afraid of disclosing our alcoholism on the theory it may cause financial harm. Approached in this way, the most ruthless creditor will sometimes surprise us. Arranging the best deal we can we let these people know we are sorry. Our drinking has made us slow to pay. We must lose our fear of creditors no matter how far we have to go, for we are liable to drink if we are afraid to face them.

Perhaps we have committed a criminal offense which might land us in jail if it were known to the authorities. We may be short in our accounts and unable to make good. We have already admitted this in confidence to another person, but we are sure we would be imprisoned or lose our job if it were known. Maybe it's only a petty offense such as padding the expense account. Most of us have done that sort of thing.

Maybe we are divorced, and have remarried but haven't kept up the alimony to number one. She is indignant about it, and has a warrant out for our arrest. That's a common form of trouble too.

Although these reparations take innumerable forms, there are some general principles which we find guiding. Reminding ourselves that we have decided to go to any lengths to find a spiritual experience, we ask that we be given strength and direction to do the right thing, no matter what the personal consequences may be. We may lose our position or reputation or face jail, but we are willing. We have to be. We must not shrink at anything.

Usually, however, other people are involved. Therefore, we are not to be the hasty and foolish martyr who would needlessly sacrifice others to save himself from the alcoholic pit. A man we know had remarried. Because of resentment and drinking, he had not paid alimony to his first wife. She was furious. She went to court and got an order for his arrest. He had commenced our way of life, had secured a position, and was getting his head above water. It would have been impressive heroics if he had walked up to the Judge and said, "Here I am."

We thought he ought to be willing to do that if necessary, but if he were in jail he could provide nothing for either family. We suggested he write his first wife admitting his faults and asking forgiveness. He did, and also sent a small amount of money. He told her what he would try to do in the future. He said he was perfectly willing to go to jail if she insisted. Of course she did not, and the whole situation has long since been adjusted.

Before taking drastic action which might implicate other people we secure their consent. If we have obtained permission, have consulted with others, asked God to help and the drastic step is indicated we must not shrink.

This brings to mind a story about one of our friends. While drinking, he accepted a sum of money from a bitterly-hated business rival, giving him no receipt for it. He subsequently denied having received the money and used the incident as a basis for discrediting the man. He thus used his own wrong-doing as a means of destroying the reputation of another. In fact, his rival was ruined.

He felt that he had done a wrong he could not possibly make right. If he opened that old affair, he was afraid it would destroy the reputation of his partner, disgrace his family and take away his means of livelihood. What right had he to involve those dependent upon him? How could he possibly make a public statement exonerating his rival?

After consulting with his wife and partner he came to the conclusion that is was better to take those risks than to stand before his Creator guilty of such ruinous slander. He saw that he had to place the outcome in God's hands or he would soon start drinking again, and all would be lost anyhow. He attended church for the first time in many years. After the sermon, he quietly got up and made an explanation. His action met wide-spread approval, and today he is one of the most trusted citizens of his town. This all happened years ago.

The chances are that we have domestic troubles. Perhaps we are mixed up with women in a fashion we wouldn't care to have advertised. We doubt if, in this respect, alcoholics are fundamentally much worse than other people. But drinking does complicate sex relations in the home. After a few years with an alcoholic, a wife gets worn out, resentful and uncommunicative. How could she be anything else? The husband begins to feel lonely, sorry for himself. He commences to look around in the night clubs, or their equivalent, for something besides liquor. Perhaps he is having a secret and exciting affair with "the girl who understands." In fairness we must say that she may understand, but what are we going to do about a thing like that? A man so involved often feels very remorseful at times, especially if he is married to a loyal and courageous girl who has literally gone through hell for him.

Whatever the situation, we usually have to do something about it. If we are sure our wife does not know, should we tell her? Not always, we think. If she knows in a general way that we have been wild, should we tell her in detail? Undoubtedly we should admit our fault. She may insist on knowing all the particulars. She will want to know who the woman is and where she is. We feel we ought to say to her that we have no right to involve another person. We are sorry for what we have done and, God willing, it shall not be repeated. More than that we cannot do; we have no right to go further. Though there may be justifiable exceptions, and though we wish to lay down no rule of any sort, we have often found this the best course to take.

Our design for living is not a one-way street. It is as good for the wife as for the husband. If we can forget, so can she. It is better, however, that one does not needlessly name a person upon whom she can vent jealousy.

Perhaps there are some cases where the utmost frankness is demanded. No outsider can appraise such an intimate situation. It may be that both will decide that the way of good sense and loving kindness is to let bygones be by-gones. Each might pray about it, having the other one's happiness uppermost in mind. Keep it always in sight that we are dealing with that most terrible human emotion-jealousy. Good generalship may decide that the problem be attacked on the flank rather than risk a face-to-face combat.

If we have no such complication, there is plenty we should do at home. Sometimes we hear an alcoholic say that the only thing he needs to do is to keep sober. Certainly he must keep sober, for there will be no home if he doesn't. But he is yet a long way from making good to the wife or parents whom for years he has so shockingly treated. Passing all understanding is the patience mothers and wives have had with alcoholics. Had this not been so, many of us would have no homes today, would perhaps be dead.

The alcoholic is like a tornado roaring his way through the lives of others. Hearts are broken. Sweet relationships are dead. Affections have been uprooted. Selfish and inconsiderate habits have kept the home in turmoil. We feel a man is unthinking when he says that sobriety is enough. He is like the farmer who came up out of his cyclone cellar to find his home ruined. To his wife, he remarked, "Don't see anything the matter here, Ma. Ain't it grand the wind stopped blowin'?"

Yes, there is a long period of reconstruction ahead. We must take the lead. A remorseful mumbling that we are sorry won't fill the bill at all. We ought to sit down with the family and frankly analyze the past as we now see it, being very careful not to criticize them. Their defects may be glaring, but the chances are that our own actions are partly responsible. So we clean house with the family, asking each morning in meditation that our Creator show us the way of patience, tolerance, kindliness and love.

The spiritual life is not a theory. *We have to live it.* Unless one's family expresses a desire to live upon spiritual principles we think we ought not to urge them. We should not talk incessantly to them about spiritual matters. They will change in time. Our behavior will convince them more than our words. We must remember that ten or twenty years of drunkenness would make a skeptic out of anyone.

There may be some wrongs we can never fully right. We don't worry about them if we can honestly say to ourselves that we would right them if we could. Some people cannot be seen—we send them an honest letter. And there may be a valid reason for postponement in some cases. But we don't delay if it can be avoided. We should be sensible, tactful, considerate and humble without being servile or scraping. As God's people we stand on our feet; we don't crawl before anyone.

If we are painstaking about this phase of our development, we will be amazed before we are half way through. We are going to know a new freedom and a new happiness. We will not regret the past nor wish to shut the door on it. We will comprehend the word serenity and we will know peace. No matter how far down the scale we have gone, we will see how our experience can benefit others. That feeling of uselessness and self-pity will disappear. We will lose interest in selfish things and gain interest in our fellows. Self-seeking will slip away. Our whole attitude and outlook upon life will change. Fear of people and of economic insecurity will leave us. We will intuitively know how to handle situations which used to baffle us. We will suddenly realize that God is doing for us what we could not do for ourselves.

Are these extravagant promises? We think not. They are being fulfilled among us—sometimes quickly, sometimes slowly. They will always materialize if we work for them.

This thought brings us to *Step Ten*, which suggests we continue to take personal inventory and continue to set right any new mistakes as we go along. We vigorously commenced this way of living as we cleaned up the past. We have entered the world of the Spirit. Our next function is to grow in understanding and effectiveness. This is not an overnight matter. It should continue for our lifetime. Continue to watch for selfishness, dishonesty, resentment, and fear. When these crop up, we ask God at once to remove them. We discuss them with someone immediately and make amends quickly if we have harmed anyone. Then we resolutely turn our thoughts to someone we can help. Love and tolerance of others is our code.

And we have ceased fighting anything or anyone—even alcohol. For by this time sanity will have returned. We will seldom be interested in liquor. If tempted, we recoil from it as from a hot flame. We react sanely and normally, and we will find that this has happened automatically. We will see that our new attitude toward liquor has been given us without any thought or effort on our part. It just comes! That is the miracle of it. We are not fighting it, neither are we avoiding temptation. We feel as though we had been placed in a position of neutrality—safe and protected. We have not even sworn off. Instead, the problem has been removed. It does not exist for us. We are neither cocky nor are we afraid. That is our experience. That is how we react so long as we keep in fit spiritual condition.

It is easy to let up on the spiritual program of action and rest on our laurels. We are headed for trouble if we do, for alcohol is a subtle foe. We are not cured of alcoholism. What we really have is a daily reprieve contingent on the maintenance of our spiritual condition. Every day is a day when we must carry the vision of God's will into all of our activities. "How can I best serve Thee—Thy will (not mine) be done." These are thoughts which must go with us constantly. We can exercise our will power along this line all we wish. It is the proper use of the will.

Much has already been said about receiving strength, inspiration, and direction from Him who has all knowledge and power. If we have carefully followed directions, we have begun to sense the flow of His Spirit into us. To some extent we have become God-conscious. We have begun to develop this vital sixth sense. But we must go further and that means more action.

Step Eleven suggests prayer and meditation. We shouldn't be shy on this matter of prayer. Better men than we are using it constantly. It works, if we have the proper attitude and work at it. It would be easy to be vague about this matter. Yet, we believe we can make some definite and valuable suggestions.

When we retire at night, we constructively review our day. Were we resentful, selfish, dishonest or afraid? Do we owe an apology? Have we kept something to ourselves which should be discussed with another person at once? Were we kind and loving toward all? What could we have done better? Were we thinking of ourselves most of the time? Or were we thinking of what we could do for others, of what we could pack into the stream of life? But we must be careful not to drift into worry, remorse or morbid reflection, for that would diminish our usefulness to others. After making our review we ask God's forgiveness and inquire what corrective measures should be taken.

On awakening let us think about the twenty-four hours ahead. We consider our plans for the day. Before we begin, we ask God to direct our thinking, especially asking that it be divorced from self-pity, dishonest or self-seeking motives. Under these conditions we can employ our mental faculties with assurance, for after all God gave us brains to use. Our thought-life will be placed on a much higher plane when our thinking is cleared of wrong motives.

In thinking about our day we may face indecision. We may not be able to determine which course to take. Here we ask God for inspiration, an intuitive thought or a decision. We relax and take it easy. We don't struggle. We are often surprised how the right answers come after we have tried this for a while.

What used to be the hunch or the occasional inspiration gradually becomes a working part of the mind. Being still inexperienced and having just made conscious contact with God, it is not probable that we are going to be inspired at all times. We might pay for this presumption in all sorts of absurd actions and ideas. Nevertheless, we find that our thinking will, as time passes, be more and more on the plane of inspiration. We come to rely upon it.

We usually conclude the period of meditation with a prayer that we be shown all through the day what our next step is to be, that we be given whatever we need to take care of such problems. We ask especially for freedom from self-will, and are careful to make no request for ourselves only. We may ask for ourselves, however, if others will be helped. We are careful never to pray for our own selfish ends. Many of us have wasted a lot of time doing that and it doesn't work. You can easily see why.

If circumstances warrant, we ask our wives or friends to join us in morning meditation. If we belong to a religious denomination which requires a definite morning devotion, we attend to that also. If not members of religious bodies, we sometimes select and memorize a few set prayers which emphasize the principles we have been discussing. There are many helpful books also. Suggestions about these may be obtained from one's priest, minister, or rabbi. Be quick to see where religious people are right. Make use of what they offer.

As we go through the day we pause, when agitated or doubtful, and ask for the right thought or action. We constantly remind ourselves we are no longer running the show, humbly saying to ourselves many times each day "Thy will be done." We are then in much less danger of excitement, fear, anger, worry, self-pity, or foolish decisions. We become much more efficient. We do not tire so easily, for we are not burning up energy foolishly as we did when we were trying to arrange life to suit ourselves.

It works—it really does.

We alcoholics are undisciplined. So we let God discipline us in the simple way we have just outlined.

But this is not all. There is action and more action. "Faith without works is dead." The next chapter is entirely devoted to *Step Twelve.*

Chapter 7

WORKING WITH OTHERS

PRACTICAL EXPERIENCE shows that nothing will so much insure immunity from drinking as intensive work with other alcoholics. It works when other activities fail. This is our *twelfth suggestion*: Carry this message to other alcoholics! You can help when no one else can. You can secure their confidence when others fail. Remember they are very ill.

Life will take on new meaning. To watch people recover, to see them help others, to watch loneliness vanish, to see a fellowship grow up about you, to have a host of friends—this is an experience you must not miss. We know you will not want to miss it. Frequent contact with newcomers and with each other is the bright spot of our lives.

Perhaps you are not acquainted with any drinkers who want to recover. You can easily find some by asking a few doctors, ministers, priests or hospitals. They will be only too glad to assist you. Don't start out as an evangelist or reformer. Unfortunately a lot of prejudice exists. You will be handicapped if you arouse it. Ministers and doctors are competent and you can learn much from them if you wish, but it happens that because of your own drinking experience you can be uniquely useful to other alcoholics. So cooperate; never criticize. To be helpful is our only aim.

When you discover a prospect for Alcoholics Anonymous, find out all you can about him. If he does not want to stop drinking, don't waste time trying to persuade him. You may spoil a later opportunity. This advice is given for his family also. They should be patient, realizing they are dealing with a sick person.

If there is any indication that he wants to stop, have a good talk with the person most interested in him—usually his wife. Get an idea of his behavior, his problems, his background, the seriousness of his condition, and his religious leanings. You need this information to put yourself in his place, to see how you would like him to approach you if the tables were turned.

Sometimes it is wise to wait till he goes on a binge. The family may object to this, but unless he is in a dangerous physical condition, it is better to risk it. Don't deal with him when he is very drunk, unless he is ugly and the family needs your help. Wait for the end of the spree, or at least for a lucid interval. Then let his family or a friend ask him if he wants to quit for good and if he would go to any extreme to do so. If he says yes, then his attention should be drawn to you as a person who has recovered. You should be described to him as one of a fellowship who, as part of their own recovery, try to help others and who will be glad to talk to him if he cares to see you.

If he does not want to see you, never force yourself upon him. Neither should the family hysterically plead with him to do anything, nor should they tell him much about you. They should wait for the end of his next drinking bout. You might place this book where he can see it in the interval. Here no specific rule can be given. The family must decide these things. But urge them not to be over-anxious, for that might spoil matters.

Usually the family should not try to tell your story. When possible, avoid meeting a man through his family. Approach through a doctor or an institution is a better bet. If your man needs hospitalization, he should have it, but not forcibly unless he is violent. Let the doctor, if he will, tell him he has something in the way of a solution.

When your man is better, the doctor might suggest a visit from you. Though you have talked with the family, leave them out of the first discussion. Under these conditions your prospect will see he is under no pressure. He will feel he can deal with you without being nagged by his family. Call on him while he is still jittery. He may be more receptive when depressed.

See your man alone, if possible. At first engage in general conversation. After a while, turn the talk to some phase of drinking. Tell him enough about your drinking habits, symptoms, and experiences to encourage him to speak of himself. If he wishes to talk, let him do so. You will thus get a better idea of how you ought to proceed. If he is not communicative, give him a sketch of your drinking career up to the time you quit. But say nothing, for the moment, of how that was accomplished. If he is in a serious mood dwell on the troubles liquor has caused you, being careful not to moralize or lecture. If his mood is light, tell him humorous stories of your escapades. Get him to tell some of his.

When he sees you know all about the drinking game, commence to describe yourself as an alcoholic.

Tell him how baffled you were, how you finally learned that you were sick. Give him an account of the struggles you made to stop. Show him the mental twist which leads to the first drink of a spree. We suggest you do this as we have done it in the chapter on alcoholism. If he is alcoholic, he will understand you at once. He will match your mental inconsistencies with some of his own.

If you are satisfied that he is a real alcoholic, begin to dwell on the hopeless feature of the malady. Show him, from your own experience, how the queer mental condition surrounding that first drink prevents normal functioning of the will power. Don't, at this stage, refer to this book, unless he has seen it and wishes to discuss it. And be careful not to brand him as an alcoholic. Let him draw his own conclusion. If he sticks to the idea that he can still control his drinking, tell him that possibly he can—if he is not too alcoholic. But insist that if he is severely afflicted, there may be little chance he can recover by himself.

Continue to speak of alcoholism as an illness, a fatal malady. Talk about the conditions of body and mind which accompany it. Keep his attention focused mainly on your personal experience. Explain that many are doomed who never realize their predicament. Doctors are rightly loath to tell alcoholic patients the whole story unless it will serve some good purpose. But you may talk to him about the hopelessness of alcoholism because you offer a solution. You will soon have your friend admitting he has many, if not all, of the traits of the alcoholic. If his own doctor is willing to tell him that he is alcoholic, so much the better. Even though your protégé may not have entirely admitted his condition, he has become very curious to know how you got well. Let him ask you that question, if he will. *Tell him exactly what happened to you.* Stress the spiritual feature freely. If the man be agnostic or atheist, make it emphatic that *he does not have to agree with your conception of God.* He can choose any conception he likes, provided it makes sense to him. *The main thing is that he be willing to believe in a Power greater than himself and that he live by spiritual principles.*

When dealing with such a person, you had better use everyday language to describe spiritual principles. There is no use arousing any prejudice he may have against certain theological terms and conceptions about which he may already be confused. Don't raise such issues, no matter what your own convictions are.

Your prospect may belong to a religious denomination. His religious education and training may be far superior to yours. In that case he is going to wonder how you can add anything to what he already knows. But he will be curious to learn why his own convictions have not worked and why yours seem to work so well. He may be an example of the truth that faith alone is insufficient. To be vital, faith must be accompanied by self sacrifice and unselfish, constructive action. Let him see that you are not there to instruct him in religion. Admit that he probably knows more about it than you do, but call to his attention the fact that however deep his faith and knowledge, he could not have applied it or he would not drink. Perhaps your story will help him see where he has failed to practice the very precepts he knows so well. We represent no particular faith or denomination. We are dealing only with general principles common to most denominations.

Outline the program of action, explaining how you made a self-appraisal, how you straightened out your past and why you are now endeavoring to be helpful to him. It is important for him to realize that your attempt to pass this on to him plays a vital part in your own recovery. Actually, he may be helping you more than you are helping him. Make it plain he is under no obligation to you, that you hope only that he will try to help other alcoholics when he escapes his own difficulties. Suggest how important it is that he place the welfare of other people ahead of his own. Make it clear that he is not under pressure, that he needn't see you again if he doesn't want to. You should not be offended if he wants to call it off, for he has helped you more than you have helped him. If your talk has been sane, quiet and full of human understanding, you have perhaps made a friend. Maybe you have disturbed him about the question of alcoholism. This is all to the good. The more hopeless he feels, the better. He will be more likely to follow your suggestions.

Your candidate may give reasons why he need not follow all of the program. He may rebel at the thought of a drastic housecleaning which requires discussion with other people. Do not contradict such views. Tell him you once felt as he does, but you doubt whether you would have made much progress had you not taken action. On your first visit tell him about the Fellowship of Alcoholics Anonymous. If he shows interest, lend him your copy of this book.

Unless your friend wants to talk further about himself, do not wear out your welcome. Give him a chance to think it over. If you do stay, let him steer the conversation in any direction he likes. Sometimes a new man is anxious to proceed at once. And you may be tempted to let him do so. This is sometimes a mistake. If he has trouble later, he is likely to say you rushed him. You will be most successful with alcoholics if you do not exhibit any passion for crusade or reform. Never talk down to an alcoholic from any moral or spiritual hilltop; simply lay out the kit of spiritual tools for his inspection. Show him how they worked with you. Offer him friendship and fellowship. Tell him that if he wants to get well you will do anything to help.

If he is not interested in your solution, if he expects you to act only as a banker for his financial difficulties or a nurse for his sprees, you may have to drop him until he changes his mind. This he may do after he gets hurt some more.

If he is sincerely interested and wants to see you again, ask him to read this book in the interval. After doing that, he must decide for himself whether he wants to go on. He should not be pushed or prodded by you, his wife, or his friends. If he is to find God, the desire must come from within.

If he thinks he can do the job in some other way, or prefers some other spiritual approach, encourage him to follow his own conscience. We have no monopoly on God; we merely have an approach that worked with us. But point out that we alcoholics have much in common and that you would like, in any case, to be friendly. Let it go at that.

Do not be discouraged if your prospect does not respond at once. Search out another alcoholic and try again. You are sure to find someone desperate enough to accept with eagerness what you offer. We find it a waste of time to keep chasing a man who cannot or will not work with you. If you leave such a person alone, he may soon become convinced that he cannot recover by himself. To spend too much time on any one situation is to deny some other alcoholic an opportunity to live and be happy. One of our Fellowship failed entirely with his first half dozen prospects. He often says that if he had continued to work on them, he might have deprived many others, who have since recovered, of their chance.

Suppose now you are making your second visit to a man. He has read this volume and says he is prepared to go through with the Twelve Steps of the program of recovery. Having had the experience yourself, you can give him much practical advice. Let him know you are available if he wishes to make a decision and tell his story, but do not insist upon it if he prefers to consult someone else.

He may be broke and homeless. If he is, you might try to help him about getting a job, or give him a little financial assistance. But you should not deprive your family or creditors of money they should have. Perhaps you will want to take the man into your home for a few days. But be sure you use discretion. Be certain he will be welcomed by your family, and that he is not trying to impose upon you for money, connections, or shelter. Permit that and you only harm him. You will be making it possible for him to be insincere.

You may be aiding in his destruction rather than his recovery.

Never avoid these responsibilities, but be sure you are doing the right thing if you assume them. Helping others is the foundation stone of your recovery. A kindly act once in a while isn't enough. You have to act the Good Samaritan every day, if need be. It may mean the loss of many nights' sleep, great interference with your pleasures, interruptions to your business. It may mean sharing your money and your home, counseling frantic wives and relatives, innumerable trips to police courts, sanitariums, hospitals, jails and asylums. Your telephone may jangle at any time of the day or night. Your wife may sometimes say she is neglected. A drunk may smash the furniture in your home, or burn a mattress. You may have to fight with him if he is violent. Sometimes you will have to call a doctor and administer sedatives under his direction. Another time you may have to send for the police or an ambulance. Occasionally you will have to meet such conditions.

We seldom allow an alcoholic to live in our homes for long at a time. It is not good for him, and it sometimes creates serious complications in a family.

Though an alcoholic does not respond, there is no reason why you should neglect his family. You should continue to be friendly to them. The family should be offered your way of life. Should they accept and practice spiritual principles, there is a much better chance that the head of the family will recover. And even though he continues to drink, the family will find life more bearable.

For the type of alcoholic who is able and willing to

get well, little charity, in the ordinary sense of the word, is needed or wanted. The men who cry for money and shelter before conquering alcohol, are on the wrong track. Yet we do go to great extremes to provide each other with these very things, when such action is warranted. This may seem inconsistent, but we think it is not.

It is not the matter of giving that is in question, but when and how to give. That often makes the difference between failure and success. The minute we put our work on a service plane, the alcoholic commences to rely upon our assistance rather than upon God. He clamors for this or that, claiming he cannot master alcohol until his material needs are cared for. Nonsense. Some of us have taken very hard knocks to learn this truth: Job or no job—wife or no wife—we simply do not stop drinking so long as we place dependence upon other people ahead of dependence on God.

Burn the idea into the consciousness of every man that he can get well regardless of anyone. The only condition is that he trust in God and clean house.

Now, the domestic problem: There may be divorce, separation, or just strained relations. When your prospect has made such reparation as he can to his family, and has thoroughly explained to them the new principles by which he is living, he should proceed to put those principles into action at home. That is, if he is lucky enough to have a home. Though his family be at fault in many respects, he should not be concerned about that. He should concentrate on his own spiritual demonstration. Argument and fault-finding are to be avoided like the plague. In many homes this is a difficult thing to do, but it must be done if any results are to be expected. If persisted in for a few months, the effect on a man's family is sure to be great. The most incompatible people discover they have a basis upon which they can meet. Little by little the family may see their own defects and admit them. These can then be discussed in an atmosphere of helpfulness and friendliness.

After they have seen tangible results, the family will perhaps want to go along. These things will come to pass naturally and in good time provided, however, the alcoholic continues to demonstrate that he can be sober, considerate, and helpful, regardless of what anyone says or does. Of course, we all fall much below this standard many times. But we must try to repair the damage immediately lest we pay the penalty by a spree.

If there be divorce or separation, there should be no undue haste for the couple to get together. The man should be sure of his recovery. The wife should fully understand his new way of life. If their old relationship is to be resumed it must be on a better basis, since the former did not work. This means a new attitude and spirit all around. Sometimes it is to the best interest of all concerned that a couple remain apart. Obviously, no rule can be laid down. Let the alcoholic continue his program day by day. When the time for living together has come, it will be apparent to both parties.

Let no alcoholic say he cannot recover unless he has his family back. This just isn't so. In some cases the wife will never come back for one reason or another. Remind the prospect that his recovery is not dependent upon people. It is dependent upon his relationship with God. We have seen men get well whose families have not returned at all. We have seen others slip when the family came back too soon.

Both you and the new man must walk day by day in the path of spiritual progress. If you persist, remarkable things will happen. When we look back, we realize that the things which came to us when we put ourselves in God's hands were better than anything we could have planned. Follow the dictates of a Higher Power and you will presently live in a new and wonderful world, no matter what your present circumstances!

When working with a man and his family, you should take care not to participate in their quarrels. You may spoil your chance of being helpful if you do. But urge upon a man's family that he has been a very sick person and should be treated accordingly. You should warn against arousing resentment or jealousy. You should point out that his defects of character are not going to disappear over night. Show them that he has entered upon a period of growth. Ask them to remember, when they are impatient, the blessed fact of his sobriety.

If you have been successful in solving your own domestic problems, tell the newcomer's family how that was accomplished. In this way you can set them on the right track without becoming critical of them. The story of how you and your wife settled your difficulties is worth any amount of criticism.

Assuming we are spiritually fit, we can do all sorts of things alcoholics are not supposed to do. People have said we must not go where liquor is served; we must not have it in our homes; we must shun friends who drink; we must avoid moving pictures which show drinking scenes; we must not go into bars; our friends must hide their bottles if we go to their houses; we mustn't think or be reminded about alcohol at all. Our experience shows that this is not necessarily so.

We meet these conditions every day. An alcoholic who cannot meet them, still has an alcoholic mind; there is something the matter with his spiritual status. His only chance for sobriety would be some place like the Greenland Ice Cap, and even there an Eskimo might turn up with a bottle of scotch and ruin everything! Ask any woman who has sent her husband to distant places on the theory he would escape the alcohol problem.

In our belief any scheme of combating alcoholism which proposes to shield the sick man from temptation is doomed to failure. If the alcoholic tries to shield himself he may succeed for a time, but he usually winds up with a bigger explosion than ever. We have tried these methods. These attempts to do the impossible have always failed.

So our rule is not to avoid a place where there is drinking, *if we have a legitimate reason for being there.* That includes bars, nightclubs, dances, receptions, weddings, even plain ordinary whoopee parties. To a person who has had experience with an alcoholic, this may seem like tempting Providence, but it isn't.

You will note that we made an important qualification. Therefore, ask yourself on each occasion, "Have I any good social, business, or personal reason for going to this place? Or am I expecting to steal a little vicarious pleasure from the atmosphere of such places?" If you answer these questions satisfactorily, you need have no apprehension. Go or stay away, whichever seems best. But be sure you are on solid spiritual ground before you start and that your motive in going is thoroughly good. Do not think of what you will get out of the occasion. Think of what you can bring to it. But if you are shaky, you had better work with another alcoholic instead!

Why sit with a long face in places where there is drinking, sighing about the good old days. If it is a happy occasion, try to increase the pleasure of those there; if a business occasion, go and attend to your business enthusiastically. If you are with a person who wants to eat in a bar, by all means go along. Let your friends know they are not to change their habits on your account. At a proper time and place explain to all your friends why alcohol disagrees with you. If you do this thoroughly, few people will ask you to drink. While you were drinking, you were withdrawing from life little by little. Now you are getting back into the social life of this world. Don't start to withdraw again just because your friends drink liquor.

Your job now is to be at the place where you may be of maximum helpfulness to others, so never hesitate to go anywhere if you can be helpful. You should not hesitate to visit the most sordid spot on earth on such an errand. Keep on the firing line of life with these motives and God will keep you unharmed.

Many of us keep liquor in our homes. We often need it to carry green recruits through a severe hangover Some of us still serve it to our friends provided they are not alcoholic. But some of us think we should not serve liquor to anyone. We never argue this question. We feel that each family, in the light of their own circumstances, ought to decide for themselves.

We are careful never to show intolerance or hatred of drinking as an institution. Experience shows that such an attitude is not helpful to anyone. Every new alcoholic looks for this spirit among us and is immensely relieved when he finds we are not witch burners. A spirit of intolerance might repel alcoholics whose lives could have been saved, had it not been for such stupidity. We would not even do the cause of temperate drinking any good, for not one drinker in a thousand likes to be told anything about alcohol by one who hates it.

Some day we hope that Alcoholics Anonymous will help the public to a better realization of the gravity of the alcoholic problem, but we shall be of little use if our attitude is one of bitterness or hostility. Drinkers will not stand for it.

After all, our problems were of our own making. Bottles were only a symbol. Besides, we have stopped fighting anybody or anything. We have to!

Chapter 8

TO WIVES

WITH FEW EXCEPTIONS, our book thus far has spoken of men. But what we have said applies quite as much to women. Our activities in behalf of women who drink are on the increase. There is every evidence that women regain their health as readily as men if they try our suggestions.

But for every man who drinks others are involved—the wife who trembles in fear of the next debauch; the mother and father who see their son wasting away.

Among us are wives, relatives and friends whose problem has been solved, as well as some who have not yet found a happy solution. We want the wives of Alcoholics Anonymous to address the wives of men who drink too much. What they say will apply to nearly everyone bound by ties of blood or affection to an alcoholic.

As wives of Alcoholics Anonymous, we would like you to feel that we understand as perhaps few can. We want to analyze mistakes we have made. We want to leave you with the feeling that no situation is too difficult and no unhappiness too great to be overcome.

We have traveled a rocky road, there is no mistake about that. We have had long rendezvous with hurt pride, frustration, self-pity, misunderstanding and fear. These are not pleasant companions. We have been driven to maudlin sympathy, to bitter resentment. Some of us veered from extreme to extreme, ever hoping that one day our loved ones would be themselves once more.

Our loyalty and the desire that our husbands hold up their heads and be like other men have begotten all sorts of predicaments. We have been unselfish and self-sacrificing. We have told innumerable lies to protect our pride and our husbands' reputations. We have prayed, we have begged, we have been patient. We have struck out viciously. We have run away. We have been hysterical. We have been terror stricken. We have sought sympathy. We have had retaliatory love affairs with other men.

Our homes have been battle-grounds many an evening. In the morning we have kissed and made up. Our friends have counseled chucking the men and we have done so with finality, only to be back in a little while hoping, always hoping. Our men have sworn great solemn oaths that they were through drinking forever. We have believed them when no one else could or would. Then, in days, weeks, or months, a fresh outburst.

We seldom had friends at our homes, never knowing how or when the men of the house would appear. We could make few social engagements. We came to live almost alone. When we were invited out, our husbands sneaked so many drinks that they spoiled the occasion. If, on the other hand, they took nothing, their self-pity made them killjoys.

There was never financial security. Positions were always in jeopardy or gone. An armored car could not have brought the pay envelopes home. The checking account melted like snow in June.

Sometimes there were other women. How heartbreaking was this discovery; how cruel to be told they understood our men as we did not!

The bill collectors, the sheriffs, the angry taxi drivers, the policemen, the bums, the pals, and even the ladies they sometimes brought home—our husbands thought we were so inhospitable. "Joykiller, nag, wet blanket"—that's what they said. Next day they would be themselves again and we would forgive and try to forget.

We have tried to hold the love of our children for their father. We have told small tots that father was sick, which was much nearer the truth than we realized. They struck the children, kicked out door panels, smashed treasured crockery, and ripped the keys out of pianos. In the midst of such pandemonium they may have rushed out threatening to live with the other woman forever. In desperation, we have even got tight ourselves—the drunk to end all drunks. The unexpected result was that our husbands seemed to like it.

Perhaps at this point we got a divorce and took the children home to father and mother. Then we were severely criticized by our husband's parents for desertion. Usually we did not leave. We stayed on and on. We finally sought employment ourselves as destitution faced us and our families.

We began to ask medical advice as the sprees got closer together. The alarming physical and mental symptoms, the deepening pall of remorse, depression and inferiority that settled down on our loved ones—

these things terrified and distracted us. As animals on a treadmill, we have patiently and wearily climbed, falling back in exhaustion after each futile effort to reach solid ground. Most of us have entered the final stage with its commitment to health resorts, sanitariums, hospitals, and jails. Sometimes there were screaming delirium and insanity. Death was often near.

Under these conditions we naturally made mistakes. Some of them rose out of ignorance of alcoholism. Sometimes we sensed dimly that we were dealing with sick men. Had we fully understood the nature of the alcoholic illness, we might have behaved differently.

How could men who loved their wives and children be so unthinking, so callous, so cruel? There could be no love in such persons, we thought. And just as we were being convinced of their heartlessness, they would surprise us with fresh resolves and new attentions. For a while they would be their old sweet selves, only to dash the new structure of affection to pieces once more. Asked why they commenced to drink again, they would reply with some silly excuse, or none. It was so baffling, so heartbreaking. Could we have been so mistaken in the men we married? When drinking, they were strangers. Sometimes they were so inaccessible that it seemed as though a great wall had been built around them.

And even if they did not love their families, how could they be so blind about themselves? What had become of their judgment, their common sense, their will power? Why could they not see that drink meant ruin to them? Why was it, when these dangers were pointed out that they agreed, and then got drunk again immediately?

These are some of the questions which race through the mind of every woman who has an alcoholic husband. We hope this book has answered some of them. Perhaps your husband has been living in that strange world of alcoholism where everything is distorted and exaggerated. You can see that he really does love you with his better self. Of course, there is such a thing as incompatibility, but in nearly every instance the alcoholic only seems to be unloving and inconsiderate; it is usually because he is warped and sickened that he says and does these appalling things. Today most of our men are better husbands and fathers than ever before.

Try not to condemn your alcoholic husband no matter what he says or does. He is just another very sick, unreasonable person. Treat him, when you can, as though he had pneumonia. When he angers you, remember that he is very ill.

There is an important exception to the foregoing. We realize some men are thoroughly bad-intentioned, that no amount of patience will make any difference. An alcoholic of this temperament may be quick to use this chapter as a club over your head. Don't let him get away with it. If you are positive he is one of this type you may feel you had better leave. Is it right to let him ruin your life and the lives of your children? Especially when he has before him a way to stop his drinking and abuse if he really wants to pay the price.

The problem with which you struggle usually falls within one of four categories:

One: Your husband may be only a heavy drinker.

His drinking may be constant or it may be heavy only on certain occasions. Perhaps he spends too much money for liquor. It may be slowing him up mentally and physically, but he does not see it. Sometimes he is a source of embarrassment to you and his friends. He is positive he can handle his liquor, that it does him no harm, that drinking is necessary in his business. He would probably be insulted if he were called an alcoholic. This world is full of people like him. Some will moderate or stop altogether, and some will not. Of those who keep on, a good number will become true alcoholics after a while.

Two: Your husband is showing lack of control, for he is unable to stay on the water wagon even when he wants to. He often gets entirely out of hand when drinking. He admits this is true, but is positive that he will do better. He has begun to try, with or without your cooperation, various means of moderating or staying dry. Maybe he is beginning to lose his friends. His business may suffer somewhat. He is worried at times, and is becoming aware that he cannot drink like other people. He sometimes drinks in the morning and through the day also, to hold his nervousness in check. He is remorseful after serious drinking bouts and tells you he wants to stop. But when he gets over the spree, he begins to think once more how he can drink moderately next time. We think this person is in danger. These are the earmarks of a real alcoholic. Perhaps he can still tend to business fairly well. He has by no means ruined everything. As we say among ourselves, *"He wants to want to stop."*

Three: This husband has gone much further than husband number two. Though once like number two he became worse. His friends have slipped away, his home is a near-wreck and he cannot hold a position. Maybe the doctor has been called in, and the weary round of sanitariums and hospitals has begun. He admits he cannot drink like other people, but does not see why. He clings to the notion that he will yet find a way to do so. He may have come to the point where he desperately wants to stop but cannot. His case presents additional questions which we shall try to answer for you. You can be quite hopeful of a situation like this.

Four: You may have a husband of whom you completely despair. He has been placed in one institution after another. He is violent, or appears definitely insane when drunk. Sometimes he drinks on the way home from the hospital. Perhaps he has had delirium tremens. Doctors may shake their heads and advise you to have him committed. Maybe you have already been obliged to put him away. This picture may not be as dark as it looks. Many of our husbands were just as far gone. Yet they got well.

Let's now go back to husband number one. Oddly enough, he is often difficult to deal with. He enjoys drinking. It stirs his imagination. His friends feel closer over a highball. Perhaps you enjoy drinking with him yourself when he doesn't go too far. You have passed happy evenings together chatting and drinking before your fire. Perhaps you both like parties which would be dull without liquor. We have enjoyed such evenings ourselves; we had a good time. We know all about liquor as a social lubricant. Some, but not all of us, think it has its advantages when reasonably used.

The first principle of success is that you should never be angry. Even though your husband becomes unbearable and you have to leave him temporarily, you should, if you can, go without rancor. Patience and good temper are most necessary.

Our next thought is that you should never tell him what he must do about his drinking. If he gets the idea that you are a nag or killjoy, your chance of accomplishing anything useful may be zero. He will use that as an excuse to drink more. He will tell you he is misunderstood. This may lead to lonely evenings for you. He may seek someone else to console him—not always another man.

Be determined that your husband's drinking is not going to spoil your relations with your children or your friends. They need your companionship and your help. It is possible to have a full and useful life, though your husband continues to drink. We know women who are unafraid, even happy under these conditions. Do not set your heart on reforming your husband. You may be unable to do so, no matter how hard you try.

We know these suggestions are sometimes difficult to follow, but you will save many a heartbreak if you can succeed in observing them. Your husband may come to appreciate your reasonableness and patience. This may lay the groundwork for a friendly talk about his alcoholic problem. Try to have him bring up the subject himself. Be sure you are not critical during such a discussion. Attempt instead, to put yourself in his place. Let him see that you want to be helpful rather than critical.

When a discussion does arise, you might suggest he

read this book or at least the chapter on alcoholism. Tell him you have been worried, though perhaps needlessly. You think he ought to know the subject better, as everyone should have a clear understanding of the risk he takes if he drinks too much. Show him you have confidence in his power to stop or moderate. Say you do not want to be a wet blanket; that you only want him to take care of his health. Thus you may succeed in interesting him in alcoholism.

He probably has several alcoholics among his own acquaintances. You might suggest that you both take an interest in them. Drinkers like to help other drinkers. Your husband may be willing to talk to one of them.

If this kind of approach does not catch your husband's interest, it may be best to drop the subject, but after a friendly talk your husband will usually revive the topic himself. This may take patient waiting, but it will be worth it. Meanwhile you might try to help the wife of another serious drinker. If you act upon these principles, your husband may stop or moderate.

Suppose, however, that your husband fits the description of number two. The same principles which apply to husband number one should be practiced. But after his next binge, ask him if he would really like to get over drinking for good. Do not ask that he do it for you or anyone else. Just would he *like* to?

The chances are he would. Show him your copy of this book and tell him what you have found out about alcoholism. Show him that as alcoholics, the writers of the book understand. Tell him some of the interesting stories you have read. If you think he will be shy of a spiritual remedy, ask him to look at the chapter on alcoholism. Then perhaps he will be interested enough to continue.

If he is enthusiastic your cooperation will mean a great deal. If he is lukewarm or thinks he is not an alcoholic, we suggest you leave him alone. Avoid urging him to follow our program. The seed has been planted in his mind. He knows that thousands of men, much like himself, have recovered. But don't remind him of this after he had been drinking, for he may be angry. Sooner or later, you are likely to find him reading the book once more. Wait until repeated stumbling convinces him he must act, for the more you hurry him the longer his recovery may be delayed.

If you have a number three husband, you may be in luck. Being certain he wants to stop, you can go to him with this volume as joyfully as though you had struck oil. He may not share your enthusiasm, but he is practically sure to read the book and he may go for the program at once. If he does not, you will probably not have long to wait. Again, you should not crowd him. Let him decide for himself. Cheerfully see him through more sprees. Talk about his condition or this book only when he raises the issue. In some cases it may be better to let someone outside the family present the book. They can urge action without arousing hostility. If your husband is otherwise a normal individual, your chances are good at this stage.

You would suppose that men in the fourth classification would be quite hopeless, but that is not so. Many of Alcoholics Anonymous were like that. Everybody had given them up. Defeat seemed certain. Yet often such men had spectacular and powerful recoveries.

There are exceptions. Some men have been so impaired by alcohol that they cannot stop. Sometimes there are cases where alcoholism is complicated by other disorders. A good doctor or psychiatrist can tell you whether these complications are serious. In any event, try to have your husband read this book. His reaction may be one of enthusiasm. If he is already committed to an institution, but can convince you and your doctor that he means business, give him a chance to try our method, unless the doctor thinks his mental condition too abnormal or dangerous. We make this recommendation with some confidence. For years we have been working with alcoholics committed to institutions. Since this book was first published, A.A. has released thousands of alcoholics from asylums and hospitals of every kind. The majority have never returned. The power of God goes deep!

You may have the reverse situation on your hands. Perhaps you have a husband who is at large, but who should be committed. Some men cannot or will not get over alcoholism. When they become too dangerous, we think the kind thing is to lock them up, but of course a good doctor should always be consulted. The wives and children of such men suffer horribly, but not more than the men themselves.

But sometimes you must start life anew. We know women who have done it. If such women adopt a spiritual way of life their road will be smoother.

If your husband is a drinker, you probably worry over what other people are thinking and you hate to meet your friends. You draw more and more into yourself and you think everyone is talking about conditions at your home. You avoid the subject of drinking, even with your own parents. You do not know what to tell the children. When your husband is bad, you become a trembling recluse, wishing the telephone had never been invented.

We find that most of this embarrassment is unnecessary. While you need not discuss your husband at length, you can quietly let your friends know the nature of his illness. But you must be on guard not to embarrass or harm your husband.

When you have carefully explained to such people that he is a sick person, you will have created a new atmosphere. Barriers which have sprung up between you and your friends will disappear with the growth of sympathetic understanding. You will no longer be self-conscious or feel that you must apologize as though your husband were a weak character. He may be anything but that. Your new courage, good nature and lack of self-consciousness will do wonders for you socially.

The same principle applies in dealing with the children. Unless they actually need protection from their father, it is best not to take sides in any argument he has with them while drinking. Use your energies to promote a better understanding all around. Then that terrible tension which grips the home of every problem drinker will be lessened.

Frequently, you have felt obliged to tell your husband's employer and his friends that he was sick, when as a matter of fact he was tight. Avoid answering these inquiries as much as you can. Whenever possible, let your husband explain. Your desire to protect him should not cause you to lie to people when they have a right to know where he is and what he is doing. Discuss this with him when he is sober and in good spirits. Ask him what you should do if he places you in such a position again. But be careful not to be resentful about the last time he did so.

There is another paralyzing fear. You may be afraid your husband will lose his position; you are thinking of the disgrace and hard times which will befall you and the children. This experience may come to you. Or you may already have had it several times. Should it happen again, regard it in a different light. Maybe it will prove a blessing! It may convince your husband he wants to stop drinking forever. And now you know that he can stop if he will! Time after time, this apparent calamity has been a boon to us, for it opened up a path which led to the discovery of God.

We have elsewhere remarked how much better life is when lived on a spiritual plane. If God can solve the age-old riddle of alcoholism, He can solve your problems too. We wives found that, like everybody else, we were afflicted with pride, self-pity, vanity and all the things which go to make up the self-centered person; and we were not above selfishness or dishonesty. As our husbands began to apply spiritual principles in their lives, we began to see the desirability of doing so too.

At first, some of us did not believe we needed this help. We thought, on the whole, we were pretty good women, capable of being nicer if our husbands stopped drinking. But it was a silly idea that we were too good to need God. Now we try to put spiritual principles to work in every department of our lives. When we do that, we find it solves our problems too; the ensuing lack of fear, worry and hurt feelings is a wonderful thing. We urge you to try our program, for nothing will be so helpful to your husband as the radically changed attitude toward him which God will show you how to have. Go along with your husband if you possibly can.

If you and your husband find a solution for the pressing problem of drink you are, of course, going to be very happy. But all problems will not be solved at once. Seed has started to sprout in a new soil, but growth has only begun. In spite of your new-found happiness, there will be ups and downs. Many of the old problems will still be with you. This is as it should be.

The faith and sincerity of both you and your husband will be put to the test. These work-outs should be regarded as part of your education, for thus you will be learning to live. You will make mistakes, but if you are in earnest they will not drag you down. Instead, you will capitalize them. A better way of life will emerge when they are overcome.

Some of the snags you will encounter are irritation, hurt feelings and resentments. Your husband will sometimes be unreasonable and you will want to criticize. Starting from a speck on the domestic horizon, great thunderclouds of dispute may gather. These family dissensions are very dangerous, especially to your husband. Often you must carry the burden of avoiding them or keeping them under control. Never forget that resentment is a deadly hazard to an alcoholic. We do not mean that you have to agree with your husband whenever there is an honest difference of opinion. Just be careful not to disagree in a resentful or critical spirit.

You and your husband will find that you can dispose of serious problems easier than you can the trivial ones. Next time you and he have a heated discussion, no matter what the subject, it should be the privilege of either to smile and say, "This is getting serious. I'm sorry I got disturbed. Let's talk about it later." If your husband is trying to live on a spiritual basis, he will also be doing everything in his power to avoid disagreement or contention.

Your husband knows he owes you more than sobriety. He wants to make good. Yet you must not expect too much. His ways of thinking and doing are the habits of years. Patience, tolerance, understanding and love are the watchwords. Show him these things in yourself and they will be reflected back to you from him. Live and let live is the rule. If you both show a willingness to remedy your own defects, there will be little need to criticize each other.

We women carry with us a picture of the ideal man, the sort of chap we would like our husbands to be. It is the most natural thing in the world, once his liquor problem is solved, to feel that he will now measure up to that cherished vision. The chances are he will not for, like yourself, he is just beginning his development. Be patient.

Another feeling we are very likely to entertain is one of resentment that love and loyalty could not cure our husbands of alcoholism. We do not like the thought that the contents of a book or the work of another alcoholic has accomplished in a few weeks that for which we struggled for years. At such moments we forget that alcoholism is an illness over which we could not possibly have had any power. Your husband will be the first to say it was your devotion and care which brought him to the point where he could have a spiritual experience. Without you he would have gone to pieces long ago. When resentful thoughts come, try to pause and count your blessings. After all, your family is reunited, alcohol is no longer a problem and you and your husband are working together toward an undreamed-of future.

Still another difficulty is that you may become jealous of the attention he bestows on other people, especially alcoholics. You have been starving for his companionship, yet he spends long hours helping other men and their families. You feel he should now be yours. The fact is that he should work with other people to maintain his own sobriety. Sometimes he will be so interested that he becomes really neglectful. Your house is filled with strangers. You may not like some of them. He gets stirred up about their troubles, but not at all about yours. It will do little good if you point that out and urge more attention for yourself. We find it a real mistake to dampen his enthusiasm for alcoholic work. You should join in his efforts as much as you possibly can. We suggest that you direct some of your thought to the wives of his new alcoholic friends. They need the counsel and love of a woman who has gone through what you have.

It is probably true that you and your husband have been living too much alone, for drinking many times isolates the wife of an alcoholic. Therefore, you probably need fresh interests and a great cause to live for as much as your husband. If you cooperate, rather than complain, you will find that his excess enthusiasm will tone down. Both of you will awaken to a new sense of responsibility for others. You, as well as your husband, ought to think of what you can put into life instead of how much you can take out. Inevitably your lives will be fuller for doing so. You will lose the old life to find one much better.

Perhaps your husband will make a fair start on the new basis, but just as things are going beautifully he dismays you by coming home drunk. If you are satisfied he really wants to get over drinking, you need not be alarmed. Though it is infinitely better that he have no relapse at all, as has been true with many of our men, it is by no means a bad thing in some cases. Your husband will see at once that he must redouble his spiritual activities if he expects to survive. You need not remind him of his spiritual deficiency—he will know of it. Cheer him up and ask him how you can be still more helpful.

The slightest sign of fear or intolerance may lessen your husband's chance of recovery. In a weak moment he may take your dislike of his high-stepping friends as one of those insanely trivial excuses to drink.

We never, never try to arrange a man's life so as to shield him from temptation. The slightest disposition on your part to guide his appointments or his affairs so he will not be tempted will be noticed. Make him feel absolutely free to come and go as he likes. This is important. If he gets drunk, don't blame yourself. God has either removed your husband's liquor problem or He has not. If not, it had better be found out right away. Then you and your husband can get right down to fundamentals. If a repetition is to be prevented, place the problem, along with everything else, in God's hands.

We realize that we have been giving you much direction and advice. We may have seemed to lecture. If that is so we are sorry, for we ourselves don't always care for people who lecture us. But what we have related is based upon experience, some of it painful. We had to learn these things the hard way. That is why we are anxious that you understand, and that you avoid these unnecessary difficulties.

So to you out there who may soon be with us—we say "Good luck and God bless you!"

Chapter 9

THE FAMILY AFTERWARD

OUR WOMEN FOLK have suggested certain attitudes a wife may take with the husband who is recovering. Perhaps they created the impression that he is to be wrapped in cotton wool and placed on a pedestal. Successful readjustment means the opposite. All members of the family should meet upon the common ground of tolerance, understanding and love. This involves a process of deflation. The alcoholic, his wife, his children, his "in-laws," each one is likely to have fixed ideas about the family's attitude towards himself or herself. Each is interested in having his or her wishes respected. We find the more one member of the family demands that the others concede to him, the more resentful they become. This makes for discord and unhappiness.

And why? Is it not because each wants to play the lead? Is not each trying to arrange the family show to his liking? Is he not unconsciously trying to see what he can take from the family life rather than give?

Cessation of drinking is but the first step away from a highly strained, abnormal condition. A doctor said to us, "Years of living with an alcoholic is almost sure to make any wife or child neurotic. The entire family is, to some extent, ill." Let families realize, as they start their journey, that all will not be fair weather. Each in his turn may be footsore and may straggle.

There will be alluring shortcuts and by-paths down which they may wander and lose their way.

Suppose we tell you some of the obstacles a family will meet; suppose we suggest how they may be avoided—even converted to good use for others. The family of an alcoholic longs for the return of happiness and security. They remember when father was romantic, thoughtful and successful. Today's life is measured against that of other years and, when it falls short, the family may be unhappy.

Family confidence in dad is rising high. The good old days will soon be back, they think. Sometimes they demand that dad bring them back instantly! God, they believe, almost owes this recompense on a long overdue account. But the head of the house has spent years in pulling down the structures of business, romance, friendship, health—these things are now ruined or damaged. It will take time to clear away the wreck. Though old buildings will eventually be replaced by finer ones, the new structures will take years to complete.

Father knows he is to blame; it may take him many seasons of hard work to be restored financially, but he shouldn't be reproached. Perhaps he will never have much money again. But the wise family will admire him for what he is trying to be, rather than for what he is trying to get.

Now and then the family will be plagued by spectres from the past, for the drinking career of almost every alcoholic has been marked by escapades, funny, humiliating, shameful or tragic. The first impulse will be to bury these skeletons in a dark closet and padlock the door. The family may be possessed by the idea that future happiness can be based only upon forgetfulness of the past. We think that such a view is self-centered and in direct conflict with the new way of living.

Henry Ford once made a wise remark to the effect that experience is the thing of supreme value in life.[1] That is true only if one is willing to turn the past to good account. We grow by our willingness to face and rectify errors and convert them into assets. The alcoholic's past thus becomes the principal asset of the family and frequently it is almost the only one!

This painful past may be of infinite value to other families still struggling with their problem. We think each family which has been relieved owes something to those who have not, and when the occasion requires, each member of it should be only too willing to bring former mistakes, no matter how grievous, out of their hiding places. Showing others who suffer how we were given help is the very thing which makes life seem so worth while to us now. Cling to the thought that, in God's hands, the dark past is the greatest possession you have—the key to life and happiness for others. With it you can avert death and misery for them.

It is possible to dig up past misdeeds so they become a blight, a veritable plague. For example, we know of situations in which the alcoholic or his wife have had love affairs. In the first flush of spiritual experience they forgave each other and drew closer together. The miracle of reconciliation was at hand. Then, under one provocation or another, the aggrieved one would unearth the old affair and angrily cast its ashes about. A few of us have had these growing pains and they hurt a great deal. Husbands and wives have sometimes been obliged to separate for a time until new perspective, new victory over hurt pride could be re-won. In most cases, the alcoholic survived this ordeal without relapse, but not always. So we think that unless some good and useful purpose is to be served, past occurrences should not be discussed.

We families of Alcoholics Anonymous keep few skeletons in the closet. Everyone knows about the others' alcoholic troubles. This is a condition which, in ordinary life, would produce untold grief; there might be scandalous gossip, laughter at the expense of other people, and a tendency to take advantage of intimate information. Among us, these are rare occurrences. We do talk about each other a great deal, but we almost invariably temper such talk by a spirit of love and tolerance.

Another principle we observe carefully is that we do not relate intimate experiences of another person unless we are sure he would approve. We find it better, when possible, to stick to our own stories. A man may criticize or laugh at himself and it will affect others favorably, but criticism or ridicule coming from another often produces the contrary effect. Members of a family should watch such matters carefully, for one careless, inconsiderate remark has been known to raise the very devil. We alcoholics are sensitive people. It takes some of us a long time to outgrow that serious handicap.

Many alcoholics are enthusiasts. They run to extremes. At the beginning of recovery a man will take, as a rule, one of two directions. He may either plunge into a frantic attempt to get on his feet in business, or he may be so enthralled by his new life that he talks or thinks of little else. In either case certain family problems will arise. With these we have had experience galore.

We think it dangerous if he rushes headlong at his economic problem. The family will be affected also, pleasantly at first, as they feel their money troubles are about to be solved, then not so pleasantly as they find themselves neglected. Dad may be tired at night and preoccupied by day. He may take small interest in the children and may show irritation when reproved for his delinquencies. If not irritable, he may seem dull and boring, not gay and affectionate as the family would like him to be. Mother may complain of inattention. They are all disappointed, and often let him feel it. Beginning with such complaints, a barrier arises. He is straining every nerve to make up for lost time. He is striving to recover fortune and reputation and feels he is doing very well.

Sometimes mother and children don't think so. Having been neglected and misused in the past, they think father owes them more than they are getting. They want him to make a fuss over them. They expect him to give them the nice times they used to have before he drank so much, and to show his contrition for what they suffered. But dad doesn't give freely of himself. Resentment grows. He becomes still less communicative. Sometimes he explodes over a trifle. The family is mystified. They criticize, pointing out how he is falling down on his spiritual program.

This sort of thing can be avoided. Both father and the family are mistaken, though each side may have some justification. It is of little use to argue and only makes the impasse worse. The family must realize that dad, though marvelously improved, is still convalescing. They should be thankful he is sober and able to be of this world once more. Let them praise his progress. Let them remember that his drinking wrought all kinds of damage that may take long to repair. If they sense these things, they will not take so seriously his periods of crankiness, depression, or apathy, which will disappear when there is tolerance, love, and spiritual understanding.

The head of the house ought to remember that he is mainly to blame for what befell his home. He can scarcely square the account in his lifetime. But he must see the danger of over-concentration on financial success. Although financial recovery is on the way for many of us, we found we could not place money first. For us, material well-being always followed spiritual progress; it never preceded.

Since the home has suffered more than anything else, it is well that a man exert himself there. He is not likely to get far in any direction if he fails to show unselfishness and love under his own roof. We know there are difficult wives and families, but the man who is getting over alcoholism must remember he did much to make them so.

As each member of a resentful family begins to see his shortcomings and admits them to the others, he lays a basis for helpful discussion. These family talks will be constructive if they can be carried on without heated argument, self-pity, self-justification or resentful criticism. Little by little, mother and children will see they ask too much, and father will see he gives too little. Giving, rather than getting, will become the guiding principle.

Assume on the other hand that father has, at the outset, a stirring spiritual experience. Overnight, as it were, he is a different man. He becomes a religious enthusiast. He is unable to focus on anything else. As soon as his sobriety begins to be taken as a matter of course, the family may look at their strange new dad with apprehension, then with irritation. There is talk about spiritual matters morning, noon and night. He may demand that the family find God in a hurry, or exhibit amazing indifference to them and say he is above worldly considerations. He may tell mother, who has been religious all her life, that she doesn't know what it's all about, and that she had better get his brand of spirituality while there is yet time.

When father takes this tack, the family may react unfavorably. They may be jealous of a God who has stolen dad's affections. While grateful that he drinks no more, they may not like the idea that God has accomplished the miracle where they failed. They often forget father was beyond human aid. They may not see why their love and devotion did not straighten him out. Dad is not so spiritual after all, they say. If he means to right his past wrongs, why all this concern for everyone in the world but his family? What about his talk that God will take care of them? They suspect father is a bit balmy!

He is not so unbalanced as they might think. Many of us have experienced dad's elation. We have indulged in spiritual intoxication. Like a gaunt prospector, belt drawn in over the last ounce of food, our pick struck gold. Joy at our release from a lifetime of frustration knew no bounds. Father feels he has struck something better than gold. For a time he may try to hug the new treasure to himself. He may not see at once that he has barely scratched a limitless lode which will pay dividends only if he mines it for the rest of his life and insists on giving away the entire product.

If the family cooperates, dad will soon see that he is suffering from a distortion of values. He will perceive that his spiritual growth is lopsided, that for an average man like himself, a spiritual life which does not include his family obligations may not be so perfect after all. If the family will appreciate that dad's current behavior is but a phase of his development, all will be well. In the midst of an understanding and sympathetic family, these vagaries of dad's spiritual infancy will quickly disappear.

The opposite may happen should the family condemn and criticize. Dad may feel that for years his drinking has placed him on the wrong side of every argument, but that now he has become a superior person with God on his side. If the family persists in criticism, this fallacy may take a still greater hold on father. Instead of treating the family as he should, he may retreat further into himself and feel he has spiritual justification for so doing.

Though the family does not fully agree with dad's spiritual activities, they should let him have his head. Even if he displays a certain amount of neglect and irresponsibility towards the family, it is well to let him go as far as he likes in helping other alcoholics. During those first days of convalescence, this will do more to insure his sobriety than anything else. Though some of his manifestations are alarming and disagreeable, we think dad will be on a firmer foundation than the man who is placing business or professional success ahead of spiritual development. He will be less likely to drink again, and anything is preferable to that.

Those of us who have spent much time in the world of spiritual make-believe have eventually seen the childishness of it. This dream world has been replaced by a great sense of purpose, accompanied by a growing consciousness of the power of God in our lives. We have come to believe He would like us to keep our heads in the clouds with Him, but that our feet ought to be firmly planted on earth. That is where our fellow travelers are, and that is where our work must be done. These are the realities for us. We have found nothing incompatible between a powerful spiritual experience and a life of sane and happy usefulness.

One more suggestion: Whether the family has spiritual convictions or not, they may do well to examine the principles by which the alcoholic member is trying to live. They can hardly fail to approve these simple principles, though the head of the house still fails somewhat in practicing them. Nothing will help the man who is off on a spiritual tangent so much as the wife who adopts a sane spiritual program, making a better practical use of it.

There will be other profound changes in the household. Liquor incapacitated father for so many years that mother became head of the house. She met these responsibilities gallantly. By force of circumstances, she was often obliged to treat father as a sick or wayward child. Even when he wanted to assert himself he could not, for his drinking placed him constantly in the wrong. Mother made all the plans and gave the directions. When sober, father usually obeyed. Thus mother, through no fault of her own, became accustomed to wearing the family trousers. Father, coming suddenly to life again, often begins to assert himself. This means trouble, unless the family watches for these tendencies in each other and comes to a friendly agreement about them.

Drinking isolates most homes from the outside world. Father may have laid aside for years all normal activities—clubs, civic duties, sports. When he renews interest in such things, a feeling of jealousy may arise. The family may feel they hold a mortgage on dad, so big that no equity should be left for outsiders. Instead of developing new channels of activity for themselves, mother and children demand that he stay home and make up the deficiency.

At the very beginning, the couple ought to frankly face the fact that each will have to yield here and there if the family is going to play an effective part in the new life. Father will necessarily spend much time with other alcoholics, but this activity should be balanced. New acquaintances who know nothing of alcoholism might be made and thoughtful consideration given their needs. The problems of the community might engage attention. Though the family has no religious connections, they may wish to make contact with or take membership in a religious body.

Alcoholics who have derided religious people will be helped by such contacts. Being possessed of a spiritual experience, the alcoholic will find he has much in common with these people, though he may differ with them on many matters. If he does not argue about religion, he will make new friends and is sure to find new avenues of usefulness and pleasure. He and his family can be a bright spot in such congregations. He may bring new hope and new courage to many a priest, minister, or rabbi, who gives his all to minister to our troubled world. We intend the foregoing as a helpful suggestion only. So far as we are concerned, there is nothing obligatory about it. As non-denominational people, we cannot make up others' minds for them. Each individual should consult his own conscience.

We have been speaking to you of serious, sometimes tragic things. We have been dealing with alcohol in its worst aspect. But we aren't a glum lot. If newcomers could see no joy or fun in our existence, they wouldn't want it. We absolutely insist on enjoying life. We try not to indulge in cynicism over the state of the nations, nor do we carry the world's troubles on our shoulders. When we see a man sinking into the mire that is alcoholism, we give him first aid and place what we have at his disposal. For his sake, we do recount and almost relive the horrors of our past. But those of us who have tried to shoulder the entire burden and trouble of others find we are soon overcome by them.

So we think cheerfulness and laughter make for usefulness. Outsiders are sometimes shocked when we burst into merriment over a seemingly tragic experience out of the past. But why shouldn't we laugh? We have recovered, and have been given the power to help others.

Everybody knows that those in bad health, and those who seldom play, do not laugh much. So let each family play together or separately, as much as their circumstances warrant. We are sure God wants us to be happy, joyous, and free. We cannot subscribe to the belief that this life is a vale of tears, though it once was just that for many of us. But it is clear that we made our own misery. God didn't do it. Avoid then, the deliberate manufacture of misery, but if trouble comes, cheerfully capitalize it as an opportunity to demonstrate His omnipotence.

Now about health: A body badly burned by alcohol does not often recover overnight nor do twisted thinking and depression vanish in a twinkling. We are convinced that a spiritual mode of living is a most powerful health restorative. We, who have recovered from serious drinking, are miracles of mental health. But we have seen remarkable transformations in our bodies. Hardly one of our crowd now shows any mark of dissipation.

But this does not mean that we disregard human health measures. God has abundantly supplied this world with fine doctors, psychologists, and practitioners of various kinds. Do not hesitate to take your health problems to such persons. Most of them give freely of themselves, that their fellows may enjoy sound minds and bodies. Try to remember that though God has wrought miracles among us, we should never belittle a good doctor or psychiatrist. Their services are often indispensable in treating a newcomer and in following his case afterward.

One of the many doctors who had the opportunity of reading this book in manuscript form told us that the use of sweets was often helpful, of course depending upon a doctor's advice. He thought all alcoholics should constantly have chocolate available for its quick energy value at times of fatigue. He added that occasionally in the night a vague craving arose which would be satisfied by candy. Many of us have noticed a tendency to eat sweets and have found this practice beneficial.

A word about sex relations. Alcohol is so sexually stimulating to some men that they have over-indulged. Couples are occasionally dismayed to find that when drinking is stopped the man tends to be impotent. Unless the reason is understood, there may be an emotional upset. Some of us had this experience, only to enjoy, in a few months, a finer intimacy than ever. There should be no hesitancy in consulting a doctor or psychologist if the condition persists. We do not know of many cases where this difficulty lasted long.

The alcoholic may find it hard to re-establish friendly relations with his children. Their young minds were impressionable while he was drinking. Without saying so, they may cordially hate him for what he has done to them and to their mother. The children are sometimes dominated by a pathetic hardness and cynicism. They cannot seem to forgive and forget. This may hang on for months, long after their mother has accepted dad's new way of living and thinking.

In time they will see that he is a new man and in their own way they will let him know it. When this happens, they can be invited to join in morning meditation and then they can take part in the daily discussion without rancor or bias. From that point on, progress will be rapid. Marvelous results often follow such a reunion.

Whether the family goes on a spiritual basis or not, the alcoholic member has to if he would recover. The others must be convinced of his new status beyond the shadow of a doubt. Seeing is believing to most families who have lived with a drinker.

Here is a case in point: One of our friends is a heavy smoker and coffee drinker. There was no doubt he over-indulged. Seeing this, and meaning to be helpful, his wife commenced to admonish him about it. He admitted he was overdoing these things, but frankly said that he was not ready to stop. His wife is one of those persons who really feels there is something rather sinful about these commodities, so she nagged, and her intolerance finally threw him into a fit of anger. He got drunk.

Of course our friend was wrong—dead wrong. He had to painfully admit that and mend his spiritual fences. Though he is now a most effective member of Alcoholics Anonymous, he still smokes and drinks coffee, but neither his wife nor anyone else stands in judgment. She sees she was wrong to make a burning issue out of such a matter when his more serious ailments were being rapidly cured.

We have three little mottoes which are apropos. Here they are:

First Things First
Live and Let Live
Easy Does It.

Note
1. Henry Ford: A pioneer of automated production, became widely known and very wealthy from manufacturing automobiles.

Chapter 10

TO EMPLOYERS

AMONG MANY employers nowadays, we think of one member who has spent much of his life in the world of big business. He has hired and fired hundreds of men. He knows the alcoholic as the employer sees him. His present views ought to prove exceptionally useful to business men everywhere.

But let him tell you:

I was at one time assistant manager of a corporation department employing sixty-six hundred men. One day my secretary came in saying that Mr. B— insisted on speaking with me. I told her to say that I was not interested. I had warned him several times that he had but one more chance. Not long afterward he had called me from Hartford on two successive days, so drunk he could hardly speak. I told him he was through—finally and forever.

My secretary returned to say that it was not Mr. B— on the phone; it was Mr. B—'s brother, and he wished to give me a message. I still expected a plea for clemency, but these words came through the receiver: "I just wanted to tell you Paul jumped from a hotel window in Hartford last Saturday. He left us a note saying you were the best boss he ever had, and that you were not to blame in any way."

Another time, as I opened a letter which lay on my

desk, a newspaper clipping fell out. It was the obituary of one of the best salesmen I ever had. After two weeks of drinking, he had placed his toe on the trigger of a loaded shotgun—the barrel was in his mouth. I had discharged him for drinking six weeks before.

Still another experience: A woman's voice came faintly over long distance from Virginia. She wanted to know if her husband's company insurance was still in force. Four days before he had hanged himself in his woodshed. I had been obliged to discharge him for drinking, though he was brilliant, alert, and one of the best organizers I have ever known.

Here were three exceptional men lost to this world because I did not understand alcoholism as I do now. What irony—I became an alcoholic myself! And but for the intervention of an understanding person, I might have followed in their footsteps. My downfall cost the business community unknown thousands of dollars, for it takes real money to train a man for an executive position. This kind of waste goes on unabated. We think the business fabric is shot through with a situation which might be helped by better understanding all around.

Nearly every modern employer feels a moral responsibility for the well-being of his help, and he tries to meet these responsibilities. That he has not always done so for the alcoholic is easily understood. To him the alcoholic has often seemed a fool of the first magnitude. Because of the employee's special ability, or of his own strong personal attachment to him, the employer has sometimes kept such a man at work long beyond a reasonable period. Some employers have tried every known remedy. In only a few instances has there been a lack of patience and tolerance. And we, who have imposed on the best of employers, can scarcely blame them if they have been short with us.

Here, for instance, is a typical example: An officer of one of the largest banking institutions in America knows I no longer drink. One day he told me about an executive of the same bank who, from his description, was undoubtedly alcoholic. This seemed to me like an opportunity to be helpful, so I spent two hours talking about alcoholism, the malady, and described the symptoms and results as well as I could. His comment was, "Very interesting. But I'm sure this man is done drinking. He has just returned from a three-months leave of absence, has taken a cure, looks fine, and to clinch the matter, the board of directors told him this was his last chance."

The only answer I could make was that if the man followed the usual pattern, he would go on a bigger bust than ever. I felt this was inevitable and wondered if the bank was doing the man an injustice. Why not bring him into contact with some of our alcoholic crowd? He might have a chance. I pointed out that I had had nothing to drink whatever for three years, and this in the face of difficulties that would have made nine out of ten men drink their heads off. Why not at least afford him an opportunity to hear my story? "Oh no," said my friend, "this chap is either through with liquor, or he is minus a job. If he has your will power and guts, he will make the grade."

I wanted to throw up my hands in discouragement, for I saw that I had failed to help my banker friend understand. He simply could not believe that his brother-executive suffered from a serious illness. There was nothing to do but wait.

Presently the man did slip and was fired. Following his discharge, we contacted him. Without much ado, he accepted the principles and procedure that had helped us. He is undoubtedly on the road to recovery. To me, this incident illustrates lack of understanding as to what really ails the alcoholic, and lack of knowledge as to what part employers might profitably take in salvaging their sick employees.

If you desire to help it might be well to disregard your own drinking, or lack of it. Whether you are a hard drinker, a moderate drinker or a teetotaler[1], you may have some pretty strong opinions, perhaps prejudices. Those who drink moderately may be more annoyed with an alcoholic than a total abstainer would be. Drinking occasionally, and understanding your own reactions, it is possible for you to become quite sure of many things which, so far as the alcoholic is concerned, are not always so. As a moderate drinker, you can take your liquor or leave it alone. Whenever you want to, you control your drinking. Of an evening, you can go on a mild bender, get up in the morning, shake your head and go to business. To you, liquor is no real problem. You cannot see why it should be to anyone else, save the spineless and stupid.

When dealing with an alcoholic, there may be a natural annoyance that a man could be so weak, stupid and irresponsible. Even when you understand the malady better, you may feel this feeling rising.

A look at the alcoholic in your organization is many times illuminating. Is he not usually brilliant, fast-thinking, imaginative and likeable? When sober, does he not work hard and have a knack of getting things done? If he had these qualities and did not drink would he be worth retaining? Should he have the same consideration as other ailing employees? Is he worth salvaging? If your decision is yes, whether the reason be humanitarian or business or both, then the following suggestions may be helpful.

Can you discard the feeling that you are dealing only with habit, with stubbornness, or a weak will? If this presents difficulty, re-reading chapters two and three, where the alcoholic sickness is discussed at length might be worth while. You, as a business man, want to know the necessities before considering the result. If you concede that your employee is ill, can he be forgiven for what he has done in the past? Can his past absurdities be forgotten? Can it be appreciated that he has been a victim of crooked thinking, directly caused by the action of alcohol on his brain?

I well remember the shock I received when a prominent doctor in Chicago told me of cases where pressure of the spinal fluid actually ruptured the brain. No wonder an alcoholic is strangely irrational. Who wouldn't be, with such a fevered brain? Normal drinkers are not so affected, nor can they understand the aberrations of the alcoholic.

Your man has probably been trying to conceal a number of scrapes, perhaps pretty messy ones. They may be disgusting. You may be at a loss to understand how such a seemingly above-board chap could be so involved. But these scrapes can generally be charged, no matter how bad, to the abnormal action of alcohol on his mind. When drinking, or getting over a bout, an alcoholic, sometimes the model of honesty when normal, will do incredible things. Afterward, his revulsion will be terrible. Nearly always, these antics indicate nothing more than temporary conditions.

This is not to say that all alcoholics are honest and upright when not drinking. Of course that isn't so, and such people often may impose on you. Seeing your attempt to understand and help, some men will try to take advantage of your kindness. If you are sure your man does not want to stop, he may as well be discharged, the sooner the better. You are not doing him a favor by keeping him on. Firing such an individual may prove a blessing to him. It may be just the jolt he needs. I know, in my own particular case, that nothing my company could have done would have stopped me for, so long as I was able to hold my position, I could not possibly realize how serious my situation was. Had they fired me first, and had they then taken steps to see that I was presented with the solution contained in this book, I might have returned to them six months later, a well man.

But there are many men who want to stop, and with them you can go far. Your understanding treatment of their cases will pay dividends.

Perhaps you have such a man in mind. He wants to quit drinking and you want to help him, even if it be only a matter of good business. You now know more about alcoholism. You can see that he is mentally and physically sick. You are willing to overlook his past performances. Suppose an approach is made something like this:

State that you know about his drinking, and that it must stop. You might say you appreciate his abilities, would like to keep him, but cannot if he continues to drink. A firm attitude at this point has helped many of us.

Next he can be assured that you do not intend to lecture, moralize, or condemn; that if this was done formerly, it was because of misunderstanding. If possible express a lack of hard feeling toward him. At this point, it might be well to explain alcoholism, the illness. Say that you believe he is a gravely ill person, with this qualification—being perhaps fatally ill, does he want to get well? You ask, because many alcoholics, being warped and drugged, do not want to quit. But does he? Will he take every necessary step, submit to anything to get well, to stop drinking forever?

If he says yes, does he really mean it, or down inside does he think he is fooling you, and that after rest and treatment he will be able to get away with a few drinks now and then? We believe a man should be thoroughly probed on these points. Be satisfied he is not deceiving himself or you.

Whether you mention this book is a matter for your discretion. If he temporizes and still thinks he can ever drink again, even beer, he might as well be discharged after the next bender which, if an alcoholic, he is almost certain to have. He should understand that emphatically. Either you are dealing with a man who can and will get well or you are not. If not, why waste time with him? This may seem severe, but it is usually the best course.

After satisfying yourself that your man wants to recover and that he will go to any extreme to do so, you may suggest a definite course of action. For most alcoholics who are drinking, or who are just getting over a spree, a certain amount of physical treatment is desirable, even imperative. The matter of physical treatment should, of course, be referred to your own doctor. Whatever the method, its object is to thoroughly clear mind and body of the effects of alcohol. In competent hands, this seldom takes long nor is it very expensive. Your man will fare better if placed in such physical condition that he can think straight and no longer craves liquor. If you propose such a procedure to him, it may be necessary to advance the cost of treatment, but we believe it should be made plain that any expense will later be deducted from his pay. It is better for him to feel fully responsible.

If your man accepts your offer, it should be pointed out that physical treatment is but a small part of the picture. Though you are providing him with the best possible medical attention, he should understand that he must undergo a change of heart. To get over drinking will require a transformation of thought and attitude. We all had to place recovery above everything, for without recovery we would have lost both home and business.

Can you have every confidence in his ability to recover? While on the subject of confidence, can you adopt the attitude that so far as you are concerned this will be a strictly personal matter, that his alcoholic derelictions, the treatment about to be undertaken, will never be discussed without his consent? It might be well to have a long chat with him on his return.

To return to the subject matter of this book: It contains full suggestions by which the employee may solve his problem. To you, some of the ideas which it contains are novel. Perhaps you are not quite in sympathy with the approach we suggest. By no means do we offer it as the last word on this subject, but so far as we are concerned, it has worked with us. After all, are you not looking for results rather than methods? Whether your employee likes it or not, he will learn the grim truth about alcoholism. That won't hurt him a bit, even though he does not go for this remedy.

We suggest you draw the book to the attention of the doctor who is to attend your patient during treatment. If the book is read the moment the patient is able, while acutely depressed, realization of his condition may come to him.

We hope the doctor will tell the patient the truth about his condition, whatever that happens to be. When the man is presented with this volume it is best that no one tell him he must abide by its suggestions. The man must decide for himself.

You are betting, of course, that your changed attitude plus the contents of this book will turn the trick. In some cases it will, and in others it may not. But we think that if you persevere, the percentage of successes will gratify you. As our work spreads and our numbers increase, we hope your employees may be put in personal contact with some of us. Meanwhile, we are sure a great deal can be accomplished by the use of the book alone.

On your employee's return, talk with him. Ask him if he thinks he has the answer. If he feels free to discuss his problems with you, if he knows you understand and will not be upset by anything he wishes to say, he will probably be off to a fast start.

In this connection, can you remain undisturbed if the man proceeds to tell you shocking things? He may, for example, reveal that he has padded his expense account or that he has planned to take your best customers away from you. In fact, he may say almost anything if he has accepted our solution which, as you know, demands rigorous honesty. Can you charge this off as you would a bad account and start fresh with him? If he owes you money you may wish to make terms.

If he speaks of his home situation, you can undoubtedly make helpful suggestions. Can he talk frankly with you so long as he does not bear business tales or criticize his associates? With this kind of employee such an attitude will command undying loyalty.

The greatest enemies of us alcoholics are resentment, jealousy, envy, frustration, and fear. Wherever men are gathered together in business there will be rivalries and, arising out of these, a certain amount of office politics. Sometimes we alcoholics have an idea that people are trying to pull us down. Often this is not so at all. But sometimes our drinking will be used politically.

One instance comes to mind in which a malicious individual was always making friendly little jokes about an alcoholic's drinking exploits. In this way he was slyly carrying tales. In another case, an alcoholic was sent to a hospital for treatment. Only a few knew of it at first but, within a short time, it was billboarded throughout the entire company. Naturally this sort of thing decreased the man's chance of recovery. The employer can many times protect the victim from this kind of talk. The employer cannot play favorites, but he can always defend a man from needless provocation and unfair criticism.

As a class, alcoholics are energetic people. They work hard and they play hard. Your man should be on his mettle to make good. Being somewhat weakened, and faced with physical and mental readjustment to a life which knows no alcohol, he may overdo. You may have to curb his desire to work sixteen hours a day. You may need to encourage him to play once in a while. He may wish to do a lot for other alcoholics and something of the sort may come up during business hours. A reasonable amount of latitude will be helpful. This work is necessary to maintain his sobriety.

After your man has gone along without drinking for a few months, you may be able to make use of his services with other employees who are giving you the alcoholic run-around—provided, of course, they are willing to have a third party in the picture. An alcoholic who has recovered, but holds a relatively unimportant job, can talk to a man with a better position. Being on a radically different basis of life, he will never take advantage of the situation.

Your man may be trusted. Long experience with alcoholic excuses naturally arouses suspicion. When his wife next calls saying he is sick, you might jump to the conclusion he is drunk. If he is, and is still trying to recover, he will tell you about it even if it means the loss of his job. For he knows he must be honest if he would live at all. He will appreciate knowing you are not bothering your head about him, that you are not suspicious nor are you trying to run his life so he will be shielded from temptation to drink. If he is conscientiously following the program of recovery he can go anywhere your business may call him.

In case he does stumble, even once, you will have to decide whether to let him go. If you are sure he doesn't mean business, there is no doubt you should discharge him. If, on the contrary, you are sure he is doing his utmost, you may wish to give him another chance. But you should feel under no obligation to keep him on, for your obligation has been well discharged already.

There is another thing you might wish to do. If your organization is a large one, your junior executives might be provided with this book. You might let them know you have no quarrel with the alcoholics of your organization. These juniors are often in a difficult position. Men under them are frequently their friends. So, for one reason or another, they cover these men, hoping matters will take a turn for the better. They often jeopardize their own positions by trying to help serious drinkers who should have been fired long ago, or else given an opportunity to get well.

After reading this book, a junior executive can go to such a man and say approximately this, "Look here, Ed. Do you want to stop drinking or not? You put me on the spot every time you get drunk. It isn't fair to me or the firm. I have been learning something about alcoholism. If you are an alcoholic, you are a mighty sick man. You act like one. The firm wants to help you get over it, and if you are interested, there is a way out. If you take it, your past will be forgotten and the fact that you went away for treatment will not be mentioned. But if you cannot or will not stop drinking, I think you ought to resign."

Your junior executive may not agree with the contents of our book. He need not, and often should not show it to his alcoholic prospect. But at least he will understand the problem and will no longer be misled by ordinary promises. He will be able to take a position with such a man which is eminently fair and square. He will have no further reason for covering up an alcoholic employee.

It boils right down to this: No man should be fired just because he is alcoholic. If he wants to stop, he should be afforded a real chance. If he cannot or does not want to stop, he should be discharged. The exceptions are few.

We think this method of approach will accomplish several things. It will permit the rehabilitation of good men. At the same time you will feel no reluctance to rid yourself of those who cannot or will not stop. Alcoholism may be causing your organization considerable damage in its waste of time, men and reputation. We hope our suggestions will help you plug up this sometimes serious leak. We think we are sensible when we urge that you stop this waste and give your worthwhile man a chance.

The other day an approach was made to the vice president of a large industrial concern. He remarked: "I'm mighty glad you fellows got over your drinking. But the policy of this company is not to interfere with the habits of our employees. If a man drinks so much that his job suffers, we fire him. I don't see how you can be of any help to us for, as you see, we don't have any alcoholic problem." This same company spends millions for research every year. Their cost of production is figured to a fine decimal point. They have recreational facilities. There is company insurance. There is a real interest, both humanitarian and business, in the well-being of employees. But alcoholism—well, they just don't believe they have it.

Perhaps this is a typical attitude. We, who have collectively seen a great deal of business life, at least from the alcoholic angle, had to smile at this gentleman's sincere opinion. He might be shocked if he knew how much alcoholism is costing his organization a year. That company may harbor many actual or potential alcoholics. We believe that managers of large enterprises often have little idea how prevalent this problem is. Even if you feel your organization has no alcoholic problem, it might pay to take another look down the line. You may make some interesting discoveries.

Of course, this chapter refers to alcoholics, sick people, deranged men. What our friend, the vice president, had in mind was the habitual or whoopee drinker. As to them, his policy is undoubtedly sound, but he did not distinguish between such people and the alcoholic.

It is not to be expected that an alcoholic employee will receive a disproportionate amount of time and attention. He should not be made a favorite. The right kind of man, the kind who recovers, will not want this sort of thing. He will not impose. Far from it. He will work like the devil and thank you to his dying day.

Today I own a little company. There are two

alcoholic employees, who produce as much as five normal salesmen. But why not? They have a new attitude, and they have been saved from a living death. I have enjoyed every moment spent in getting them straightened out.

Note
1. Teetotaler: a person who does not drink alcohol.

Chapter 11

A VISION FOR YOU

FOR MOST normal folks, drinking means conviviality, companionship and colorful imagination. It means release from care, boredom and worry. It is joyous intimacy with friends and a feeling that life is good. But not so with us in those last days of heavy drinking. The old pleasures were gone. They were but memories. Never could we recapture the great moments of the past. There was an insistent yearning to enjoy life as we once did and a heartbreaking obsession that some new miracle of control would enable us to do it. There was always one more attempt—and one more failure.

The less people tolerated us, the more we withdrew from society, from life itself. As we became subjects of King Alcohol, shivering denizens of his mad realm, the chilling vapor that is loneliness settled down. It thickened, ever becoming blacker. Some of us sought out sordid places, hoping to find understanding companionship and approval. Momentarily we did—then would come oblivion and the awful awakening to face the hideous Four Horsemen—Terror, Bewilderment, Frustration, Despair. Unhappy drinkers who read this page will understand!

Now and then a serious drinker, being dry at the moment says, "I don't miss it at all. Feel better. Work better. Having a better time." As ex-problem drinkers, we smile at such a sally. We know our friend is like a boy whistling in the dark to keep up his spirits. He fools himself. Inwardly he would give anything to take half a dozen drinks and get away with them. He will presently try the old game again, for he isn't happy about his sobriety. He cannot picture life without alcohol. Some day he will be unable to imagine life either with alcohol or without it. Then he will know loneliness such as few do. He will be at the jumping-off place. He will wish for the end.

We have shown how we got out from under. You say, "Yes, I'm willing. But am I to be consigned to a life where I shall be stupid, boring and glum, like some righteous people I see? I know I must get along without liquor, but how can I? Have you a sufficient substitute?"

Yes, there is a substitute and it is vastly more than that. It is a fellowship in Alcoholics Anonymous. There you will find release from care, boredom and worry. Your imagination will be fired. Life will mean something at last. The most satisfactory years of your existence lie ahead. Thus we find the fellowship, and so will you.

"How is that to come about?" you ask. "Where am I to find these people?"

You are going to meet these new friends in your own community. Near you, alcoholics are dying helplessly like people in a sinking ship. If you live in a large place, there are hundreds. High and low, rich and poor, these are future fellows of Alcoholics Anonymous. Among them you will make lifelong friends. You will be bound to them with new and wonderful ties, for you will escape disaster together and you will commence shoulder to shoulder your common journey. Then you will know what it means to give of yourself that others may survive and rediscover life. You will learn the full meaning of "Love thy neighbor as thyself."

It may seem incredible that these men are to become happy, respected, and useful once more. How can they rise out of such misery, bad repute and hopelessness? The practical answer is that since these things have happened among us, they can happen with you. Should you wish them above all else, and be willing to make use of our experience, we are sure they will come. The age of miracles is still with us. Our own recovery proves that!

Our hope is that when this chip of a book is launched on the world tide of alcoholism, defeated drinkers will seize upon it, to follow its suggestions. Many, we are sure, will rise to their feet and march on. They will approach still other sick ones and fellowships of Alcoholics Anonymous may spring up in each city and hamlet, havens for those who must find a way out.

In the chapter "Working With Others" you gathered an idea of how we approach and aid others to health. Suppose now that through you several families have adopted this way of life. You will want to know more of how to proceed from that point. Perhaps the best way of treating you to a glimpse of your future will be to describe the growth of the fellowship among us. Here is a brief account:

Years ago, in 1935, one of our number made a journey to a certain western city. From a business standpoint, his trip came off badly. Had he been successful in his enterprise, he would have been set on his feet financially which, at the time, seemed vitally important. But his venture wound up in a law suit and bogged down completely. The proceeding was shot through with much hard feeling and controversy.

Bitterly discouraged, he found himself in a strange place, discredited and almost broke. Still physically weak, and sober but a few months, he saw that his predicament was dangerous. He wanted so much to talk with someone, but whom?

One dismal afternoon he paced a hotel lobby wondering how his bill was to be paid. At one end of the room stood a glass covered directory of local churches. Down the lobby a door opened into an attractive bar. He could see the gay crowd inside. In there he would find companionship and release. Unless he took some drinks, he might not have the courage to scrape an acquaintance and would have a lonely week-end.

Of course he couldn't drink, but why not sit hopefully at a table, a bottle of ginger ale before him? After all, had he not been sober six months now? Perhaps he could handle, say, three drinks—no more! Fear gripped him. He was on thin ice. Again it was the old, insidious insanity—that first drink. With a shiver, he turned away and walked down the lobby to the church directory. Music and gay chatter still floated to him from the bar.

But what about his responsibilities—his family and the men who would die because they would not know how to get well, ah—yes, those other alcoholics? There must be many such in this town. He would phone a clergyman. His sanity returned and he thanked

God. Selecting a church at random from the directory, he stepped into a booth and lifted the receiver.

His call to the clergyman led him presently to a certain resident of the town, who, though formerly able and respected, was then nearing the nadir of alcoholic despair. It was the usual situation: home in jeopardy, wife ill, children distracted, bills in arrears and standing damaged. He had a desperate desire to stop, but saw no way out, for he had earnestly tried many avenues of escape. Painfully aware of being somehow abnormal, the man did not fully realize what it meant to be alcoholic.*

When our friend related his experience, the man agreed that no amount of will power he might muster could stop his drinking for long. A spiritual experience, he conceded, was absolutely necessary, but the price seemed high upon the basis suggested. He told how he lived in constant worry about those who might find out about his alcoholism. He had, of course, the familiar alcoholic obsession that few knew of his drinking. Why, he argued, should he lose the remainder of his business, only to bring still more suffering to his family by foolishly admitting his plight to people from whom he made his livelihood? He would do anything, he said, but that.

Being intrigued, however, he invited our friend to his home. Some time later, and just as he thought he was getting control of his liquor situation, he went on a roaring bender. For him, this was the spree that ended all sprees. He saw that he would have to face

*This refers to Bill's first visit with Dr. Bob. These men later became co-founders of A.A. This resulted in A.A.'s first group, in Akron, Ohio, in 1935.

his problems squarely that God might give him mastery.

One morning he took the bull by the horns and set out to tell those he feared what his trouble had been. He found himself surprisingly well received, and learned that many knew of his drinking. Stepping into his car, he made the rounds of people he had hurt. He trembled as he went about, for this might mean ruin, particularly to a person in his line of business.

At midnight he came home exhausted, but very happy. He has not had a drink since. As we shall see, he now means a great deal to his community, and the major liabilities of thirty years of hard drinking have been repaired in four.

But life was not easy for the two friends. Plenty of difficulties presented themselves. Both saw that they must keep spiritually active. One day they called up the head nurse of a local hospital. They explained their need and inquired if she had a first class alcoholic prospect.

She replied, "Yes, we've got a corker. He's just beaten up a couple of nurses. Goes off his head completely when he's drinking. But he's a grand chap when he's sober, though he's been in here eight times in the last six months. Understand he was once a well-known lawyer in town, but just now we've got him strapped down tight." *

Here was a prospect all right but, by the description, none too promising. The use of spiritual principles in

*This refers to Bill's and Dr. Bob's first visit to A.A. Number Three.

such cases was not so well understood as it is now. But one of the friends said, "Put him in a private room. We'll be down."

Two days later, a future fellow of Alcoholics Anonymous stared glassily at the strangers beside his bed. "Who are you fellows, and why this private room? I was always in a ward before."

Said one of the visitors, "We're giving you a treatment for alcoholism."

Hopelessness was written large on the man's face as he replied, "Oh, but that's no use. Nothing would fix me. I'm a goner. The last three times, I got drunk on the way home from here. I'm afraid to go out the door. I can't understand it."

For an hour, the two friends told him about their drinking experiences. Over and over, he would say: "That's me. That's me. I drink like that."

The man in the bed was told of the acute poisoning from which he suffered, how it deteriorates the body of an alcoholic and warps his mind. There was much talk about the mental state preceding the first drink.

"Yes, that's me," said the sick man, "the very image. You fellows know your stuff all right, but I don't see what good it'll do. You fellows are somebody. I was once, but I'm a nobody now. From what you tell me, I know more than ever I can't stop." At this both the visitors burst into a laugh. Said the future Fellow Anonymous: "Damn little to laugh about that I can see."

The two friends spoke of their spiritual experience and told him about the course of action they carried out.

He interrupted: "I used to be strong for the church,

but that won't fix it. I've prayed to God on hangover mornings and sworn that I'd never touch another drop but by nine o'clock I'd be boiled as an owl."

Next day found the prospect more receptive. He had been thinking it over. "Maybe you're right," he said. "God ought to be able to do anything." Then he added, "He sure didn't do much for me when I was trying to fight this booze racket alone."

On the third day the lawyer gave his life to the care and direction of his Creator, and said he was perfectly willing to do anything necessary. His wife came, scarcely daring to be hopeful, though she thought she saw something different about her husband already. He had begun to have a spiritual experience.

That afternoon he put on his clothes and walked from the hospital a free man. He entered a political campaign, making speeches, frequenting men's gathering places of all sorts, often staying up all night. He lost the race by only a narrow margin. But he had found God—and in finding God had found himself.

That was in June, 1935. He never drank again. He too, has become a respected and useful member of his community. He has helped other men recover, and is a power in the church from which he was long absent.

So, you see, there were three alcoholics in that town, who now felt they had to give to others what they had found, or be sunk. After several failures to find others, a fourth turned up. He came through an acquaintance who had heard the good news. He proved to be a devil-may-care young fellow whose parents could not make out whether he wanted to stop drinking or not. They were deeply religious people, much shocked by their son's refusal to have anything to do with the church. He suffered horribly from his sprees, but it seemed as if nothing could be done for him. He consented, however, to go to the hospital, where he occupied the very room recently vacated by the lawyer.

He had three visitors. After a bit, he said, "The way you fellows put this spiritual stuff makes sense. I'm ready to do business. I guess the old folks were right after all." So one more was added to the Fellowship.

All this time our friend of the hotel lobby incident remained in that town. He was there three months. He now returned home, leaving behind his first acquaintance, the lawyer and the devil-may-care chap. These men had found something brand new in life. Though they knew they must help other alcoholics if they would remain sober, that motive became secondary. It was transcended by the happiness they found in giving themselves for others. They shared their homes, their slender resources, and gladly devoted their spare hours to fellow-sufferers. They were willing, by day or night, to place a new man in the hospital and visit him afterward. They grew in numbers. They experienced a few distressing failures, but in those cases they made an effort to bring the man's family into a spiritual way of living, thus relieving much worry and suffering.

A year and six months later these three had succeeded with seven more. Seeing much of each other, scarce an evening passed that someone's home did not shelter a little gathering of men and women, happy in their release, and constantly thinking how they might present their discovery to some newcomer. In addition to these casual get-togethers, it became customary to set apart one night a week for a meeting to be attended by anyone or everyone interested in a spiritual way of life. Aside from fellowship and sociability, the prime object was to provide a time and place where new people might bring their problems.

Outsiders became interested. One man and his wife placed their large home at the disposal of this strangely assorted crowd. This couple has since become so fascinated that they have dedicated their home to the work. Many a distracted wife has visited this house to find loving and understanding companionship among women who knew her problem, to hear from the lips of their husbands what had happened to them, to be advised how her own wayward mate might be hospitalized and approached when next he stumbled.

Many a man, yet dazed from his hospital experience, has stepped over the threshold of that home into freedom. Many an alcoholic who entered there came away with an answer. He succumbed to that gay crowd inside, who laughed at their own misfortunes and understood his. Impressed by those who visited him at the hospital, he capitulated entirely when, later, in an upper room of this house, he heard the story of some man whose experience closely tallied with his own. The expression on the faces of the women, that indefinable something in the eyes of the men, the stimulating and electric atmosphere of the place, conspired to let him know that here was haven at last.

The very practical approach to his problems, the absence of intolerance of any kind, the informality, the genuine democracy, the uncanny understanding which these people had were irresistible. He and his wife would leave elated by the thought of what they could now do for some stricken acquaintance and his family. They knew they had a host of new friends; it seemed they had known these strangers always. They had seen miracles, and one was to come to them. They had visioned the Great Reality—their loving and All Powerful Creator.

Now, this house will hardly accommodate its weekly visitors, for they number sixty or eighty as a rule. Alcoholics are being attracted from far and near. From surrounding towns, families drive long distances to be present. A community thirty miles away has fifteen fellows of Alcoholics Anonymous. Being a large place, we think that some day its Fellowship will number many hundreds.*

But life among Alcoholics Anonymous is more than attending gatherings and visiting hospitals. Cleaning up old scrapes, helping to settle family differences, explaining the disinherited son to his irate parents, lending money and securing jobs for each other, when justified—these are everyday occurrences. No one is too discredited or has sunk too low to be welcomed cordially—if he means business. Social distinctions, petty rivalries and jealousies—these are laughed out of countenance. Being wrecked in the same vessel, being restored and united under one God, with hearts and minds attuned to the welfare of others, the things which matter so much to some people no longer signify much to them. How could they?

Under only slightly different conditions, the same thing is taking place in many eastern cities. In one of

*Written in 1939.

these there is a well-known hospital for the treatment of alcoholic and drug addiction. Six years ago one of our number was a patient there. Many of us have felt, for the first time, the Presence and Power of God within its walls. We are greatly indebted to the doctor in attendance there, for he, although it might prejudice his own work, has told us of his belief in ours.

Every few days this doctor suggests our approach to one of his patients. Understanding our work, he can do this with an eye to selecting those who are willing and able to recover on a spiritual basis. Many of us, former patients, go there to help. Then, in this eastern city, there are informal meetings such as we have described to you, where you may now see scores of members. There are the same fast friendships, there is the same helpfulness to one another as you find among our western friends. There is a good bit of travel between East and West and we foresee a great increase in this helpful interchange.

Some day we hope that every alcoholic who journeys will find a Fellowship of Alcoholics Anonymous at his destination. To some extent this is already true. Some of us are salesmen and go about. Little clusters of twos and threes and fives of us have sprung up in other communities, through contact with our two larger centers. Those of us who travel drop in as often as we can. This practice enables us to lend a hand, at the same time avoiding certain alluring distractions of the road, about which any traveling man can inform you.*

Thus we grow. And so can you, though you be but

*Written in 1939. In 2012 there are over 116,000 groups. There is A.A. activity in 180 countries, with an estimated membership of over two million.

one man with this book in your hand. We believe and hope it contains all you will need to begin.

We know what you are thinking. You are saying to yourself: "I'm jittery and alone. I couldn't do that." But you can. You forget that you have just now tapped a source of power much greater than yourself. To duplicate, with such backing, what we have accomplished is only a matter of willingness, patience and labor.

We know of an A.A. member who was living in a large community. He had lived there but a few weeks when he found that the place probably contained more alcoholics per square mile than any city in the country. This was only a few days ago at this writing. (1939) The authorities were much concerned. He got in touch with a prominent psychiatrist who had undertaken certain responsibilities for the mental health of the community. The doctor proved to be able and exceedingly anxious to adopt any workable method of handling the situation. So he inquired, what did our friend have on the ball?

Our friend proceeded to tell him. And with such good effect that the doctor agreed to a test among his patients and certain other alcoholics from a clinic which he attends. Arrangements were also made with the chief psychiatrist of a large public hospital to select still others from the stream of misery which flows through that institution.

So our fellow worker will soon have friends galore. Some of them may sink and perhaps never get up, but if our experience is a criterion, more than half of those approached will become fellows of Alcoholics Anonymous. When a few men in this city have found themselves, and have discovered the joy of helping others to face life again, there will be no stopping until everyone in that town has had his opportunity to recover—if he can and will.

Still you may say: "But I will not have the benefit of contact with you who write this book." We cannot be sure. God will determine that, so you must remember that your real reliance is always upon Him. He will show you how to create the fellowship you crave.*

Our book is meant to be suggestive only. We realize we know only a little. God will constantly disclose more to you and to us. Ask Him in your morning meditation what you can do each day for the man who is still sick. The answers will come, if your own house is in order. But obviously you cannot transmit something you haven't got. See to it that your relationship with Him is right, and great events will come to pass for you and countless others. This is the Great Fact for us.

Abandon yourself to God as you understand God. Admit your faults to Him and to your fellows. Clear away the wreckage of your past. Give freely of what you find and join us. We shall be with you in the Fellowship of the Spirit, and you will surely meet some of us as you trudge the Road of Happy Destiny.

May God bless you and keep you—until then.

*Alcoholics Anonymous will be glad to hear from you.
Address: PO Box 459, Grand Central Station, New York, NY 10163.

DOCTOR BOB'S NIGHTMARE

A co-founder of Alcoholics Anonymous. The birth of our Society dates from his first day of permanent sobriety, June 10, 1935.

To 1950, the year of his death, he carried the A.A. message to more than 5,000 alcoholic men and women, and to all these he gave his medical services without thought of charge.

In this prodigy of service, he was well assisted by Sister Ignatia at St. Thomas Hospital in Akron, Ohio, one of the greatest friends our Fellowship will ever know.

I WAS BORN in a small New England village of about seven thousand souls. The general moral standard was, as I recall it, far above the average. No beer or liquor was sold in the neighborhood, except at the State liquor agency where perhaps one might procure a pint if he could convince the agent that he really needed it. Without this proof the expectant purchaser would be forced to depart empty handed with none of what I later came to believe was the great panacea for all human ills. Men who had liquor shipped in from Boston or New York by express were looked upon with great distrust and disfavor by most of the good townspeople. The town was well supplied with churches and schools in which I pursued my early educational activities.

My father was a professional man of recognized ability and both my father and mother were most active in church affairs. Both father and mother were considerably above the average in intelligence.

Unfortunately for me, I was the only child, which perhaps engendered the selfishness which played such an important part in bringing on my alcoholism.

From childhood through high school I was more or less forced to go to church, Sunday School and evening service, Monday night Christian Endeavor and sometimes to Wednesday evening prayer meeting. This had the effect of making me resolve that when I was free from parental domination, I would never again darken the doors of a church. This resolution I kept steadfastly for the next forty years, except when circumstances made it seem unwise to absent myself.

After high school came four years in one of the best colleges in the country where drinking seemed to be a major extra-curricular activity. Almost everyone seemed to do it. I did it more and more, and had lots of fun without much grief, either physical or financial. I seemed to be able to snap back the next morning better than most of my fellow drinkers, who were cursed (or perhaps blessed) with a great deal of morning-after nausea. Never once in my life have I had a headache, which fact leads me to believe that I was an alcoholic almost from the start. My whole life seemed to be centered around doing what I wanted to do, without regard for the rights, wishes, or privileges of anyone else; a state of mind which became more and more predominant as the years passed. I was graduated "summa cum laude" in the eyes of the drinking fraternity, but not in the eyes of the Dean.

The next three years I spent in Boston, Chicago, and Montreal in the employ of a large manufacturing concern, selling railway supplies, gas engines of all sorts, and many other items of heavy hardware. During these years, I drank as much as my purse permitted, still without paying too great a penalty, although I was beginning to have morning jitters at times. I lost only a half day's work during these three years.

My next move was to take up the study of medicine, entering one of the largest universities in the country. There I took up the business of drinking with much greater earnestness than I had previously shown. On account of my enormous capacity for beer, I was elected to membership in one of the drinking societies, and soon became one of the leading spirits. Many mornings I have gone to classes, and even though fully prepared, would turn and walk back to the fraternity house because of my jitters, not daring to enter the classroom for fear of making a scene should I be called on for recitation.

This went from bad to worse until Sophomore spring when, after a prolonged period of drinking, I made up my mind that I could not complete my course, so I packed my grip and went South to spend a month on a large farm owned by a friend of mine. When I got the fog out of my brain, I decided that quitting school was very foolish and that I had better return and continue my work. When I reached school, I discovered the faculty had other ideas on the subject. After much argument they allowed me to return and take my exams, all of which I passed creditably. But they were much disgusted and told me they would attempt to struggle along without my presence. After many painful discussions, they finally gave me my credits and I migrated to another of the leading universities of the country and entered as a Junior that fall.

There my drinking became so much worse that the boys in the fraternity house where I lived felt forced to send for my father, who made a long journey in the vain endeavor to get me straightened around. This had little effect however for I kept on drinking and used a great deal more hard liquor than in former years.

Coming up to final exams I went on a particularly strenuous spree. When I went in to write the examinations, my hand trembled so I could not hold a pencil. I passed in at least three absolutely blank books. I was, of course, soon on the carpet and the upshot was that I had to go back for two more quarters and remain absolutely dry, if I wished to graduate. This I did, and proved myself satisfactory to the faculty, both in deportment and scholastically.

I conducted myself so creditably that I was able to secure a much coveted internship in a western city, where I spent two years. During these two years I was kept so busy that I hardly left the hospital at all. Consequently, I could not get into any trouble.

When those two years were up, I opened an office downtown. I had some money, all the time in the world, and considerable stomach trouble. I soon discovered that a couple of drinks would alleviate my gastric distress, at least for a few hours at a time, so it was not at all difficult for me to return to my former excessive indulgence.

By this time I was beginning to pay very dearly physically and, in hope of relief, voluntarily incarcerated myself at least a dozen times in one of the local sanitariums. I was between Scylla and Charybdis now, because if I did not drink my stomach tortured me, and if I did, my nerves did the same thing. After three years of this, I wound up in the local hospital where they attempted to help me, but I would get my friends to smuggle me a quart, or I would steal the alcohol about the building, so that I got rapidly worse.

Finally my father had to send a doctor out from my home town who managed to get me back there in some way, and I was in bed about two months before I could venture out of the house. I stayed about town a couple of months more and then returned to resume my practice. I think I must have been thoroughly scared by what had happened, or by the doctor, or probably both, so that I did not touch a drink again until the country went dry.

With the passing of the Eighteenth Amendment I felt quite safe. I knew everyone would buy a few bottles, or cases, of liquor as their exchequers permitted, and that it would soon be gone. Therefore it would make no great difference, even if I should do some drinking. At that time I was not aware of the almost unlimited supply the government made it possible for us doctors to obtain, neither had I any knowledge of the bootlegger who soon appeared on the horizon. I drank with moderation at first, but it took me only a relatively short time to drift back into the old habits which had wound up so disastrously before.

During the next few years, I developed two distinct phobias. One was the fear of not sleeping, and the other was the fear of running out of liquor. Not being a man of means, I knew that if I did not stay sober enough to earn money, I would run out of liquor. Most of the time, therefore, I did not take the morning drink which I craved so badly, but instead would fill up on large doses of sedatives to quiet the jitters, which distressed me terribly. Occasionally, I would yield to the morning craving, but if I did, it would be only a few hours before I would be quite unfit for work. This would lessen my chances of smuggling some home that evening, which in turn would mean a night of futile tossing around in bed followed by a morning of unbearable jitters. During the subsequent fifteen years I had sense enough never to go to the hospital if I had been drinking, and very seldom did I receive patients. I would sometimes hide out in one of the clubs of which I was a member, and had the habit at times of registering at a hotel under a fictitious name. But my friends usually found me and I would go home if they promised that I should not be scolded.

If my wife was planning to go out in the afternoon, I would get a large supply of liquor and smuggle it home and hide it in the coal bin, the clothes chute, over door jambs, over beams in the cellar and in cracks in the cellar tile. I also made use of old trunks and chests, the old can container, and even the ash container. The water tank on the toilet I never used, because that looked too easy. I found out later that my wife inspected it frequently. I used to put eight or twelve ounce bottles of alcohol in a fur lined glove and toss it onto the back airing porch when winter days got dark enough. My bootlegger had hidden alcohol at the back steps where I could get it at my convenience. Sometimes I would bring it in my pockets, but they were inspected, and that became too risky. I used also to put it up in four ounce bottles and stick several in my stocking tops. This worked nicely until my wife and I went to see Wallace Beery in "Tugboat Annie," after which the pant-leg and stocking racket were out!

I will not take space to relate all my hospital or sanitarium experiences.

During all this time we became more or less ostracized by our friends. We could not be invited out because I would surely get tight and my wife dared not invite people in for the same reason. My phobia for sleeplessness demanded that I get drunk every night, but in order to get more liquor for the next night, I had to stay sober during the day, at least up to four o'clock. This routine went on with few interruptions for seventeen years. It was really a horrible nightmare, this earning money, getting liquor, smuggling it home, getting drunk, morning jitters, taking large doses of sedatives to make it possible for me to earn more money, and so on ad nauseam. I used to promise my wife, my friends, and my children that I would drink no more—promises which seldom kept me sober even through the day, though I was very sincere when I made them.

For the benefit of those experimentally inclined, I should mention the so-called beer experiment. When beer first came back, I thought that I was safe. I could drink all I wanted of that. It was harmless; nobody ever got drunk on beer. So I filled the cellar full, with the permission of my good wife. It was not long before I was drinking at least a case and a half a day. I put on thirty pounds of weight in about two months, looked like a pig, and was uncomfortable from shortness of breath. It then occurred to me that after one was all smelled up with beer nobody could tell what had been drunk, so I began to fortify my beer with straight alcohol. Of course, the result was very bad, and that ended the beer experiment.

About the time of the beer experiment I was thrown in with a crowd of people who attracted me because of their seeming poise, health, and happiness. They spoke with great freedom from embarrassment, which I could never do, and they seemed very much at ease on all occasions and appeared very healthy. More than these attributes, they seemed to be happy. I was self conscious and ill at ease most of the time, my health was at the breaking point, and I was thoroughly miserable. I sensed they had something I did not have, from which I might readily profit. I learned that it was something of a spiritual nature, which did not appeal to me very much, but I thought it could do no harm. I gave the matter much time and study for the next two and a half years, but still got tight every night nevertheless. I read everything I could find, and talked to everyone who I thought knew anything about it.

My wife became deeply interested and it was her interest that sustained mine, though I at no time sensed that it might be an answer to my liquor problem. How my wife kept her faith and courage during all those years, I'll never know, but she did. If she had not, I know I would have been dead a long time ago. For some reason, we alcoholics seem to have the gift of picking out the world's finest women. Why they should be subjected to the tortures we inflict upon them, I cannot explain.

About this time a lady called up my wife one Saturday afternoon, saying she wanted me to come over that evening to meet a friend of hers who might help me. It was the day before Mother's Day and I had come home plastered, carrying a big potted plant which I set down on the table and forthwith went upstairs and passed out. The next day she called again. Wishing to be polite, though I felt very badly, I said, "Let's make the call," and extracted from my wife a promise that we would not stay over fifteen minutes.

We entered her house at exactly five o'clock and it was eleven fifteen when we left. I had a couple of shorter talks with this man afterward, and stopped drinking abruptly. This dry spell lasted for about three weeks; then I went to Atlantic City to attend several days' meeting of a national society of which I was a member. I drank all the scotch they had on the train and bought several quarts on my way to the hotel. This was on Sunday. I got tight that night, stayed sober Monday till after the dinner and then proceeded to get tight again. I drank all I dared in the bar, and then went to my room to finish the job. Tuesday I started in the morning, getting well organized by noon. I did not want to disgrace myself so I then checked out. I bought some more liquor on the way to the depot. I had to wait some time for the train. I remember nothing from then on until I woke up at a friend's house, in a town near home. These good people notified my wife, who sent my newly made friend over to get me. He came and got me home and to bed, gave me a few drinks that night, and one bottle of beer the next morning.

That was June 10, 1935, and that was my last drink. As I write nearly four years have passed.

The question which might naturally come into your mind would be: "What did the man do or say that was different from what others had done or said?" It must be remembered that I had read a great deal and talked to everyone who knew, or thought they knew anything about the subject of alcoholism. But this was a man who had experienced many years of frightful drinking, who had had most all the drunkard's experiences known to man, but who had been cured by the very means I had been trying to employ, that is to say the spiritual approach. He gave me information about the subject of alcoholism which was undoubtedly helpful. *Of far more importance was the fact that he was the first living human with whom I had ever talked, who knew what he was talking about in regard to alcoholism from actual experience. In other words, he talked my language.* He knew all the answers, and certainly not because he had picked them up in his reading.

It is a most wonderful blessing to be relieved of the terrible curse with which I was afflicted. My health is good and I have regained my self-respect and the respect of my colleagues. My home life is ideal and my business is as good as can be expected in these uncertain times.

I spend a great deal of time passing on what I learned to others who want and need it badly. I do it for four reasons:

1. Sense of duty.
2. It is a pleasure.
3. Because in so doing I am paying my debt to the man who took time to pass it on to me.
4. Because every time I do it I take out a little more insurance for myself against a possible slip.

Unlike most of our crowd, I did not get over my craving for liquor much during the first two and one-half years of abstinence. It was almost always with me. But at no time have I been anywhere near yielding. I used to get terribly upset when I saw my friends drink and knew I could not, but I schooled myself to believe that though I once had the same privilege, I had abused it so frightfully that it was withdrawn. So it doesn't behoove me to squawk about it for, after all, nobody ever had to throw me down and pour liquor down my throat.

If you think you are an atheist, an agnostic, a skeptic, or have any other form of intellectual pride which keeps you from accepting what is in this book, I feel sorry for you. If you still think you are strong enough to beat the game alone, that is your affair. But if you really and truly want to quit drinking liquor for good and all, and sincerely feel that you must have some help, we know that we have an answer for you. It never fails, if you go about it with one half the zeal you have been in the habit of showing when you were getting another drink.

Your Heavenly Father will never let you down!

SPIRITUAL EXPERIENCE

The terms "spiritual experience" and "spiritual awakening" are used many times in this book which, upon careful reading, shows that the personality change sufficient to bring about recovery from alcoholism has manifested itself among us in many different forms.

Yet it is true that our first printing gave many readers the impression that these personality changes, or religious experiences, must be in the nature of sudden and spectacular upheavals. Happily for everyone, this conclusion is erroneous.

In the first few chapters a number of sudden revolutionary changes are described. Though it was not our intention to create such an impression, many alcoholics have nevertheless concluded that in order to recover they must acquire an immediate and overwhelming "God-consciousness" followed at once by a vast change in feeling and outlook.

Among our rapidly growing membership of thousands of alcoholics such transformations, though frequent, are by no means the rule. Most of our experiences are what the psychologist William James calls the "educational variety" because they develop slowly over a period of time. Quite often friends of the newcomer are aware of the difference long before he is himself. He finally realizes that he has undergone a profound alteration in his reaction to life; that such a change could hardly have been brought about by himself alone. What often takes place in a few months could seldom have been accomplished by years of self discipline. With few exceptions our members find that they have tapped an unsuspected inner resource which they presently identify with their own conception of a Power greater than themselves.

Most of us think this awareness of a Power greater than ourselves is the essence of spiritual experience. Our more religious members call it "God-consciousness."

Most emphatically we wish to say that any alcoholic capable of honestly facing his problems in the light of our experience can recover, provided he does not close his mind to all spiritual concepts. He can only be defeated by an attitude of intolerance or belligerent denial.

We find that no one need have difficulty with the spirituality of the program. *Willingness, honesty and open mindedness are the essentials of recovery. But these are indispensable.*

> "There is a principle which is a bar against all information, which is proof against all arguments and which cannot fail to keep a man in everlasting ignorance—that principle is contempt prior to investigation."
>
> —HERBERT SPENCER[1]

Note

1. Extensive research reveals that in all likelihood Spencer never said or wrote this. This quotation seems to have evolved in the course of numerous attributions to an observation written by British theologian William Paley.
   Full documentation is available at http://anonpress.org/spencer

The following is the fifth chapter, "How It Works" from The Original Manuscript of Alcoholics Anonymous. It was this version that was distributed to friends and colleagues of The Fellowship's founders to get comments and suggestions on what to change before sending it to the printer.

Rarely have we seen a person fail who has thoroughly followed our directions. Those who do not recover are people who cannot or will not completely give themselves to this simple program, usually men and women who are constitutionally incapable of being honest with themselves. There are such unfortunates. They are not at fault; they seem to have been born that way. They are naturally incapable of grasping and developing a way of life which demands rigorous honesty. Their chances are less than average. There are those, too, who suffer from grave emotional and mental disorders, but many of them do recover if they have the capacity to be honest.

Our stories disclose in a general way what we used to be like, what happened, and what we are like now. If you have decided you want what we have and are willing to go to any length to get it — then you are ready to follow directions.

At some of these you may balk. You may think you can find an easier, softer way. We doubt if you can. With all the earnestness at our command, we beg of you to be fearless and thorough from the very start. Some of us have tried to hold on to our old ideas and the result was nil until we let go absolutely.

Remember that you are dealing with alcohol — cunning, baffling, powerful! Without help it is too much for you. But there is One who has all power — That One is God. You must find Him now!

Half measures will avail you nothing. You stand at the turning point. Throw yourself under His protection and care with complete abandon.

Now we think you can take it! Here are the steps we took, which are suggested as your Program of Recovery:

1. Admitted we were powerless over alcohol — that our lives had become unmanageable.
2. Came to believe that a Power greater than ourselves could restore us to sanity.
3. Made a decision to turn our will and our lives over to the care and direction of God as we understood Him.
4. Made a searching and fearless moral inventory of ourselves.
5. Admitted to God, to ourselves, and to another human being the exact nature of our wrongs.
6. Were entirely willing that God remove all these defects of character.
7. Humbly, on our knees, asked Him to remove our shortcomings — holding nothing back.
8. Made a list of all persons we had harmed, and became willing to make complete amends to them all.
9. Made direct amends to such people wherever possible, except when to do so would injure them or others.
10. Continued to take personal inventory and when we were wrong promptly admitted it.
11. Sought through prayer and meditation to improve our contact with God, praying only for knowledge of His will for us and the power to carry that out.

12. Having had a spiritual experience as the result of this course of action, we tried to carry this message to others, especially alcoholics, and to practice these principles in all our affairs.

You may exclaim, "What an order! I can't go through with it." Do not be discouraged. No one among us has been able to maintain anything like perfect adherence to these principles. We are not saints. The point is, that we are willing to grow along spiritual lines. The principles we have set down are guides to progress. We claim spiritual progress rather than spiritual perfection.

Our description of the alcoholic, the chapter to the agnostic, and our personal adventures before and after, have been designed to sell you three pertinent ideas:

(a) That you are alcoholic and cannot manage your own life.
(b) That probably no human power can relieve your alcoholism.
(c) That God can and will.

If you are not convinced on these vital issues, you ought to re-read the book to this point or else throw it away!

If you are convinced, you are now at step three, which is that you make a decision to turn your will and your life over to God as you understand Him. Just what do we mean by that, and just what do we do?

The first requirement is that you see that any life run on self-will can hardly be a success. On that basis we are almost always in collission* with something or somebody, even though our motives may be good. Most people try to live by self-propulsion. Each person is like an actor who wants to run the whole show: is forever trying to arrange the lights, the ballet, the scenery and the rest of the players in his own way. If his arrangements would only stay put, if only people would do as he wishes, the show would be great. Everybody, including himself, would be pleased. Life would be wonderful. In trying to make these arrangements our actor may sometimes be quite virtuous. He may be kind, considerate, patient, generous; even modest and self-sacrificing. On the other hand, he may be mean, egotistical, selfish and dishonest. But, as with most humans, he is more likely to have varied traits.

What usually happens? The show doesn't come off very well. He begins to think life doesn't treat him right. He decides to exert himself some more. He becomes, on the next occasion, still more demanding or gracious, as the case may be. Still the play does not suit him. Admitting he may be somewhat at fault, he is sure that other people are more to blame. He becomes angry, indignant, self-pitying. What is his basic trouble? Is he not really a self-seeker even when trying to be kind? Is he not a victim of the delusion that he can wrest satisfaction and happiness out of this world if he only manages well? Is it not evident to all the rest of the players that these are the things he wants? And do not his actions make each of them wish to retaliate, snatching all they can get out of the show? Is he not, even in his best moments, a producer of confusion rather than harmony?

Our actor is self-centered — ego-centric, as people like to call it nowadays. He is like the retired business man who lolls in the Florida sunshine in the winter complaining of the sad state of the nation; the preacher who sighs over the sins of the twentieth century; politicians and reformers who are sure all would be Utopia if the rest of the world would only behave; the outlaw safe cracker who thinks society has wronged him; and the alcoholic who has lost all and is locked up. Whatever their protestations, are not these people mostly concerned with themselves, their resentments, or their self-pity?

Selfishness — self-centeredness! That, we think, is the root of our troubles. Driven by a hundred forms of fear, self-delusion, self-seeking, and self-pity, we step on the toes of our fellows and they retaliate. Sometimes they hurt us, seemingly, without provocation, but we invariably find that at some time in the past we have made decisions based on self, which later placed us in a position to be hurt.

So our troubles, we think, are basically of our own making. They arise out of ourselves, and the alcoholic is almost the most extreme example that could be found of self-will run riot, though he usually doesn't think so. Above everything, we alcoholics must be rid of this selfishness. We must, or it kills us! God makes that possible. And there is no way of entirely getting rid of self without Him.

You may have moral and philosophical convictions galore, but you can't live up to them even though you would like to. Neither can you reduce your self-centeredness much by wishing or trying on your own power. You must have God's help.

This is the how and why of it. First of all, quit playing God yourself. It doesn't work. Next, decide that hereafter in this drama of life, God is going to be your Director. He is the Principal; you are to be His agent. He is the Father, and you are His child. Get that simple relationship straight. Most good ideas are simple and this concept is to be the keystone of the new and triumphant arch through which you will pass to freedom.

When you sincerely take such a position, all sorts of remarkable things follow. You have a new Employer. Being all powerful, He must necessarily provide what you need, if you keep close to Him and perform His work well. Established on such a footing you become less and less interested in yourself, your little plans and designs. More and more you become interested in seeing what you can contribute to life. As you feel new power flow in, as you enjoy peace of mind, as you discover you can face life successfully, and as you become conscious of His presence, you begin to lose your fear of today, tomorrow, or the hereafter. You will have been reborn.

Get down upon your knees and say to your Maker, as you understand Him: "God, I offer myself to Thee — to build with me and to do with me as Thou wilt. Relieve me of the bondage of self, that I may better do Thy will. Take away my difficulties, that victory over them may bear witness to those I would help of Thy Power, Thy Love, and Thy Way of life. May I do Thy will always!" Think well before taking this step. Be sure you are ready; that you can at last abandon yourself utterly to Him.

It is very desirable that you make your decision with an understanding person. It may be your wife, your best friend, your spiritual adviser, but remember it is better to meet God alone that* with one who might misunderstand. You must decide this for yourself. The wording of your decision is, of course, quite optional so long as you express the idea, voicing it without reservation. This decision is only a beginning, though if honestly and humbly made, an effect, sometimes a very great one, will be felt at once.

Next we launch out on a course of vigorous action, the first step of which is a personal housecleaning, which you have never in all probability attempted. Though your decision is a vital and crucial step, it can have little permanent effect unless at once followed by a strenuous effort to face, and to be rid of, the things in yourself which have been blocking you. Your liquor is but a symptom. Let's now get down to basic causes and conditions.

Therefore, you start upon a personal inventory. This is step four. A business which takes no regular inventory usually goes broke. Taking a commercial inventory is a fact-finding and fact-facing process. It is an effort to discover the truth about the stock in trade. Its object is to disclose damaged or unsalable goods, to get rid of them promptly and without regret. If the owner of the business is to be successful, he cannot fool himself about values.

We do exactly the same thing with our lives. We take stock honestly. First, we search out the flaws in our make-up which have caused our failure. Being convinced that self, manifested in various ways, is what has defeated us, we consider its common manifestations.

Resentment is the "number one" offender. It destroys more alcoholics than anything else. From it stem all forms of spiritual disease, for we have been not only mentally and physically ill, we have been spiritually sick. When the spiritual malady is overcome, we straighten out mentally and physically. In dealing with resentments, we set them on paper. List people, institutions or principles with whom you are angry. Ask yourself why you are angry. In most cases it will be found that your self-esteem, your pocketbook, your ambitions, your personal relationships (including sex) are hurt or threatened. So you are sore. You are "burned up."

On your grudge list set opposite each name your injuries. Is it your self-esteem, your security, your ambitions, your personal, or your sex relations, which have been interfered with?

Be as definite as this example:

I'm resentful at:	The Cause	Affects my:
Mr. Brown	His attention to my wife.	Sex relations. Self-esteem (fear)
	Told my wife of my mistress.	Sex relations. Self-esteem (fear)
	Brown may get my job at the office.	Security. Self-esteem (fear)
Mrs.Jones	She's a nut -- she snubbed me. She committed her husband for drinking.	Personal relationship. Self-esteem (fear)
	He's my friend	
	She's a gossip.	
My employer	Unreasonable-Unjust - Overbearing - Threatens to fire me for drinking and padding my expense account.	Self-esteem(fear) Security.
My wife	Misunderstands and nags. Likes Brown. Wants house put in her name.	Pride - Personal sex relations - Security (fear)

Go on through the list back through your lifetime. Nothing counts but thoroughness and honesty. When you are finished consider it carefully.

The first thing apparent to you is that this world and its people are often quite wrong. To conclude that others are wrong is as far as most of us ever get. The usual outcome is that people continue to wrong you and you stay sore. Sometimes it is remorse and then you are sore at yourself. But the more you fight and try to have your way, the worse matters get. Isn't that so? As in war, victors only seem to win. Your moments of triumph are short-lived.

It is plain that a way of life which includes deep resentment leads only to futility and unhappiness. To the precise extent that we permit these, do we squander the hours that might have been worth while. But with the alcoholic whose only hope is the maintenance and growth of a spiritual experience, this business of resentment is infinitely grave. We find that it is fatal. For when harboring such feelings we shut ourselves off from the sunlight of the Spirit. The insanity of alcohol returns and we drink again. And with us, to drink is to die.

If we are to live, we must be free of anger. The grouch and the brainstorm are not for us. They may be the dubious luxury of normal men, but for alcoholics these things are poison.

Turn back to your list, for it holds the key to your future. You must be prepared to look at it from an entirely different angle. You will begin to see that the world and its people really dominate you. In your present state, the wrongdoing of others, fancied or real, has power to actually kill you. How shall you escape? You see that these resentments must be mastered, but how? You cannot wish them away any more than alcohol.

This is our course: realize at once that the people who wronged you are spiritually sick.

Though you don't like their symptoms and the way these disturb you, they, like yourself, are sick, too. Ask God to help you show them the same tolerance, pity, and patience that you would cheerfully grant a friend who has cancer. When a person next offends, say to yourself "This is a sick man. How can I be helpful to him? God save me from being angry. Thy will be done."

Never argue. Never retaliate. You wouldn't treat sick people that way. If you do, you destroy your chance of being helpful. You cannot be helpful to all people, but at least God will show you how to take a kindly and tolerant view of each and every one.

Take up your list again. Putting out of your mind the wrongs others have done, resolutely look for your own mistakes. Where have you been selfish, dishonest, self-seeking and frightened? Though a situation may not be entirely your fault, disregard the other person involved entirely. See where vou have been to blame. This is your inventory, not the other man's. When you see your fault write it down on the list. See it before you in black and white. Admit your wrongs honestly and be willing to set these matters straight.

You will notice that the word fear is bracketed alongside the difficulties with Mr. Brown, Mrs. Jones, your employer, and your wife. This short word somehow touches about every aspect of our lives. It is an evil and corroding thread; the fabric of our existence is shot through with it. It sets in motion trains of circumstances which bring us misfortune we feel we don't deserve. But did not we, ourselves, set the ball rolling? Sometimes we think fear ought to be classed with stealing as a sin. It seems to cause more trouble.

Review your fears thoroughly. Put them on paper, even though you have no resentment in connection with them. Ask yourself why you have them. Isn't it because self-reliance has failed you? Self-reliance was good as far as it went, but it didn't go far enough. Some of us once had great self-confidence, but it didn't fully solve the fear problem, or any other. When it made us cocky, it was worse.

Perhaps there is a better way — we think so. For you are now to go on a different basis; the basis of trusting and relying upon God. You are to trust infinite God rather than your finite self. You are in the world to play the role he assigns. Just to the extent that you do as you think He would have you, and humbly rely on Him, does He enable you to match calamity with serenity.

You must never apologize to anyone for depending upon your Creator. You can laugh at those who think spirituality the way of weakness. Paradoxically, it is the way of strength. The verdict of the ages is that faith means courage. All men of faith have courage. They trust their God. Never apologize for God. Instead let Him demonstrate, through you, what He can do. Ask Him to remove your fear and direct your attention to what He would have you be. At once, you will commence to outgrow fear.

Now about sex. You can probably stand an overhauling there. We needed it. But above all, let's be sensible on this question. It's so easy to get way off the track. Here we find human opinions running to extremes — absurd extremes, perhaps. One set of voices cry that sex is a lust of our lower nature, a base necessity of procreation. Then we have the voices who cry for sex and more sex; who bewail the institution of marriage; who think that most of the troubles of the race are traceable to sex causes. They think we do not have enough of it, or that it isn't the right kind. They see its significance everywhere. One school would allow man no flavor for his fare and the other would have us all on a straight pepper diet. We want to stay out of this controversy. We do not want to be the arbiter of anyone's sex conduct. We all have sex problems. We'd hardly be human if we didn't. What can we do about them?

Review your own conduct over the years past. Where have you been selfish, dishonest, or inconsiderate? Whom did you hurt? Did you unjustifiably arouse jealousy, suspicion or bitterness? Where you were at fault, what should you have done instead? Get this all down on paper and look at it.

In this way you can shape a sane and sound ideal for your future sex life. Subject each relation to this test — is it selfish or not? Ask God to mold your ideals and help you to live up to them. Remember always that your sex powers are God-given, and therefore good, neither to be used lightly or selfishly nor to be despised and loathed.

Whatever your ideal may be, you must be willing to grow toward it. You must be willing to make amends where you have done harm, provided that you will not bring about still more harm in so doing. In other words, treat sex as you would any other problem. In meditation, ask God what you should do about each specific matter. The right answer will come, if you want it.

God alone can judge your sex situation. Counsel with

persons is often desirable, but let God be the final judge. Remember that some people are as fanatical about sex as others are loose. Avoid hysterical thinking or advice.

Suppose you fall short of the chosen ideal and stumble. Does this mean you are going to get drunk? Some people will tell you so. If they do, it will be only a half-truth. It depends on you and your motive. If you are sorry for what you have done, and have the honest desire to let God take you to better things, you will be forgiven and will have learned your lesson. If you are not sorry, and your conduct continues to harm others, you are quite sure to drink. We are not theorizing. These are facts out of our experience.

To sum up about sex: earnestly pray for the right ideal, for guidance in each questionable situation, for sanity, and for the strength to do the right thing. If sex is very troublesome, throw yourself the harder into helping others. Think of their needs and work for them. This will take you out of yourself. It will quiet the imperious urge, when to yield would mean heartache.

If you have been thorough about your personal inventory, you have written down a lot by this time. You have listed and analyzed your resentments. You have begun to comprehend their futility and their fatality. You have commenced to see their terrible destructiveness. You have begun to learn tolerance, patience and good will toward all men, even your enemies, for you know them to be sick people. You have listed the people you have hurt by your conduct, and you are willing to straighten out the past if you can.

In this book you read again and again that God

did for us what we could not do for ourselves. We hope you are convinced now that He can remove the self-will that has blocked you off from Him. You have made your decision. You have made an inventory of the grosser handicaps you have. You have made a good beginning, for you have swallowed and digested some big chunks of truth about yourself. Are you willing to go on?

---

*Accurately reflects the original text.

The entire "Original Manuscript," including the stories, is available in our Study Edition which is available in softcover for $6.25.

http://anonpress.org

Abandoned 15, 45, 48, 59, 63, 164
Abated 137
derived from: abate (uh bAYt') v.
– to reduce in amount, degree, intensity, etc.; lessen; diminish: to abate a tax; to abate one's enthusiasm.
– Law. (a). to stop or suppress (an action, nuisance, etc.). (b). to annul (a writ).
– to deduct or subtract: to abate part of the price.
Aberrations 140
derived from: aberration (ab'uh rAY'shuhn) n.
– deviation from the usual, normal, or right course.
– deviation from the ordinary, usual, or normal type.
– deviation from truth or moral rectitude.
Abide 144
abide (uh bId') v.
– to remain; continue; stay: Abide with me.
– to have one's abode; dwell; reside.
– to continue in a particular condition; last; endure.
Abilities 8, 26, 30, 37, 41, 54, 141, 143
Abjectly 54
derived from: abject (ab'jekt) adj.
– utterly hopeless, miserable, or wretched: abject poverty.
– contemptible; despicable; base-spirited: an abject coward.
– servile; submissive; slavish.
Able xxix, 46, 51, 74, 86, 97, 127, 144, 146, 155, 158
Abnormal xviv, 23, 30, 114, 122, 140, 155
Absolute 14, 25
Absolutely xxvi, 17, 24, 29, 58, 120, 155
absolutely (ab'suh lUt'lEE) adv.
– completely; perfectly; unqualifiedly.
– positively; certainly.
– in an absolute condition or manner.
Abstainer 39
abstainer (ab stAY'nuhr) n.
– a person who abstains, esp. from the drinking of alcoholic beverages.
Abstinence 139
Accept 25, 39, 47, 48, 96, 143
Acceptance 14, 30, 48, 96, 143
acceptance (ak sep'tuhns) n.
– the act of taking or receiving something offered.
– favorable reception; approval; favor.
– the act of assenting or believing: acceptance of a theory.
Accepted xxviii, 14, 47, 80, 134, 139, 145
Accepting xxvii, 31, 47
Accomplished 18, 25, 31, 50, 91, 100, 111, 128, 144, 148, 163
Account xxvi, 29, 65, 78, 92, 102, 124, 145
Accounted 40
Acquaintance 74, 76, 112, 131, 150, 154, 159, 161
Acquired xxvii, 26, 33, 40
Act 31, 95, 97, 112, 113, 147
Action xxviii, 9, 17, 42, 61, 63, 72-73, 76, 80, 93, 94, 98, 140, 157
Activities 72, 104, 129, 131
Actor 60, 61
Actually 29, 49, 55, 66, 94, 115
Acute 157
acute (uh kyUt') adj.
– sharp or severe in effect; intense: acute pain.
– extremely great or serious; critical: an acute shortage of oil.
– (of disease) brief and severe (disting. from chronic).
Addiction xxvii, 162
Adherence 60
Admit xxviii-xxx, 30, 37-38, 78, 81, 93, 99, 110, 127, 135, 164
Admitted 11, 13, 59, 67, 72, 78, 92, 135
Admitting 77
Adopt 114, 130, 143, 163
Adopted 11, 153
Advantages xiii, 110, 125, 146
Adventure 60
Advertised 81
Advice 70, 73, 96, 106, 121
Advised 160

THE ANONYMOUS PRESS INDEX

Affairs 19, 60, 105, 120, 124
Affected 18, 33, 125, 126, 140
Affectionate 126
Affections 35, 82, 104, 107, 128
Affiliation 28
Afflicted xiv, xxvii, 92, 116
Afraid 78, 80, 85, 86, 116
Afterward 47, 133, 136, 141, 159
Against 41, 47, 49, 93
Aggrieved 24
aggrieved (uh grEEvd') adj.
– wronged, offended, or injured.
– Law. deprived of legal rights or claims.
– troubled; worried; disturbed.
Aghast 9
aghast (uh gast') adj.
– struck with overwhelming shock or amazement; filled with sudden fright or horror.
Agitated 87
Agnostic 28, 44-46, 49, 52, 60, 93
agnostic (ag nos'tik) n.
– a person who holds that the existence of the ultimate cause, as a god or God, and the essential nature of things are unknown and unknowable.
– of or pertaining to agnostics or agnosticism.
Agnostically 53
Agree 31, 35, 43, 50, 73, 93, 108, 129, 148, 155
Agreement 131
Aimlessly 10
Airplane 41, 52
Alcohol xxviii, xxix, xxxi, 8, 13, 24, 26, 33, 38, 48, 58-60, 66, 76, 84, 85, 98, 101-102, 108, 114, 119, 133, 134, 140, 143, 146
Alcoholic xxv-xxxii, 2, 7, 9, 14-16, 20-23, 25, 27, 29-30, 32-36, 39, 42-45, 48, 56, 60, 62, 64, 66, 73, 78, 79, 82, 88, 89, 91, 92, 94, 100, 102, 103, 107-109, 111-114, 117-119, 122-125, 130-131, 134-139, 141-142, 145-150, 152, 154, 163
Alcoholics Anonymous xiii, xxv, xxix, 104, 113, 114, 125, 135, 152, 153, 156, 157, 161-163
Alcoholism xiii, xxv, xxix, 17, 28, 34, 35, 38, 40, 42-44, 53, 56, 73, 74, 78, 85, 92, 94, 107, 112, 114-116, 118, 127, 131, 138, 141, 144, 147-149, 151-153, 155, 157
Ale 6, 154
Alexander, Jack xviii
Alibis 23
derived from: alibi (al'uh bI') n.
– Law. the defense by an accused person of having been elsewhere when an offense was committed.
– an excuse, esp. to avoid blame.
– a person used as one's excuse.
Alimony 79
Allergy xxvi, xxviii, xxx
allergy (al'er gEE) n.
– a condition of unusual sensitivity to a substance or substances which, in like amounts, do not effect others.
Allowed xxvii, 69
Alloy 2
alloy (al'oi) n.
– a substance composed of two or more metals, or of a metal or metals with a nonmetal, intimately mixed, as by fusion or electrodeposition.
– a less costly metal mixed with a more valuable one.
– standard; quality; fineness.
Alluring 123
alluring (uh loor'ing) adj.
– very attractive or tempting; enticing; seductive.
– fascinating; charming.
Almost 7, 24-25, 51-52, 60, 72, 105, 123-125, 142, 145
Alone 20, 34, 63, 75, 91, 96, 105, 113, 119, 158, 163
Alpha 49
alpha (al'fuh) n.
– the first letter of the Greek alphabet.
– the first; beginning.
– (cap.) the brightest star in a constellation: Alpha Centauri.
Alternative 25, 44

Altruistic xxvi, xxviii
derived from: altruism
(al'trU iz'uhm) n.
– the principle or practice of unselfish concern for the welfare of others (opposed to egoism).
– behavior by an animal that may be to its disadvantage but that benefits others of its kind.
Always 31, 36-37, 44, 60, 69, 74, 81, 105, 121, 125, 127
Amazing xxvii, 83, 128
Ambitious 32, 64, 65
Amends 8, 59, 69, 84
amends (uh mendz') n.
– reparation or compensation for a loss, damage, or injury of any kind; recompense.
– Idiom "make amends" to compensate, as for an injury, loss, or insult.
America 17, 26, 50, 51, 138
Amused 4, 49
Analysis 55, 70, 83, 104
Anger 37, 66, 88, 108, 135
Angry 18, 61, 64, 67, 106, 111, 113, 124
Animals 107
Annihilation 18
derived from: annihilate
(uh nI'uh lAYt') v.
– to reduce to utter ruin or nonexistence; destroy utterly.
– to destroy the collective existence or main body of; wipe out: to annihilate an army.
– to defeat completely; vanquish: Our team was annihilated in the playoffs.
Annoyance 139
Anonymous 19, 157
Answer xxxi, 7, 18, 20, 22, 35, 42, 56, 86, 110, 115, 138, 144, 153, 160, 164
Answered xviii, 13
Antagonism 48
Antipathy 12
antipathy (an tip'uh thEE) n.
– a natural, basic, or habitual repugnance; aversion.
– an instinctive contrariety or opposition in feeling.
– an object of natural aversion or habitual dislike.
Anti-religious 45
Anti-social 21
Anxious 74, 95, 121, 163
Any lengths 58, 76, 79, 90
Anyone 19, 69, 83-84, 98-99, 135, 139, 160
Anything xxvi, 28, 36-37, 56, 64, 75, 81, 84, 90, 93, 95, 100, 103, 111, 115, 125, 127, 145, 155, 158
Anywhere 26
Apart xxx, 43, 99, 159
Apathy 127
apathy (ap'uh thEE) n.
– absence or suppression of passion, emotion, or excitement.
– lack of interest in or concern for things that others find moving or exciting.
Apologize 68, 86, 115
Appeals xxix, xiii, 34
Appearance 39, 49
Appears xxviii, 9, 22, 28, 30, 57, 110
Applause 3
Applies 47, 93, 104, 115
Apply xxvii, 52, 104, 112, 116
Appointed 3, 74
Appointment xxx, 120
Appraise 82
Appreciated 40, 47, 111, 129, 141, 146
Appreciation 1, 102, 128
Approach xxvii, xxvi, xxix, 12, 13, 18, 19, 25, 43, 46, 50, 53, 56, 75-78, 90-91, 95, 112, 141, 144, 148, 153, 160, 162
Approve 74, 125, 130
Apropos 135
apropos (ap'ruh pO') adv.
– at the right time; opportunely.
– by the way.
– being appropriate and timely: apropos remarks.
Aptitudes 21
derived from: aptitude (ap'ti tUd') n.
– innate ability; talent: an aptitude for mathematics.
– readiness or quickness in learning; intelligence.
– suitability; fitness.

Arbiter 69
Argument 19, 49, 67, 98, 115, 126, 129, 132
Armistice 8
Arouse 89, 93, 100, 134, 146
Arousing 113
Arrange 60, 88
Arrangements 61, 163
Arranging 78, 122
Arrears 155
derived from: arrear (uh rEEr') n.
– Usually, "arrears." the state of being late in repaying a debt: to be in arrears with mortgage payments.
– Often, "arrears." a debt that remains unpaid.
Arrest 155
Ashamed 39
Ask 52, 75, 76, 87, 100, 101, 106, 112, 116, 120, 127, 144, 164
Askance 46
askance (uh skans') adv.
– with a side glance; sidewise; obliquely.
– with suspicion or disapproval; skeptically: The company may view askance your plan for early retirement.
Asked 20, 51, 56, 59, 68, 69, 80
Asking 47, 83, 89, 107
Assert 23, 130, 131
Assets 89, 124
Assistance 78, 96, 98, 136
Associates 15, 145
Association 28
Assumed 47, 97, 100, 128
Assuming 34
Assumption 48
Assure xxxi, 47, 89, 142
Astonishingly xxviii, 30
Astonishment xviii
Asylum 7, 15, 31, 35, 36, 38, 97
asylum (uh sI'luhm) n.
– (esp. formerly) an institution for the maintenance and care of the mentally ill, orphans, or other persons requiring specialized assistance.
– an inviolable refuge, as formerly for criminals and debtors; sanctuary.
– a. a refuge granted an alien by a sovereign state on its own territory.
b. a temporary refuge granted political offenders, esp. in a foreign embassy.
Atheist 10, 44, 49, 52, 55, 93
atheist (AY'thEE ist) n.
– a person who denies or disbelieves the existence of a supreme being or beings.
Attachment 137
Attempt 33, 94, 111, 125, 151
Attempted 32, 64, 141
Attend 87, 102
Attended xxv, 56, 80, 141, 161
Attention 1, 23, 65, 68, 90, 93, 107, 119, 143, 144, 149
Attitude 18, 19, 25, 27, 50, 55, 72, 77, 84-86, 99, 103, 117, 122, 143-145, 149, 150
Attractive 39, 154, 161
Attributes 53
Attuned 161
Authority 74, 78, 163
Automatically 85
Avail 24, 59
Available 74, 96, 134
Average xxviii, 17, 43, 58, 129
Avocation xiii
avocation (av'uh kAY'shuhn) n.
– something a person does in addition to a principal occupation, esp. for pleasure; hobby.
– a person's regular occupation or calling; vocation.
– Archaic. diversion or distraction.
Avoid 43, 67, 70, 72, 83, 91, 97, 98, 101, 113-115, 118, 123, 126
Avoided 126
Avoiding 85, 117
Awakening 86, 151
Aware 19, 109, 155
Awe 4, 46
Bad 29, 43, 76, 115, 132, 140
Bad-intentioned 108
Badly 20, 43, 133
Baffling 23, 26, 34, 51, 58, 62, 84, 92, 107
Balance 11, 21, 39, 131

Balked 58
derived from: balk (bôk) v.
– to refuse curtly and firmly (usually followed by at): He balked at making the speech.
– to stop short and stubbornly refuse to go on.
– to commit a balk in baseball.
Balmy 128
balmy (bä'mEE) adj.
– mild and refreshing; soft; soothing: balmy weather.
– Informal. crazy; foolish; eccentric.
Bankruptcy 34
Bar 6, 36, 41, 101
Barriers 56, 115, 126
Barroom 31
Base 68
Based 121, 124
Basic 52, 61
Basically 62
Basis 9, 33, 39, 50, 60, 68, 79, 99, 118, 120, 135, 146
Battle 6, 103
Beating 6
Beauty 50
Became 13, 59
Bed 8, 19, 41, 56, 157
Bedevilments 52
derived from: bedevil (bi dev'uhl) v.
– to torment or harass maliciously or diabolically.
– to possess as if with a devil; bewitch.
– to cause confusion or doubt in; muddle; confound.
Beer 1, 5, 20, 24, 31, 142
Beg 49, 58, 105
Begged 26
Begin 21, 22, 47, 75, 80, 109, 125, 126
Beginning 8, 19, 34, 37, 63, 71, 131
Behavior 7, 22, 37, 90, 107
Belief xxvi, 13, 28, 32, 45, 75, 101, 133
Believe xxv, xxvi, xxx, 12, 17, 25, 29, 31, 32, 39, 40, 45-49, 53, 54, 57, 59, 70, 86, 93, 116, 130, 135, 142, 143, 149, 163
Believed xxxii, 26
Belladonna 7
Belligerent 570
belligerent (buh lij'uhr uhnt) adj.
– waging war; engaged in warfare.
– showing readiness to fight; aggressively hostile; truculent: a belligerent tone.
– a state or nation at war.
Belonging 74
Bender 5, 23, 142
Benefactor 11
Beneficial 77, 134
Benefit 84
Beset 51
Best 55, 63, 72, 80, 102, 136, 137, 145
Better 63, 77
Betting 144
Bewilderment 151
Biased 51
Bidding 76
Bill 16, 106
Binds 16
Binge 90, 112
Bitter 7, 25, 39, 105
Bitterly 56, 79, 154
Bitterness 15, 103
Black 67
Blame 67, 123, 127, 136, 138
Blameless 17
Bleak 8
Bless 9, 164
Blessed 100
Blessing 116, 141
Blight 124
blight (blIt) n.
– a. the rapid and extensive discoloration, wilting, and death of plant tissues.
b. any of various plant diseases so characterized.
– any cause of impairment or frustration.
– the state or result of being deteriorated or ruined: urban blight.
Blind 10, 13, 107
Bodies 28, 39, 49
Bodily 7, 22, 30
Body xiii, xxvi, 20, 23, 92, 133, 157
Bogged 154
derived from: bog (bog) n.
– wet, spongy ground with soil

composed mainly of decayed vegetable matter.
– an area or stretch of such ground.
– to sink in or as if in a bog (often followed by down): We were bogged down with a lot of work.
Bondage 63
Book xiii, xviii, xxvii, xxxi, xxxii, 16, 19, 31, 33, 45, 47, 49, 55, 87, 92, 95, 104, 108, 112, 114, 118, 133, 143-144, 147-148, 163-164
Booze 158
Bore 13, 151-152
Boring 126, 152
Boss 11, 36, 136
Bothered 45
Bottles 5, 22, 32, 101
Bottom 75
Bounds 129, 152
Bout 23, 52
Brain xxvi, xxxi, 7, 39, 86, 140
Brainstorm 66, 138
brainstorm (brain'storm') n.
– a series of sudden, violent cerebral disturbances.
– a sudden inspiration, idea, or plan: humorous term.
Brand xxx, 77, 92, 128, 159
Brawl 4
Break xxviii, 38, 73
Bridge 53, 56
Brief 12, 30, 31, 57
Bright 21, 89, 132
Bristle 48
bristle (bris'uhl) n.
– one of the short, stiff, coarse hairs of certain animals, esp. hogs, used in making brushes.
– anything resembling these hairs.
– to stand or rise stiffly, like bristles.
Broad 55, 75
Broke 4, 64, 96, 154
Broken 8
Broker 2
Brokerage 4, 5
Brotherhood 11
Brother-in-law 7
Brotherly 16, 136, 139
Build 21, 47, 63
Building 75, 123
Built 56
Bull 156
Bums 106
Burden 117, 132
Bury 123
Business xiii,xxix, 2, 5, 15, 31, 32, 34, 39, 56, 64, 76, 79, 101, 102, 109, 114, 123, 125, 130, 136-137, 140-141, 145, 147-148, 153, 155
Businessmen xxvi
But for the grace of God 25
Calamity 46, 55, 56, 68, 116
calamity (kuh lam'i tEE) n.
– a great misfortune or disaster; catastrophe.
– grievous affliction; misery: the calamity of war.
Called xxxi, 27, 37, 61, 77, 78, 109, 110, 136
Calm 78
Camaraderie 17
camaraderie (kä'muh rä'duh rEE) n.
– comradeship; good-fellowship.
Canada 4
Cancer 18
Cannot xxvi, xxviii-xxx, 22, 38, 44, 47, 55, 58, 64, 67, 74, 81, 83, 95, 96, 98, 99, 101, 110, 114, 139, 141, 146, 148, 159, 164
Capacity xxv, 8, 54, 58
Capital 12
Capitulated 160
derived from: capitulate
(kuh pich'uh lAYt') v.
– to surrender unconditionally or on stipulated terms.
– to give up resistance; yield: to capitulate to someone's pleas.
Cared 10, 13, 26, 59, 81, 100, 151
Careers 32, 123
Careful 38, 4l, 65, 75, 83, 85-87, 103, 115, 116, 125
Carom 4
carom (kar'uhm) n.
– a shot in billiards or pool in which the cue ball hits two balls in succession.
– any hit and rebound.
– to make a carom.

THE ANONYMOUS PRESS INDEX

Cases xxv, xxvii-xxxi, 24, 27, 32, 33, 43, 61, 64, 82, 83, 93, 99, 120, 125, 144
Casting 48
Casual 24, 27, 48, 159
Catapulted 8
derived from: catapult
(kat'uh pult) n.
– an ancient military engine for hurling stones, arrows, etc.
– a device for launching an airplane from the deck of a ship.
– to hurl or be hurled from or as if from a catapult.
Caught 1, 4
Cause xxx, 65, 68, 78, 103
Cease 34
Celebrated 26, 50
Central 25
Ceremonies 28
Certain xxv, 8, 12, 15, 20, 22-24, 26, 27, 33, 43, 50, 53, 58, 72, 75, 93, 96, 109, 122
Certainty 8, 56
Cessation 122
cessation (se sAY'shuhn) n.
– a temporary or complete stopping; discontinuance: a cessation of hostilities.
Chance 5, 53
Chances 23, 34, 58, 67, 80, 83, 92, 95, 96, 97, 100, 111, 120, 135, 138, 145, 148
Changed 117
Changes xxix, xxx, 21, 50-52, 55, 75, 83, 84, 102, 130, 143, 145
Chapter xxx, 28, 44, 60, 72, 108, 112, 149, 153
Character 26, 34, 73, 75, 76, 100, 102, 115
Characterized 30, 52
Charity 98
Chat 143
Chattered 3
Cheap 2
Check 37, 109
Cheer 44, 67, 120
Cheerfulness 132
Cheery 8
Chicago 140
Chicanery 11
chicanery (shi kAY'nuh rEE) n.
– the use of sly or evasive language, reasoning, etc. to trick or deceive.
– a tricky or deceitful maneuver; subterfuge.
Chief xxv, 163
Childhood 10, 45
Childishness 130
Children xxviii, 18, 62, 106-108, 111, 114-116, 122, 126, 131, 134, 155
Chocolate 134
Choice 24, 28, 53, 73
Choose 12, 34, 74, 93
Christ 11
Chronic xxviii, xxx, xxxi, 27
Church 10, 27, 59, 80, 154, 155, 159
Cipher 10
cipher (sI'fuhr) n.
– zero.
– any of the Arabic numerals or figures.
– a person or thing of no value or importance; nonentity.
Circumstances 57, 67, 87, 100, 103, 130, 133
Cities 19
City 6, 153, 163
Civic 131
Classification xxx
Clean 14, 98
Cleaned 84, 161
Clear 55, 60, 94, 143, 164
Cleared xxvi, 7, 86
Clemency 13
clemency (klem'uhn sEE) n.
– the disposition to show forbearance, compassion, or forgiveness in judging or punishing; leniency; mercy.
– an act or deed of mercy or leniency.
– (of the weather) mildness or temperateness.
Clings 110, 124
Close 19, 36, 106
Closed 4, 27
Closer 110
Clothes 2, 58

Club 108, 131
Cock-Sureness 6
derived from: cocksure (kok'shoor) adj.
– absolutely sure; certain.
– overconfident.
Cocktails 41
Cocky 68
Code 45, 84
Coffee 135
Collapse 6, 50
Collapsed 56
Combating 7, 101
Combined 7, 22
Come xxvii, xxix, 11, 15, 22, 38, 41, 43, 50, 55, 59, 85, 99, 120, 133, 145
Comfort xxix, 45, 47
Coming 4, 9, 73, 120
Command 58
Commenced xxv, 2, 15, 25, 33, 41, 43, 46, 47, 70, 79, 81, 91, 98, 135
Commendable 35
Commission 3
Commitment 9, 31, 36
Committed 16, 35, 65, 78, 110, 114
Common 13, 22, 64, 77, 79, 94, 95, 131, 153
Communities 15, 137, 152, 156, 158, 162-163
Companions 104
Companionship 111, 151, 160
Competent xxv, 18, 89
Complete 12, 24, 52, 59, 73-74, 76
Completely xxv, 9, 27, 58, 123, 154
Complicate 81, 82, 97, 114
Comprehend xiii, 22, 70, 83, 146
Con xxx
Concealed 8, 22
Concede 30, 40, 122, 140, 155
Concept 62
Conception xxv, 12, 27, 45-47, 49, 50, 93
Concern xxv, 12, 19, 28, 36, 62, 98, 139, 144, 148, 163
Concerning 1, 21
Conclude 65, 80
Concluded 19, 53
Conclusion 43, 92, 146
Condemn 50, 108, 142
condemn (kuhn dem') v.
– to express an unfavorable or adverse judgment on; indicate strong disapproval of; censure.
– to sentence to punishment, esp. a severe punishment: to condemn a murderer to death.
– to pronounce to be guilty.
Condition xxxi, 9, 18, 26, 32, 35, 39, 42, 64, 77, 85, 86, 90, 93, 97, 98, 101, 107, 111, 114, 122, 134, 143, 144
Conduct 38, 70
Confession 25, 74
Confidence 6, 14, 18, 26, 40, 54, 74, 75, 78, 89, 114, 123, 143
Confined 26, 56
Confronted 53
Confused 93
Confusion 61
Conquer 44
Conquering 98
Conscience 95, 132
conscience (kon'shuhns) n.
– the inner sense of what is right or wrong in one's conduct or motives, impelling one toward right action: to follow the dictates of conscience.
– the complex of ethical and moral principles that controls or inhibits the actions or thoughts of an individual.
– an inhibiting sense of what is prudent.
Conscientiously 58
derived from: conscientious (kon'shEE en'shuhs) adj.
– meticulous; careful; painstaking.
– governed by or done according to conscience; scrupulous: a conscientious judge.
Consciousness 24, 25, 51, 55, 59, 63, 98, 130, 147
Consents 80
Consequences 24, 37, 41, 79
Consider 65
Considerably 22, 29, 30, 34, 46, 64, 86
Considerate 61, 99

Consigned 152
derived from: consign
(kuhn sIn') v.
– to hand over or deliver; assign.
– to transfer to another's custody or charge; entrust.
– to banish or set apart; relegate: to consign unpleasant thoughts to oblivion.
Console 14
Consternation 35
consternation
(kon'stuhr nAY'shuhn) n.
– a sudden, alarming amazement or dread that results in utter confusion; dismay.
Constitutionally 58
constitutionally
(kon'sti tU'shuh nl EE) adv.
– in respect to physical makeup.
– in respect to mental or emotional makeup: constitutionally shy.
– with respect to a constitution.
Construction 2, 54, 127
Constructive 86, 93
Consult 94, 114, 126
Consulting 80, 134
Consummation 25
derived from: consummate
(kon'suh mAYt) v.
– to bring to a state of perfection; fulfill.
– to bring to a state of completion, as an arrangement or agreement.
– to complete (the union of a marriage) by the first marital sexual intercourse.
Consumption 21, 25
Contact 35, 46, 59, 89, 131, 138, 139, 144, 164
Contempt 10
Contention 19, 49, 118
Contingent 85
Continue 3, 38, 44, 59, 66, 70, 92, 96, 97, 99, 111
Contradict 94
Contrary 147
Contribute xxvii, 63
Contrition 126
contrition (kuhn trish'uhn) n.
– sincere penitence or remorse.
– sorrow for sin with a true purpose of amendment.
Control xxvi, xxix, 5, 21, 26, 30-32, 44, 52, 92, 109, 117, 139, 151, 155
Controlled drinking 30, 31, 32
Controversial 19
Controversies 69
Convalescence 129
convalescence
(kon'vuh les'uhns) n.
– the gradual recovery of health and strength after illness.
– the period during which one is convalescing.
Convalescing 127, 129
derived from: convalesce
(kon'vuh les') v.
– to recover health and strength after illness.
Conversation 27, 91, 95
Converted 123
Convictions 27, 29, 56, 62, 77, 93
Convince 28, 30, 40, 55, 60, 70, 83, 95, 107, 135
Cooperate 89, 109, 113, 129
Cornerstone 47, 56
Could xxvi, xxxi, 3, 4, 6, 7, 9, 10, 15, 20, 25, 26, 30, 32, 34, 37, 40, 43, 45, 47, 51, 54, 55, 57-60, 62-64, 66, 80, 81, 84, 86, 93, 107, 131, 132, 151, 155, 161
Couldn't xxvii, 36, 52-54, 154
Counsel 69, 119
Counseling 97
Countenance 161
countenance (koun'tn uhns) n.
– appearance, esp. the expression of the face: a sad countenance.
– the face; visage.
– calm facial expression; composure.
Countless 30
Courage 6, 53, 68, 81, 115, 132, 154
Course xxv, xxvi, xxx, 2, 4, 9, 12, 34, 52, 54, 63, 66, 74, 79, 81, 86, 99, 108, 114, 128, 142, 143, 144, 146
Court 9, 79, 97
Cowardly 46
Crankiness 127
Craving xxix, xviii, 134, 143, 164

Crawl 83
Crazy 5, 38
Created 54, 97, 122
Creations 49
Creative 12, 23, 46, 49, 164
Creator 13, 25, 28, 33, 56, 68, 72, 75, 76, 78, 80, 158, 161
Creditors 96
Creeds 49
Criminals 78
Crisis 53
Criterion 163
criterion (krI tEEr'EE uhn) n.
– a standard of judgment or criticism; a rule or principle for evaluating or testing something.
Critical 13, 100, 111, 117
Criticize 77, 83, 89, 100, 106, 118, 125, 126, 129, 145, 146
Crowd 24, 33, 113, 133, 138, 154, 160
Crucial 64
Cruel 107
Crusade 95
crusade (krU sAYd') n.
– (often cap.) any of the military expeditions undertaken by the Christians of Europe in the 11th, 12th, and 13th centuries to recover the Holy Land from the Muslims.
– any war carried on under papal sanction.
– any vigorous movement on behalf of a cause.
Crux 35
crux (kruks) n.
– the central or pivotal point; essence: the crux of the matter.
– a perplexing, unresolved difficulty.
– a cross.
Cry 68, 69, 98
Cunning 58
Cure 138
Cured 85, 135
Curious 9, 20, 37, 93
Cursing 6
Cycle 23
Cynical xxviii
cynical (sin'i kuhl) adj.
– distrusting or disparaging the motives or sincerity of others.
– showing contempt for accepted standards of honesty or morality, esp. by actions that exploit the scruples of others.
– bitterly or sneeringly distrustful, contemptuous, or pessimistic.
Cynically 49
Cynicism 132
cynicism (sin'uh siz'uhm) n.
– cynical disposition, character, or belief.
– a cynical remark.
– (cap.) the doctrines of the Cynics.
Czar 12
Dad 123, 126-129
Daily xxviii, 134
Damn 157
Dances 101
Danger xxx, 88
Dangerous 117, 126
Dangerously 21, 34
Dared 6, 8
Daring 158
Dark 8, 75, 110, 124
Dazed 160
Dead 11, 15, 33, 88, 135
Deadly 16
Deal 5, 23, 58, 64, 78, 90-91, 93, 94, 107, 113, 125, 133, 142, 144, 149
Dealt 18
Death 21, 24, 30, 31, 33, 44, 75, 107, 154
Debacle 22
debacle (duh bä'kuhl) n.
– a disaster or fiasco.
– a general rout or dispersal of troops.
– a breaking up of ice in a river.
Debate xxx
Debauch 8, 104
debauch (di bôch') v.
– to corrupt (another's virtue or chastity) by sensuality, intemperance, etc.; seduce.
– to subvert (honesty, integrity, or the like).
– Archaic. to corrupt (allegiance, loyalty, or the like).
Decide 28, 32, 36, 38, 41, 58-62, 64, 71, 75, 79, 82, 86, 90, 95, 96, 103, 113, 140, 147

Decision 21
Dedicated 160
Deep 25, 35, 55, 66, 93, 158
Defeat 11, 42, 64, 115
Defeated 153
Defects 50, 59, 72, 83, 99, 100, 118
derived from: defect (dEE fekt) n.
– a fault or shortcoming; imperfection.
– lack of something essential; deficiency: a defect in hearing.
Defects of character 50, 59, 72, 99, 100, 118
Defend 146
Defense 24, 42, 43
Deficiencies 13, 120
Definite xxviii, 32, 65, 87
Deflation 122
Delighted 75
Delinquencies 126
Delirium 13
delirium (di lEEr'EE uhm) n.
– a temporary disturbance of consciousness characterized by restlessness, excitement, and delusions or hallucinations.
– a state of violent excitement or emotion.
Delusion 30, 61
Demands 58, 61, 122, 123, 143
Democracy 17
Demonstrate 14, 19, 25, 33, 49, 55, 68, 77, 98, 99, 133
Demoralization 30
derived from: demoralize
(di môr'uh lIz') v.
– to deprive (a person or persons) of spirit, courage, discipline, etc.; destroy the morale of.
– to throw (a person) into disorder or confusion; bewilder.
– to corrupt or undermine the morals of.
Denial 10, 20-23, 30, 31
Denied 80
Denizens 151
derived from: denizen
(den'uh zuhn) n.
– an inhabitant; resident.
– a person who regularly frequents a place; habitué.
– Brit. an alien admitted to residence and to certain rights of citizenship.
Denomination xiv, 74, 87, 93, 94
Deny 96
Depend 68, 70, 80
Dependable 54
Dependence 46, 98, 100
Deportment 18
deportment (di pôrt'muhnt) n.
– conduct; behavior.
Depression xxxi, 37, 39, 52, 56, 106, 127, 133
Depressive xxx
Deprived 96
Deranged 14
Derelictions 143
derived from: dereliction
(der'uh lik'shuhn) n.
– deliberate or conscious neglect; negligence; delinquency; dereliction of duty.
– the act of abandoning something.
– the state of being abandoned.
Describe xxv, 19, 22, 29, 35, 52, 93, 153
Description 112
Desert 9, 38
Deserted xxxi
Desertion 106
Deserve 67, 73
Design 63, 81
Designating xiii
Desire xiv, xxix, 7, 18, 24, 32, 34, 63, 70, 77, 83, 95, 105, 115, 139, 146, 155
Despair 8, 15, 50, 110, 151, 155
Despaired xxix
Despairing xxviii
Desperate xxxi, 7, 28, 29, 35, 96, 108, 110, 155
Despised 69
Despite 10, 12, 31
Destination 162
Destiny 54, 164
Destitution 106
destitution (des ti too'shun) n.
– the state of being destitute; want; lack.
– complete poverty; indigence
Destroy 27, 64, 67
Destruction 14, 48, 70, 80, 97
Detail xxvii, xxx, 20, 81
Deter 24
Deterioration xxxi, 157

Determination 4
Devil 11, 125, 149, 159
Diagnosis xxxi, 31
Die 24
Died 10
Different 9, 12, 30, 66, 68, 98, 107, 108, 116, 117, 128
Differentiate xxviii, xxx
Difficult 18, 21, 32, 44, 45, 47, 48, 67, 72, 94, 95, 99, 100, 104, 110, 111, 119, 121, 127, 134, 138, 140, 156
Difficulties xxviii, 63
Diffident 76
derived from: diffidence
(dif'fi dense) adj.
– lack of self-confidence; want of confidence in one's own power, ability, correctness or wisdom; hesitancy to assert oneself; shyness.
– distrust; doubt of the power, ability, or disposition of others.
Dilemma 28, 45
Diligently 55
Dimension 8, 25
Diminish 86
Dimly 107
Dinner 9, 41
Direct 48, 59, 68, 86, 124
Directing xxviii
Directions 8, 10, 13, 20, 46, 49, 50, 79, 85, 95, 120, 121, 125, 131, 158
Directly 11, 140
Director 62
Directors 138
Directory 154, 155
Disagree 102, 117
Disagreeable 130
Disagreement 118
Disappointed 9, 126
Disaster 17, 27, 44
Discard 52, 140
Discharged 137, 139, 141, 147
Discipline 88
Disclose 29, 57, 58, 64, 74, 78, 164
Discontented xxviii
Discord 122
Discouraged 60, 96, 138, 154
Discovered 2, 17, 20*, 28, 46, 54, 63, 64*, 72*, 90*, 99*, 106*, 159*, 164*
Discrediting 80, 161
Discretion 96, 142
Discuss 18, 45, 72, 84, 86, 87, 91, 99, 115, 125, 143, 144
Discussion 19, 20, 111, 118, 127, 134
Disease 18*, 44*, 64, 92*, 107*, 115*, 118*, 139*, 142*
disease (di zEEz') n.
– a disordered or abnormal condition of an organ or other part of an organism resulting from the effect of genetic or developmental errors, infection, nutritional deficiency, toxicity, or unfavorable environmental factors; illness; sickness.
– any harmful condition, as of society.
Disgusted 4, 18, 21
Dishonest 21, 61, 67, 69, 84, 86
Disillusionment 56
derived from: disillusion
(dis'i lU'zhuhn) v.
– to free from or deprive of illusion, belief, idealism, etc.; disenchant.
– a freeing or a being freed from illusion or conviction; disenchantment.
Dislike 77, 120
Dismal 154
Dismay 120, 134
Disorder 58, 114
Disposition 21, 35
Dispute 11, 117
Dissensions 117
derived from: dissension
(di en'shuhn) n.
– strong disagreement; a contention or quarrel; discord.
– difference in sentiment or opinion; disagreement.
Dissipation 133
dissipation (dis'uh pAY'shuhn) n.
– the act of dissipating.
– the state of being dissipated; dispersion; disintegration.
– a wasting by misuse: the dissipation of a fortune.
Distinction 44, 161
Distorted 108, 129
Distressing 159
Disturbed 2, 28, 67, 94, 118
Diverted 50

THE ANONYMOUS PRESS INDEX

Divine 43
Divorce 35, 38, 79, 99, 106
Doctor xxvi, xxix, 6, 11, 14, 18, 20-22, 26-27, 39, 73, 89, 91, 92, 97, 110, 114, 133, 140, 143, 144, 162
Does 11, 88, 90, 94, 109, 135, 147
Doggerel 1
  doggerel (dô'guhr uhl) adj.
  – comic or burlesque, and usually loose or irregular in measure.
  – crude; having no aesthetic value; poorly written.
Dollars 5, 73
Dominate 27, 66, 134
Done 11, 13, 67, 70, 76-78, 81, 114, 138, 140, 142, 159
Doomed xxix, xxx, 44, 92, 101
Doubt 10, 13, 19, 33, 43, 45, 48, 53, 72, 94, 135
Doubted xxxi, 11, 52, 87
Downfall 137
Dramatic 55
Drank 4, 7, 15, 32, 126, 158
Drastically 11, 42, 76, 80, 94
Dreamed 25
Dreary 9
Drink 2, 3, 5, 8, 9, 13, 15, 17, 21-24, 30, 31, 33, 37, 41, 43, 51, 57, 70, 75, 92, 93, 97, 102, 104, 105, 107, 110, 117, 130, 140, 142, 146, 152, 154
Drinker xxviii, 1, 9, 18, 21, 23, 31, 34, 89, 112, 114, 135, 153
Drinking xxxi, xxx, 1, 2, 4, 7, 19-21, 23, 24, 30-36, 40, 44, 72, 73, 78-81, 89-92, 98, 101-103, 109, 111, 115, 116, 120, 122, 129, 131, 134, 137-139, 141, 145, 146, 151, 156-157
Drive 2, 36, 62, 74
Driven 105
Dr. Jekyll 21
Dropped 4, 19, 95
Drugged 142, 162
Drunk 1, 4-6, 21, 22, 26, 31, 34-37, 73, 90, 97, 106, 108, 110, 120, 136
Drunkenness 3, 83
Dry 41
Dubious 49
  dubious (dU'bEE uhs) adj.
  – marked by or occasioning doubt; equivocal: a dubious reply.
  – of doubtful quality or propriety; questionable: a dubious compliment.
  – of uncertain outcome.
Dues xiv
Dull 126
Dying 149
Eagerness 96
Earnestly xiii, 46
Earnestness 16, 37, 58
Earth 130
Ease xxix, 75
Easier 118
Easily xxix, 37
Easy Does It 135
Eat 102
Economic 84, 121
Economics 2, 17
Education 56, 93, 117
Effect 42, 46, 47, 64, 143
Effective 19, 25, 43, 135
Effectiveness 84
Efficient 88
Effort xxxi
Egocentric 61
Egoism 73
Egotistical 61
Electric 160
Electricity 48
Electrons 48, 54
Elements 13, 17, 57
Emanate 55
  emanate (em'uh nAYt') v.
  – to flow out, issue forth; originate.
  – to send forth; emit.
Embarrassment 115
Embittered 56
  derived from: embitter (em bit'uhr) v.
  – to make bitter; cause to feel bitterness.
  – to make bitter or more bitter in taste.
Emerged xxxi, 117
Emerging xxix
Emotional 27, 52, 58
Emotionally xxx

Emphatic 93
emphatic (em fat'IK) adj.
– forcible; impressive; strong.
– using emphasis in speaking, etc.
– expressed, felt, or done with emphasis.
Emphatically 47, 142
Employed 27, 86
Employee 140, 144, 149
Employer 18, 67, 115, 136, 137, 146
Employment 4, 106
Enables 55, 68
Encourage xxviii, 91, 95
Endeavoring 94
Endless 8
Endlessly 5
Endured 18
Enemy 77, 78
Energetic 146
Energy 88, 115
Engaged 75, 131
Engagement 21, 105
England 1
Engulfs 18
Enjoyed 63, 110
Entertain 118
Enthralled 126
Enthusiasm 15, 102, 113, 119, 125, 128
Entire xxvii, xxx, 18, 22
Entirely xxix, xxx, 20, 42, 44, 45, 47, 59, 62, 67, 73, 88, 96, 129
Environment xxx, 21
Environs 15
environs (en vI'ruhnz) n.
– the surrounding parts or districts, as of a city; outskirts; suburbs.
– surroundings; environment.
– the nearby area or space; vicinity.
Episodes 73
Epoch xxvi
epoch (ep'uhk) n.
– a period of time marked by distinctive features, noteworthy events, changed conditions, etc.: an epoch of peace.
– the beginning of a distinctive period in the history of anything.
– a point of time distinguished by a particular event or state of affairs; a memorable date.
Eradicated xxx
derived from: eradicate
(i rad'i kAYt') v.
– to remove or destroy utterly; extirpate: to eradicate smallpox.
– to erase by rubbing or by means of a chemical solvent.
– to pull up by the roots: to eradicate weeds.
Erroneous 569
erroneous (uh rO'nEE uhs) adj.
– containing error; mistaken; incorrect.
– straying from what is right or proper.
Errors 124
Escape xxx, 9, 17, 28, 94, 152
Eskimo 101
Especially 45, 72, 86, 87, 108, 119
Essential xxix
Essentially xxviii, 14
Established xviii, 14, 24, 63, 74
Evade 53
Evangelist 89
Evening 41, 105, 159
Event 114, 164
Eventually 123, 130
Everything xxxi
Evidence 40, 42, 48, 53, 104, 110, 111
Evil 67
Evolutionists 10
Exactly 36, 45, 64, 93
Examine 53, 73
Example 62, 93, 145
Exceedingly 163
Except xxx, 27, 31, 39, 43
Exception 27, 148
Exceptionally 136, 137
Exceptions 81, 104, 108, 114
Excess 119
Exchequers 175
derived from: exchequer
(eks'chek uhr) n.
– a treasury, as of a state or nation.
– (in Great Britain).
a. (often cap.) the governmental department in charge of the public revenues.
b. (formerly) an office administering the royal revenues and determining all cases affecting them.
c. (cap.) an ancient common-law

court trying cases affecting crown revenues: now merged with King's Bench.
– Informal. financial resources; funds.
Excitement 1, 88
Exciting 81
Exclusive 4, 46
Excuses 23, 37, 40, 75, 77, 120
Executive 137, 138, 147
Exercise 37, 40, 85
Exert 127
Exhausted 156
Exhilarating 3
Existence 8, 51, 67
Existing 46, 152
Exists 17, 27, 85
Exonerating 80
derived from: exonerate
(ig zon'uh rAYt') v.
– to clear from accusation, guilt, or blame.
– to relieve from an obligation, duty, or task.
Expect 38, 74, 95, 99, 101, 120, 126, 149
Experience xxvii-xxxi, 14, 19, 22, 28, 29, 33, 39, 42, 44, 46, 50, 55, 70, 72, 84, 85, 89, 91, 92, 96, 101, 103, 116, 121, 124, 125, 128, 130, 132, 134, 137, 146, 153, 155, 157, 158-160, 163
Experimentation 31, 35
Expert 20
Explain 45, 102
Explanation 26, 75, 94, 156
Expressed 12, 46, 77
Expression 20, 47, 83, 160
Ex-problem drinker 18, 20, 151
Extent xxvi, 27, 34, 66, 68, 162
Extraordinary xxv, 28
Extravagant 84
Extreme 3, 37, 62, 68, 90, 98, 105, 125, 143
Faced xxv, xxix, 35, 44, 48, 53, 63, 64, 78, 86, 102, 106, 131, 151, 155, 163
Facilitated 11
Facilities 145
Fact 17, 18, 24, 25, 27, 44, 51, 55, 70, 72, 93, 119, 131, 148, 163, 164
Fact-facing 64
Fact-finding 64, 98
Failed 1, 2, 11, 33, 35, 51, 55, 58, 68, 78, 89, 93, 96, 127, 138, 151
Failures 24, 50, 56, 98, 158, 159
Fair 137
Faith xiv, 10, 15, 16, 28, 46, 47, 49, 50, 51, 53-55, 68, 70, 81, 93, 94, 117, 122
Faith without works is dead 14, 76, 88
Faithful 54
Fallacious 23
fallacious (fuh lAY'shuhs) adj.
– containing a fallacy; logically unsound: fallacious arguments.
– deceptive; misleading: fallacious testimony.
– disappointing; delusive: a fallacious peace.
False xxviii
Familiar xxx, 23, 36, 155
Families 15, 23, 35, 74, 79, 80, 83, 90, 96, 98, 99, 107, 119, 122-124, 126, 127, 129, 153-155
Fanatics 77
Farmer 82
Fast-moving 37
Fast-thinking 139
Fatal 56, 66, 142
Fatality 70
Fatally 92
Father 14, 39, 62, 104, 115, 123, 126, 127, 131
Fatigue 135
Fault 58, 61, 67, 69, 78, 79, 81, 98, 131, 163
Favor 141
Favorably xxx
Favorite 149
Favorites 146
Fear 1, 8, 52, 62, 63, 67, 68, 73, 75, 78, 84, 104, 116, 120, 145, 154
Feared 6
Fearless 58, 59
Fearlessly 53
Fearlessness 10, 73
Feeling 12, 42, 48, 54, 77, 84, 104, 118, 140, 142

Feelings 117
Feels xiv, 45, 75, 76, 81, 85, 91, 103, 115, 126, 139, 143, 147, 149
Fees 18
Feet 15, 130, 154
Fellow 2, 25, 30, 38, 62, 148, 152, 163
Fellowship xiii, 15, 89, 94-96, 152, 153, 159, 160, 162, 163
Felt 28
Female alcoholic 33
Fences 35
Fettered 51
derived from: fetter (fet'uhr) n.
– a chain or shackle placed on the feet.
– Usually, "fetters." anything that confines or restrains.
– to put fetters upon.
Feuds 15, 78
Fever 1, 3
Fictitious 176
fictitious (fik tish'uhs) adj.
– created, taken, or assumed for the sake of concealment; not genuine; false: fictitious names.
– of, pertaining to, or consisting of fiction; created by the imagination: a fictitious hero.
Fierce resentment 18
Fight xxx, 5, 41, 84, 85, 97, 158
Final 70
Finally 38
Financial 2, 18, 41, 78, 95, 96, 105, 123, 127, 154
Finished 4, 65
Finite 68
Fired 139, 157
Firing xxviii, 141
Firmly 130
First Things First 127*, 130*, 135, 143*, 153*
Five proposals 75
Fixed 51, 56, 122, 157
Flattered 1
Flaws 64
Fleeting 46
Flight xxvi, 2, 6, 51, 55
Flimsy 28
Florida 61
Flower 50, 54, 85
Flush 124
Flying 51
Focus 128
Followed 42, 63, 94, 100, 134, 137, 147
Fooling 55, 142, 152
Foolish 37, 39, 88, 155
Footing 12, 63
Footsteps 137
Forces 27, 137
Forcibly 91
Ford, Henry 124
Forebodings 2
Forever 5, 34, 60, 106
Forget 82, 106, 135, 147
Forgetfulness 124
Forgive 70, 106, 134
Forgiving 77, 79, 86, 140
Former 78, 99, 142, 162
Forthwith 179
forthwith (fôrth with') adv.
– immediately: The action is suspended forthwith.
Fortunate 15, 18, 19
Fortune 2, 126
Fought 66
Foundation 75, 130
Four horsemen 151
Fourth dimension 8, 25
Frailties 49
derived from: frailty (frAYl'tEE) n.
– the quality or state of being frail.
– a fault resulting from moral weakness.
Frankly xxxi, 131, 135, 146
Frankness 82
Frantic xviii, 97, 125
Fraternity 35
Fred 39
Free xxx, 66, 75
Freed xxvii
Freedom 62, 83, 87, 160
Freely 14, 19, 93, 133, 163
Friction 28
Friend 2, 4, 12, 13, 16, 18, 23, 27, 28, 56, 63, 67, 74, 77, 80, 87, 90, 94, 95, 102, 105, 115, 120, 149, 152, 155, 157, 161, 162, 163

THE ANONYMOUS PRESS INDEX

Friendly xxx, 37, 41, 53, 97, 99, 135, 145
Friends 89, 104, 111, 114, 147, 156, 159
Friendship 95, 97, 123
Frightening 67
Frustration 56, 129, 145, 151
Fuller 120
Fun 4, 16, 38, 132
Functioning 92
Fundamental 55, 120
Further 85, 95, 148
Futile 107, 176
  futile (fyUt'l) adj.
  – incapable of producing any result; ineffective; useless; not successful: Attempts to swim across the stormy channel were futile.
  – trifling; frivolous.
Futility 25, 66
Future xxxi, 69, 77, 79, 124, 152, 157
Gallantly 130
  derived from: gallant (gal'uhnt) adj.
  – brave, spirited, or noble-minded: a gallant knight; a gallant attempt.
  – exceptionally polite and attentive to women; chivalrous.
  – stately; grand: a gallant pageant.
Gastric xxxi, 174
  gastric (gas'trik) adj.
  – pertaining to the stomach.
Gaunt 128
  gaunt (gônt) adj.
  – extremely thin and bony; haggard and drawn, as from hunger or weariness.
  – bleak, desolate, or grim: the gaunt landscape of the tundra.
Gay 160
  gay (gAY) adj.
  – having or showing a merry, lively mood: gay spirits.
  – bright or showy: gay colors.
  – given to or abounding in social or other pleasures: a gay social season.
General 94
Generally 18
Generation 52
Generous 61
Genius 21
Gentleman 20
Genuine 160
Gin 5, 6, 7, 8, 9
Ginger Ale 41, 154
Giving 98, 122, 128, 129, 152, 153, 159, 164
Glass 24
God 10-14, 14-15, 28-29, 45-47, 49, 51-57, 59, 60, 62-63, 67-69, 70-72, 75-77, 80, 81, 84-88, 95, 98, 100, 116, 117, 120, 121, 123-124, 128-130, 133, 155, 156, 158, 161-162, 164
Gold 128-129
Golf 3
Good xxvi, 14, 19, 26, 48, 62, 72, 81, 82, 90, 94, 112, 121, 124, 133
Good Samaritan 97
Good will 70, 77
Goose 7
Gooseflesh 54
  gooseflesh (goose' flesh) n.
  – a bristling of the hair on the skin, as from cold or fear. Also called goose pimples or goose bumps.
Gorge 56
  gorge (gôrj) n.
  – a narrow cleft with steep, rocky walls, esp. one through which a stream runs.
  – a small canyon.
  – a gluttonous meal.
Gossip 125
Grace of God 25
Gracious 61
Grant 76
Grasping 58
Grateful 53, 128
Gratify 144
Grave 33, 58
Great Fact 164
Great Reality 55, 161
Greater Power 45-48, 50, 55, 59, 93
Grievous 124
  grievous (grEE'vuhs) adj.
  – causing grief or great sorrow: a grievous loss.

– causing serious harm; flagrant; atrocious: a grievous offense.
– characterized by great pain or suffering: arrested for causing grievous bodily harm.
Grosser handicaps 71
Grounded xxviii
Groundwork 111
Groups xxvi-xxxi
Grow 60, 162
Growing xxvi, 124
Growth xxvi, 66, 84, 115, 117, 129
Grudge 65
Guard 115
Guides 60
Guiding 49, 128
Guilty 80
Habit xxviii, 20, 91, 102, 118, 140, 148
Half measures availed us nothing 59
Half-truth 70
Handicapped xiii, 48, 71, 89
Hanger-on 5
Hangover 158
Happened 50, 52, 58, 93
Happens 78, 134
Happily 5, 39, 74
Happiness 8, 49, 50, 82, 123, 124, 159
Happy 102, 117, 130, 133, 152, 156, 164
Hard 6, 20, 74, 116, 139, 142, 146
Hardly 6, 39, 60, 69, 136, 161
Harm 69, 70, 96
Harmed 59
Harmonious 17
Harmony 61
Hartford 136
Hate 114
Hated 77
Hazy 24
Head 23, 129, 130, 156
Headache 23
Healing 57
Health xxv, 31, 104, 132
Hear 59
Hearing 50
Heart 7, 9, 11, 73, 82, 161
Heart-breaking 43, 107, 111, 151
Heaven 25, 31
Hell 27, 56, 81
Hellish 6
Help xxx, 52, 63, 75, 95, 97, 129, 130, 137, 138, 161, 164
Helped 94, 131, 139, 142
Helpful xiv, 18, 67, 77, 89, 100, 102, 117, 127, 135, 138, 145, 146
Helpfulness 102, 162
Hemorrhage xxxi
hemorrhage (hem'uhr ij) n.
– a profuse discharge of blood.
– the loss of assets, esp. in large amounts.
– to bleed profusely.
Hereafter 62, 63
Heresies 51
derived from: heresy
(her'uh sEE) n.
– religious opinion or doctrine at variance with the orthodox or accepted doctrine.
– the maintaining of such an opinion or doctrine.
– the willful and persistent rejection of any article of faith by a baptized member of the Roman Catholic church.
Heroic 1
Hesitate 102, 133
Hiding 124
High 4, 123
Highball 41, 110
Higher-Power 43, 85, 100
Highly 122
High-Powered 22, 152
Him (God) 11-13, 43-47, 57, 59, 60, 63, 68, 85, 130, 164
Holier than thou 18
Home 1, 39, 43, 82, 97, 98, 101, 102, 110, 114, 145, 155, 160
Honest xiv, xxix, 32, 45, 58, 70, 73, 83, 146
Honestly 11, 25, 44, 47, 55, 57, 63, 64, 67, 83
Honesty 13, 58, 65, 73
Honored 75
Hope xiii, xxxi, 44, 45, 66, 73, 163
Hopeful 110, 154, 158
Hopeless xxv, 10, 17, 20, 26, 42-44, 92, 94, 96, 113
Hopelessness 6, 25, 43, 92, 153, 157

Hoping 44, 147, 151
Horribly 114, 159
Horror 6
Hospital xxvii, xxviii, 1, 7, 8, 14, 15, 22, 32, 38-41, 43, 56, 89, 97, 107, 110, 114, 145, 156, 158-160, 162, 163
Hospitalization xxvi, 91
Hostility 113
Hotel 41, 136
House 5, 31, 83, 130, 161
Housecleaning 63, 73, 94
Household 130
How It Works 58-60
Human 11, 24, 43, 45, 49, 50, 52, 55, 60, 61, 68, 69, 72, 133
Humanitarian 140
Humanly 50
Humble 12, 73, 83
Humbling 72
Humbly 13, 57, 59, 63, 68
Humiliated 32
Humiliating 40
Humiliation 22, 24, 40, 123
Humility 12, 13, 63, 73
Humorous 91
Hungry 36
Hurt 62, 69, 74, 125, 143, 156
Husband 81, 105, 106, 108-111, 114, 115, 117-120, 122, 125, 158, 160
Hydrotherapy 7
Hysterically 90
Ideals xxviii, 70, 118
Ideas 27, 52, 60, 92, 111, 116, 122, 123
Identify 22, 28
Ignorance 2, 20, 107
Ill 7, 20, 21, 77, 108, 122, 140, 142, 155
Illness 18, 30, 44, 92, 107, 115, 118, 122, 139, 142, 155
Illuminating 75, 139
Illusion 30
Illustration 38, 139
Imaginable 31
Imagination 110, 152
Imaginative 139
Imagine 54, 152
Imagined 2
Immediate 56, 84, 99
Immune 33
Immunity 89
Immutable 10
immutable (i myU'tuh buhl) adj.
– not mutable; unchangeable; changeless.
Impair 20, 114
Impasse 127
Imperative xxvi, 14, 143
Importance xxvii
Important xxx, 3, 19, 51, 74, 94, 101, 108, 120, 146, 154
Impose 149
Imposed 53, 138
Impossible 15, 18, 22, 25, 34, 44, 46, 48, 101
Impotent 134
Impressing xxv
Impression xxix, 122
Impressive 79
Imprisoned 78
Improved 127
Impulse 123
Inability 31, 33, 34
Inadequacy xxix, 45, 46
Incapable 58
Incapacitated 130
Incident 80, 139, 159
Inclined 53, 73
Includes 61, 65, 66, 101
Incompatible 98, 108, 130
Incomprehensible 30, 37
Inconsiderate 69, 82, 108, 125
Inconsistencies 92
Inconsistency 73, 98
Incredible 7, 8, 21, 49, 141, 153
Indecision 86
Indescribably 17
Indicates 28, 40, 80, 141
Indication 90
Indignant 62, 79
Indispensable 76, 133
Individual xix, 13, 17, 24, 27, 28, 31, 37, 39, 46, 48, 77, 113, 132
Indulged 128, 132
Inevitably 37, 120, 138
Inexperience 87
Inexplicably 9
Inferiority 106
Infidelity 3

THE ANONYMOUS PRESS INDEX

Infinite 56, 68, 124
Infinitely 43, 66, 120
Infinitum 31
Information 39, 90, 125
Informed 7, 18
Inherent xxvi
Inherited 35
Inhospitable 106
Injured 38, 59
Injuries 65
Injurious xxviii
Injustice 77, 138
In-laws 122
Innermost 30
Innumerable 79, 97, 105
  innumerable
    (in noo'mer a ble) adj.
  – countless, without number.
  – not to be counted.
  – too many to be numbered.
Insane 37, 38, 110
Insanely 21, 37, 120
Insanity 8, 24, 30, 37, 38, 40, 56, 66, 107, 154
Insecurity 18, 84
Insidious 8, 154
  insidious (in sid'E us) adj.
  – characterized by treachery or slyness; crafty; wily.
  – operating in a slow or not easily apparent manner.
  – more dangerous than seems evident.
Insincere 96
Insist 92, 96, 132, 136
Insisted 53, 151
Insistence 92
Inspirational 31, 85, 86, 87
Inspired 4
Inspiring xxvii
Institution 64, 69, 91, 103, 110, 114, 138, 163
Instruct 93
Instructive 40
Insufficient 37, 72, 93
Insurance 137, 149
Insure 88
Intellect 51
Intellectual 10
Intelligent xxx, 35, 38, 49
Interest xxviii, xxix, 10, 63, 77, 84, 90, 95, 99, 111, 112, 119, 122, 126, 131, 160
Interfered 65, 97, 148
Interpretation 53
Intervals 30, 90, 95
Intervention 137
Intimate 18, 74, 82, 125, 134
Intimated 39
Intolerable 25
Intolerance 50, 103, 120, 135, 160
Intolerant 50
Intoxicated 21, 128
Intrigued 155
Intuitively 84, 86
Invariably 62, 73, 125
Invented 115
Inventory 59, 64-69, 67, 71, 72, 75, 76
Invited 105
Involves 18, 38, 67, 79, 80, 81, 104, 122, 140
Inwardly 11, 152
Irrational 140
Irresistible 160
Irresponsibility 129
Irritable xxviii, 105
Irritated 10, 23, 36, 126
Irritation 117, 128
Isolate 131
Issue 113, 135
Jack Alexander xviii
Jag 9
  jag (jag) n.
  – a period of unrestrained indulgence in an activity; spree; binge: a crying jag.
  – a state of intoxication from liquor.
Jail 78, 79, 107
Jails 97
James, William 28
Jaywalking 37, 38
Jealous 119, 128
Jealousy 37, 69, 82, 100, 131, 145, 161
Jekyll, Dr. 21
Jeopardize 147
Jeopardy 105
Jim 37
Jitters 32, 37

THE ANONYMOUS PRESS INDEX

Jittery xxvi, 3, 91, 163
Job 4, 95, 96, 98, 102, 148, 161
Join 28, 134
Joined 17
Journey 153
Joy 15, 17, 128, 132, 164
Joykiller 106
Joyous 133
Judge 70
Judgment 26, 40, 107
Justifiable 81
Justification 37, 126
Justified 37
Keep 82
Key 66, 106, 124
Keystone 62
Kicked 106
Kill 6, 20, 62, 66
Killjoy 105, 111
Kind 61
Kindliness 83
Kindly 67, 97
Kindness 7
Kitty Hawk 51
Knowledge 32, 36, 85
Lack 109, 139, 142
Langley's, Prof. 51
Laugh 6, 68, 125, 132, 157, 160
Laughter 132
Laurels 85
Laws 2, 10, 49
Lawyer 156, 158
Lay 11, 77, 95
Laymen xxvi
Leadership xviii, 1
Leading xxvii, 77
Leads 66, 83, 92, 111
Learn 7, 47, 93, 117, 147
Learned 28, 44, 70, 73, 92
Leave 20, 84, 104, 111
Leaving 51
Lectures 18, 120, 142
Lend 94, 161
Less 58, 63
Lethargy 23
Levity 16
Liberation 52, 53
Licked 4
Lies 105, 115
Life xxxi, 1, 8, 15, 25, 43, 44, 49, 54, 60, 61, 63, 66, 73, 75, 84, 108, 114, 122-126, 128, 131, 132, 133, 136, 146, 147, 151-153, 158, 159, 161, 164
Lifelong 42, 152
Lifted 14
Light 73, 91, 103
Lightly 69
Likeable 139
Likely 38, 61
Limitation 10
Limited xxviii, 31
Liquor xxviii, 1, 3, 5, 7, 20, 21, 34, 64, 81, 84, 85, 100, 102, 109, 110, 120, 130, 139, 143, 152, 155
Listened 14
Literally 81
Little xxvi, xxix, 2, 8, 19, 41, 53, 64, 99
Live 4, 19, 62, 66, 69, 74, 93, 96, 97, 105, 106, 117, 118
Live and Let Live 118, 135
Living xiii, 2, 4, 13, 15, 28, 50, 51, 54, 58, 81, 84, 98, 99, 133
Loaded 137
Loath 92
loath (lowth) adj.
– hateful; odious.
– unwilling; reluctant; averse.
Lobby 159
Logical 49, 53
Lolls 61
Lone 3
Loneliness 8, 89, 151, 152
Lonely 1, 81, 111
Longshoreman 52
longshoreman (long' shore' man) n.
– a person who works on a waterfront loading and unloading ships.
Lose 53, 84, 116, 123
Lost 1, 23, 30, 38, 73, 137
Love 1, 54, 63, 84, 105, 106, 118, 119, 122, 124, 125, 127, 128, 153
Loved 54
Loving 82, 160, 161
Lower 6, 68
Lubricant 110

THE ANONYMOUS PRESS INDEX

Lucid 90
lucid (loo'sid) adj.
– shining; bright; resplendent.
– clear; transparent.
– sane; mentally sound.
Lucrative 35
Lukewarm 113
Lunacy 3
lunacy (loo'na see) n.
– originally, intermittent insanity, formerly supposed to change in intensity with the phases of the moon.
– great folly; utter foolishness.
Lunar 52
lunar (lU'nuhr) adj.
– of or pertaining to the moon: the lunar orbit.
– measured by the moon's revolutions: a lunar month.
– resembling the moon; round or crescent-shaped.
Lurking 33
Lust 68
Madly 22
Madness 6
Maelstrom 2
maelstrom (mAYl'struhm) n.
– a powerful whirlpool often hazardous to approach.
– a tumultuous state of affairs.
– a powerful current off the NW coast of Norway.
Maintain 8, 60
Maintenance 66, 146
Majestic 2
Make-believe 130
Make-up 55, 64
Making 62
Maladjusted xxvi
Malady 23, 64, 92, 138, 139
Malicious 145
malicious (muh lish'uhs) adj.
– full of or showing malice; spiteful.
Man 53, 77, 82, 91, 93, 96, 100, 120, 127, 130, 132, 134, 138, 140, 141, 143, 146, 148, 157, 160
Manage 1, 6, 60, 61
Management 2
Manager 136, 149
Manhood xxxii
Manic-depressive xxx
Manifestation xxx
Manifested 64, 130
Mankind 11, 48
Manual 3
Manuscript 133
Married 39, 69
Marshalled 45
derived from: marshal (mär'shuhl) n.
– to arrange in proper or effective order: to marshal facts.
– to array, as for battle.
– to usher or lead ceremoniously.
Martyr 79
martyr (mär'tuhr) n.
– a person who willingly suffers death rather than renounce his or her religion.
– a person who is put to death or suffers on behalf of a cause.
– a person who undergoes severe or constant suffering.
Marvelous 6, 134
Mass 54
Master 98
Mastered 66, 85
Material 48, 49, 51
Materialize 84
Material needs 98
Material world 49
Mathematical 51
Matter 66, 69, 83, 85, 93, 98, 101, 108, 111, 118, 128, 132, 141, 142, 161, 163
Maudlin 105
maudlin (maud'lin) adj.
– foolishly and tearfully or weakly sentimental.
– tearfully sentimental from too much drink.
Maximum xxviii, 102
Measures xxviii, 15, 118, 123
Mechanisms 6
Medical xxvii, 19, 73, 106, 143
Medicine 6
Meditation 59, 69, 83, 85, 87, 134, 164
Meeting 159
Members xviii, 27, 43, 122, 124, 125, 127, 135

Membership 28
Memories 10, 73
Memorize 87
Memory 24
Mental xxix-xxxi, 6, 22, 33, 35, 42, 54, 56, 64, 92, 114
Mental defense 43
Mental faculties 86
Mental twist 93
Mercifully 4
Message 60, 89, 136
Methods 31, 101, 163
Middle of the road 25
Mild 37
Millennium 3, 49
millennium (mi len'EE uhm) n.
– a period of 1000 years.
– "the millennium" the period of 1000 years during which Christ will reign on earth. Rev. 20:1-7.
– a period of general righteousness and happiness.
Mind xiii, 6, 10, 11, 20, 23, 24, 27, 41, 42, 43, 51, 55, 67, 87, 108, 157
Mind Universal 12
Ministers 10, 56, 61, 87, 89, 132
Miracle 11, 57, 85, 124, 128, 153, 161
Miracles 133, 151
Miraculous 25, 50, 55
Misdeeds 124
Miserable 8
Misery 15, 52
Misgiving xxvii, 76
Mistake 67, 84, 104, 107, 117, 119, 126
Misunderstanding 18, 20, 63, 111, 142
Moderate 20, 21, 34, 39, 109, 139
Modern 51
Modestly 2
Momentarily 151
Money 3, 4, 7, 54, 79, 97, 98, 109, 123, 126, 127, 145, 161
Montreal 4
Mood 91
Moral xxvii, xxxi, 11, 44, 45, 59, 95, 137
Moralize 91, 142
Morass 8
morass (muh ras') n.
– a tract of low, soft, wet ground.
– a marsh or bog.
– something that is confusing or troublesome or from which it is difficult to free oneself.
Morbid 86
morbid (môr'bid) adj.
– suggesting an unhealthy mental state or attitude; unwholesomely gloomy, sensitive, etc.
– gruesome; grisly.
– affected by, caused by, causing, or characteristic of disease.
Morning 6, 7, 22, 83, 87, 105, 158
Morphine 22
Mortgage 5
Mother-in-law 5
Motive xxvii, 54, 70, 102, 155
Motives 86
Motorcycle 2
Mottoes 135
Murmur 46
murmur (mûr'muhr) n.
– a low and indistinct continuous sound, as of a brook or the wind, or of distant voices.
– a mumbled expression of discontent.
– an abnormal continuous or periodic sound heard within the body by auscultation, esp. one originating in the heart valves.
Must xvi, xxv
Must abide 144
Must act 113
Must admit xxix
Must apologize 115
Must be xxviii, 21, 63
Must be accompanied by action 93
Must be careful 86
Must be convinced 135
Must be done 99, 130
Must be entirely honest 73
Must be hard on ourselves 74
Must be honest 146
Must be many 154
Must be no reservations 14, 33
Must be on a better basis 99
Must be on guard 115
Must be rid of selfishness 62
Must be weak 20
Must be willing 69
Must believe xxvi

Must carry 117
Must carry the vision 85
Must change 143
Must come from a Higher Power 43
Must come from within 95
Must confess 74
Must decide 144
Must decide for himself 95
Must decide these things 90
Must feel xxix
Must find a way out 153
Must find spiritual basis of life 44
Must get along 152
Must go further 85
Must go with us 85
Must have 29
Must have depth xxviii
Must help xxix
Must help others 159
Must keep sober 82
Must keep spiritually active 156
Must listen 101
Must lose fear 78
Must make amends 69
Must never 111
Must not expect 118
Must not miss 89
Must not postpone 75
Must not shrink 80
Must not shrink at anything 79
Must or it kills us 62
Must present to others xxv
Must realize 127
Must redouble 120
Must rely on God 164
Must remember 83, 127
Must say 81
Must see danger 127
Must start anew 114
Must stop 141
Must stop drinking xxix
Must take the lead 83
Must try to repair damage 99
Must turn 14
Must walk in the path of spiritual progress 100
Mustn't 101
Nadir 155
nadir (nAY'duhr) n.
– the point on the celestial sphere directly beneath a given position or observer and diametrically opposite the zenith.
– the lowest point; point of greatest adversity or despair.
Napoleon 4
Narrow 158
Nation 61
Natural 31, 53, 118
Naturally 58, 99, 107, 145
Nature 59, 115
Near 8, 57
Nearly 17, 104
Nearness 75
Necessarily 33
Necessary 27, 73, 142
Necessity 19, 34, 74
Need 8, 20, 26, 50, 76, 102, 119, 156
Needed 45, 47, 116
Needless 146
Needlessly 82
Needs 70, 91
Neglect 129
Nervous xxxi, 32, 35
Nervousness 37
Neurotic 122
neurotic (noo rot'ik) adj.
– of, pertaining to, or characteristic of neurosis.
– a neurotic person.
Neutrality 85
neutrality (nU tral'i tEE) n.
– the state of being neutral.
– the policy or status of a nation that does not participate in a war between other nations.
– neutral status, as of a seaport during a war.
Never 30, 31, 50, 51, 57, 77, 97, 105, 111, 123, 158
Nevertheless 26, 40, 87
New 11, 14, 28, 46, 50, 52, 83, 126, 131, 134, 135, 161
New England 1
Newcomers 15, 72, 89, 100, 132, 133, 159
New York 9, 41
Night 2, 3, 6, 8, 21, 41, 46, 56, 81, 86, 97, 100, 126, 128, 134
Nightclubs 101

Nightmare 73
Nil 58
Nominal 42
nominal (nom'uh nl) adj.
– being such in name only; so-called; putative: the nominal head of the country.
– (of a price, fee, etc.) named as a matter of form, being trifling in comparison with the actual value: a nominal price.
– of, pertaining to, or constituting a name or names.
Non-alcoholic 31, 39, 44
Non-denominational 132
Non-spiritual 34
Normal xxviii, xxx, 35, 38, 66, 113
Normal drinker 31, 140
Normally 17, 33
Nothing 19, 25, 40, 41, 49, 53, 54, 59, 65, 75, 79, 89, 91, 105
Now xxviii, xxxii, 20, 55, 59, 76, 163
Number 31, 109, 110, 153, 162
Numbers 16, 33
Nurse 95
Nurses 156
Oasis 9
oasis (O AY'sis) n.
– a fertile area in a desert region, usually having a spring or well.
– a refuge, as from work or stress; haven.
Oath 31
Obeyed 131
Obligation 94
Obligations 129
Obliged 115, 125
Oblivion 19
Observations 20, 23
Observe 49, 73
Observed 49, 73
Obsession 23, 30, 155
Obstacles 123
Obstinacy 48
obstinacy (ob'stuh nuh sEE) n.
– the quality or state of being obstinate; stubbornness.
– an instance of being obstinate; an obstinate act, viewpoint, etc.
Obviously 18, 45, 99, 164
Occasion 61, 101, 102, 105, 124
Occasional 87
Occasionally 78, 97, 134
Oddly 110
Offender 64
Offense 78
Officers 1
Often xxvi, xxviii, 48, 74
Oldest xxvii
Omega 49
omega (O mAY'guh) n.
– the 24th and last letter of the Greek alphabet.
– the last of any series; the end.
Ominous 1
ominous (om'uh nuhs) adj.
– portending evil or harm; foreboding; threatening; inauspicious.
– having the significance of an omen.
Omnipotence 133
derived from: omnipotent
(om nip'uh tuhnt) adj.
– infinite in power, as God.
– having very great or unlimited authority or power.
– an omnipotent being.
Once an alcoholic 33
Once in a while 97
Only xiv, 95
Open 6, 46
Open minded 48
Opinion 20, 117
Opinions 19, 22
Opportunity 19, 77
Optional 63
Ordinary 98, 125, 148
Organization xiii
Ostracized 177
derived from: ostracize
(os'truh sIz') v.
– to exclude, by general consent, from society, privileges, etc.
– to banish (a person) from his or her native country; expatriate.
– (in ancient Greece) to banish (a citizen) temporarily by popular vote.
Ought 103, 112
Ourselves 24, 37, 38, 46, 49, 50, 59, 62, 63, 64, 67, 68, 72, 76, 106, 121
Outgrow 125

Outlaw 62
Outlines 53, 94
Outsiders 131, 160
Outward 48
Overcome xxx, 72
Overtake 3
Overwhelming xiii, 56
Owe 86
Painful 121, 135, 155
Pains 53, 124
Painstakingly 83
Pall 106
  pall (pawl) v.
  – to lose strength, life, spirit, or taste; to become insipid.
Panacea 171
  panacea (pan'uh sEE'uh) n.
  – a remedy for all ills; cure-all.
  – a solution for all difficulties.
Pandemonium 106
  pandemonium (pande mo'nee um) n.
  – the abode of all demons: in *Paradise Lost* it is the palace built under Satan's orders as the capital of Hell.
  – Hell.
  – any place or scene of wild disorder, or confusion.
Panels 106
Paradoxically 68
  derived from: paradox (par'uh doks') n.
  – a seemingly contradictory or absurd statement that expresses a possible truth.
  – a self-contradictory and false proposition.
  – a person, thing, or situation, exhibiting an apparently contradictory nature.
Paralyzing 18, 116
Paramount xxvii, xxix
Parents 4, 18, 74, 115, 158
Parties 31, 99, 101, 146
Partners 41, 80
Pass 9, 87, 94, 99, 164
Passed xxxi, 25, 62, 110
Passengers of a shipwreck 17, 161
Passion 85
Past 62, 69, 70, 76, 77, 83, 84, 94, 123-126, 132, 140, 147, 151, 164
Path 15, 58, 72, 100, 116
Pathetic 134
Pathological xxxi
  pathological (path'uh loj'i kuhl) adj.
  – of or pertaining to pathology.
  – caused or affected by disease.
  – characterized by an unhealthy compulsion: a pathological liar.
Patience 70, 82, 83, 90, 105, 107, 108, 111, 112, 118, 138, 163
Patients xxvii, xxxi, 43, 61, 67, 90, 92, 112, 118, 144, 162
Patterns 22, 138
Paul 136
Pause 87, 119
Pay 78, 99, 129
Peace 16, 63, 75, 84
Penalty 99
People 7, 20, 22, 30, 34, 49, 51, 55, 58, 59, 61, 64, 66, 67, 70, 73-76, 78, 83, 84, 87, 89, 94, 109, 114, 146, 155, 158
Perceive 129
Perfection 60, 129
Perfectly 49, 60, 79
Permission 80
Persevered 73, 144
  derived from: persevere (pûr'suh vEEr') v.
  – to persist in pursuing something in spite of obstacles or opposition.
Persistent 30, 99, 100, 129
Personal xiii, 10, 29, 40, 52, 59, 60, 64, 65, 67, 70, 72, 84, 92, 137, 144
Personality 39
Persons 30, 34, 59, 60, 63, 70, 72, 74, 76, 78, 81, 90, 93, 96, 108, 116, 133, 135, 142
Perspective 5, 125
Persuade 2, 9, 29
Persuader 48
Pertinent 60
Petty 78
Phase xviii, 91, 129
Phenomenon xxviii, xxix, 27, 37
Philosophic 2
Philosophical 62
Philosophically 45

Philosophy 23, 44, 45
Phone 136
Physical xxvii, xxxi, 6, 7, 31, 36, 56, 90, 106, 143
Physically 21, 64, 109, 141, 154
Physician xxvi, xxix, xxx, 7, 31
Picture 32, 101, 110, 143, 146, 152
Pieces 33, 119
Pioneering xvii
Pity 15, 67
Place 75, 90, 101, 130, 143
Placed 24, 62, 86, 110
Plague 98
Plagued 15, 123
Plan xxv, 63, 86
Planned 100
Planning 33
Planted 130
Plattsburg 1
Plausibility 23
Play 61, 68, 94, 132, 146
Players 60, 61
Pleasures 97, 101, 151
Plight 155
plight (plIt) n.
– a distressing condition or situation: to be left in a sorry plight.
Pneumonia 108
pneumonia (noo mOn'yuh) n.
– inflammation of the lungs with congestion.
– an acute infection of the lungs caused by the bacterium Streptococcus pneumoniae.
Pocket our pride 75
Point 24, 29, 34, 53, 56, 95, 100, 108, 119, 135, 142
Pointless 23
Poison 6
Poisoning 157
Policeman 106
Political 17, 158
Politicians 61
Positions 2, 3, 25, 36, 62, 63, 79, 110, 116, 148
Positive 21, 22, 40, 108
Possible xxv, 40, 59, 62, 80, 91, 92, 117, 139, 142, 143
Potential 33, 39, 149
Potomac River 51
Powerful 24, 28, 33, 49, 58, 63, 113, 130, 161
Powerless 45*, 59
powerless (pou'uhr lis) adj.
– unable to produce an effect; ineffective.
– lacking power to act; helpless.
Powers xxvii, xxviii, xxxi, 10-13, 16, 22, 24, 33, 43, 45, 46-48, 50, 53, 55, 56, 59, 60, 62, 63, 66, 85, 93, 107, 114, 118
Practical 9, 24, 32, 48, 89, 113, 130, 153, 160
Practice 49, 72, 97, 162
Praise 127
Pray xxxii, 70, 82, 105
Prayer 13, 59, 63*, 67*, 76, 85, 86*, 87
prayer (prâr) n.
– a devout petition to God or an object of worship.
– a spiritual communion with God or an object of worship, as in supplication, thanksgiving, or adoration.
– the act or practice of praying to God or an object of worship.
Praying 59
Preachers 10
Precede 35, 40, 44, 49, 72, 91, 95, 98, 145, 154, 163
Precepts 93
derived from: precept (prEE'sept) n.
– a commandment or direction given as a rule of action or conduct.
– an injunction as to moral conduct; maxim.
– a direction for performing a technical operation.
Precipitates xxx
derived from: precipitate
(pri sip'i tAYt) v.
– to hasten the occurrence of; bring about prematurely or suddenly: to precipitate a crisis.
– to fling or hurl down.
– to cast violently or abruptly: to precipitate oneself into a struggle.
Precisely 37, 49, 66, 79
Precisely how we recovered xiii
Predicament 92, 105

Prejudice 47, 49, 55, 93, 139, 162
Prejudices 1, 12, 45, 46, 77, 89
Preoccupied 126
Prepared 66, 75, 96
Preposterous 51
preposterous (pri pos'tuhr uhs) adj.
– completely contrary to nature, reason, or common sense; senseless; foolish.
Prescribed 26
Presence 51, 56, 63, 162
Present xiii, 39, 100, 110, 136, 139
Presented xxvii, 144
Presently 30, 38, 155
President 149
Pride 7, 8, 12, 25, 65, 75, 104, 105, 116, 125, 160*
Priest 87, 89
Principal 62, 124
Principle 112, 115
Principles 14, 19, 42, 47, 60, 64, 79, 83, 87, 93, 94, 97, 116, 121, 128*, 130, 139, 156
Private 157
Privilege xxvii, 51
Probably 60, 76
Probed 142
Problems xxvi, xxix, 13, 15, 17, 19, 23, 26, 29, 32, 35, 39, 40, 52, 55, 68, 69, 75, 87, 90, 94, 98-101, 103, 104, 108, 111, 113, 116, 117, 126, 131, 133, 139, 144, 148, 149, 156, 160
Procedure xxviii, 143
Process 25, 42, 48
Procrastination 197
Prodded 95
derived from: prod (prod) v.
– to poke or jab with or as if with something pointed.
– to rouse or incite as if by poking; nag; goad.
– the act of prodding; a poke or jab.
Prodigious 5
prodigious (pruh dij'uhs) adj.
– extraordinary in size, amount, extent, etc.
– arousing admiration or amazement: a prodigious feat.
– abnormal; monstrous.
Prodigy 171
prodigy (prod'i jEE) n.
– a person, esp. a child or young person, having extraordinary talent or ability: a musical prodigy.
– something that excites wonder or amazement.
– something abnormal or monstrous.
Professional 15, 73
Professor 51
Proffered 10
derived from: proffer (pro'fur) v.
– to offer for acceptance; to make an offer of.
Profit xxvii, 51
Program 9, 19, 58, 59, 72, 73, 126, 127
Progress 60, 94, 134
Prominent xxv, 163
Promise 53
Promised 13, 38, 84
Promises 5, 38, 63*, 70-71*, 75*, 84, 88*, 100*, 148, 164*
Promises, The 83-84
Promising 5, 21, 39, 156
Promotion 115
Promptly xvii, 64
Proof 48
Prophesied 41
derived from: prophesy (prof'uh sI') v.
– to foretell or predict.
– to indicate beforehand.
– to utter in prophecy or as a prophet. esp. by divine inspiration.
Prosaic 48
prosaic (prO zAY'ik) adj.
– commonplace or dull; matter-of-fact; unimaginative: a prosaic mind.
– of or like prose rather than poetry.
Protect 146
Protege 92
protégé (prO'tuh zhAY') n.
– a person under the patronage, protection, or care of someone interested in his or her career or welfare.
Prove xiii, 2, 31, 32, 47, 51, 54, 141

Provided 27, 43, 46, 48, 63, 69, 79, 93, 98, 102, 146, 147, 160
Providence 101
providence (prov'i duhns) n.
– (often cap.) the foreseeing care and guidance of God or nature over the creatures of the earth.
– (cap.) God, esp. when conceived as exercising such care and guidance in directing human affairs.
– a manifestation of divine care or direction.
Provocation 62, 124, 146
provocation
(prov'uh kAY'shuhn) n.
– the act of provoking.
– something that provokes, esp. by inciting, instigating, angering, or irritating.
Psychiatric 19
derived from: psychiatry
(si kl'uh trEE) n.
– the branch of medicine concerned with the study, diagnosis, and treatment of mental disorders.
Psychiatrists 18, 26, 114, 133, 163
Psychic xxix
Psychologist 28, 73, 74, 133
Psychology xxvii, xxxi
Publication xiii
Publicly xiii
Purpose xiii, 10, 50, 77, 92, 130
Qualified 32
Qualities 140
Quarrels 100, 147
Queer 38, 92
queer (kwEEr) adj.
– strange or odd from a conventional viewpoint; unusually different; singular; eccentric.
– of a questionable nature or character; suspicious; shady: something queer in the wording of the document.
– not physically right or well; giddy, faint, or qualmish.
Queried 9
derived from: query (kwEEr'EE) n.
– a question; an inquiry.
– mental reservation; doubt.
Questionable 70
Questions 20, 34, 56, 98, 108
Quicksand 8
Quiet 94
Quit 20, 34, 39, 90, 91, 141
Quitting 34
Rabbi 132
rabbi (rab'I) n.
– the chief religious official of a synagogue who performs ritualistic, educational, and other functions as spiritual leader of the congregation.
– a title of respect for a Jewish scholar or teacher.
– a Jewish scholar qualified to rule on questions of Jewish law.
Races 49
Racket 158
Radically 117, 146
Rancor 111, 134
rancor (rang'kuhr) n.
– bitter resentment or ill will; malice.
Ranting 9
Rarely 58
Reacts 19, 21, 26, 37, 43, 81
Read xxxii, 70, 95, 96, 112, 113, 114, 133, 144, 147
Reader xxv, 27, 34, 48
Readily 48
Readiness 52, 74
Readjustment 122, 146
Ready 58, 59
Real alcoholic 30, 31
Real purpose 77
Reality xxvi, 50, 55, 130
Reason 21, 23, 24, 30, 35-37, 42, 48, 53, 54, 97, 99, 101, 110, 140, 147
Reasonable 48, 53, 137, 146
Reasoning 54
Reasons 51, 72, 73, 94
Rebel 94
Reborn 63
Reconciled 72
derived from: reconcile
(rek'uhn sIl') v.
– to cause (a person) to accept or be resigned to something not desired.
– to cause to become friendly or peaceable again: to reconcile hostile persons.
– to compose or settle (a quarrel, dispute, etc.).

Reconciliation 124
Reconstruction 83
Recover 19, 26, 27, 29, 30, 39, 45, 58, 89, 96, 126, 133, 135, 142, 149, 158, 162, 164
Recovered xiii, xxv, xxxi, 17, 20, 29, 44, 90, 96, 113, 132, 133, 146
Recovering 122
Recovery xxv, xxix, 36, 59, 73, 90, 94, 96, 97, 99, 113, 120, 125, 127, 139, 143, 145, 147, 153
Rectify 124
rectify (rek'tuh fI') v.
– to make, put, or set right; remedy; correct: to rectify an error.
– to put right by adjustment or calculation, as an instrument or a course at sea.
– to purify (esp. a spirit or liquor) by repeated distillation.
Reduce 62
Re-emphasize 39
Reference 3, 48
Referring 67
Reflected 27, 37, 86, 118
Reformers 61
Refusal 158
Regained 15, 26, 30, 104
Regard xxv, 117
Regardless 98, 99
Regret 64, 83
Rehabilitation xxv, xxviii, xxxi, 7
Rejected 45
Relapse 5*, 23*, 26, 31, 35, 90*, 112*, 120, 125*, 139, 142, 155
Relating xxxi, 155
Relations 98, 111, 134
Relationship 13, 28, 29, 52, 64, 72, 82, 99, 100, 164
Relatively 146
Relatives 97, 104
Relax 86
Released 114, 128, 151, 152, 154
Reliance 164
Relieve 63, 124, 132
Religion 9, 49, 74, 93, 132
Religious xiv, 9, 27, 28, 43, 56, 71, 77, 87, 90, 93, 128, 131, 158
Rely xxvi, 31, 98
Relying 68
Remain xiii, 15, 32-34, 155, 159
Remained xxxi
Remark 125
Remarried 79
Remedy xxvi, 31, 118
Remember 36, 41, 58, 73, 76, 83, 89, 100, 108, 123, 133, 140, 164
Remind 120
Reminding 79, 87, 99, 101
Remonstrances 3
derived from: remonstrance
(ri mon'struhns) n.
– an act or instance of remonstrating.
– a protest: deaf to remonstrances.
Remorse 6, 66, 81, 83, 86, 106
Remove 59, 68, 71, 76, 84, 85
Rendezvous 104
rendezvous (rän'duh vU) n.
– an agreement to meet at a certain time and place.
– the meeting itself.
– a place designated for a meeting or assembling, esp. of troops or ships.
Renewing 5
Renews 131
Repair 76, 127
Reparation 98
reparation (rep'uhrAY'shuhn) n.
– the making of amends for wrong or injury done.
– Usually, "reparations." compensation payable by a defeated nation to the victor for damages or loss suffered during war.
– restoration to good condition.
Repeatedly 47
Repeats 35, 81
Repel 103
Repetition 120
Replaced 130
Representation 17
Reprieve 85
reprieve (ri prEEv') v.
– to delay the impending punishment or sentence of (a condemned person).
– to relieve temporarily from any evil.
– a respite from impending punishment, esp. from execution.

THE ANONYMOUS PRESS INDEX

Reproached 123
derived from: reproach (ri prOch') v.
– to find fault with (a person, group, etc.); blame; censure.
– to criticize severely; upbraid.
– to be a cause of blame or discredit to.
Reproved 126
derived from: reprove (ri prUv') v.
– to criticize or correct, esp. gently.
– to express strong disapproval of; censure.
– to disprove or refute.
Reputation 73, 80, 105, 126
Request xxvi, 13, 87
Requirement 60, 94
Requirements 50
Requires xxviii, xxix, 12, 50, 72
Resentful 81
Resentment 15, 18, 64, 66, 68, 70, 79, 84, 86, 100, 105, 116, 117, 119, 122, 126, 127, 145
Resentments 62, 100
Reservation 33, 63
Reserve 18, 51
Resign 31, 148
Resist xxxi, 12
Resistant 155
Resolutely 84
derived from: resolute (rez'uh lUt') adj.
– firmly set in purpose or opinion; determined; resolved.
– characterized by firmness and determination.
Resolutions xxx, 34
Resolve 5
Respect xxx, 19,43
Respective 19, 91
Respond 96
Responsibilities 97, 120, 130, 137, 154
Restless xxviii
Restored 57, 59
Resulting xxix
Results xiv, 4, 9, 78, 99, 134, 138, 144
Retaliate 61, 62, 67, 105
Retaliation 67, 103
Retired 32, 33, 61
Retreat 129
Revealed 48
Revelation 57
Reverse 114
Review 75, 86
Reviewing 35, 68, 75
Revolutionary 14, 50
Revolutionized 25
Revulsion 5, 7, 141
revulsion (ri vul'shuhn) n.
– a strong feeling of repugnance, distaste, or dislike; disgust; loathing.
– a sudden and violent change of feeling or response in sentiment, taste, etc.
– the act of drawing something back or away.
Rid 62, 64
Ridiculous 38
Right 69, 74, 81, 83, 86, 87, 100
Righteous 152
Rigorous 58, 145
rigorous (rig'uhr uhs) adj.
– characterized by rigid severity: rigorous laws.
– severely exact; precise: rigorous research.
– extremely inclement; harsh: rigorous weather.
Rise 45, 153
Rising 123
Rival 80
Rivalries 161
Road 104, 114, 129, 164
Roaring 82, 155
Robust 33
Rocketed 25
Rough 15, 72
Ruin 101, 107, 108
Ruined 80, 82, 109
Ruinous 80
ruinous (rU'uh nuhs) adj.
– bringing or tending to bring ruin; destructive; disastrous: a ruinous war.
– fallen into ruin; dilapidated.
– extremely expensive.
Rule 81
Rumor 9
Run 60
Run-around 146
Running 68, 88

Rushed 95
Rushes 10
Ruthless 78
Ruthlessly 13
Sacrifice xxx
Sacrifice self 93
Sad 18, 61
Safe 62, 85
Safely xxviii
Saints 60
Saloon 35
Salvaging 139, 140
Sane 14, 53, 69, 85, 130
Sanitariums 31, 97, 107
derived from: sanitarium (san'i târ'EE uhm) n.
– an institution for the preservation of health; health resort.
Sanity 7, 37*, 57, 59, 70, 84, 154
Sash 6
sash (sash) n.
– a fixed or movable framework, as in a window or door, in which panes of glass are set.
Satisfaction xxvii, 8, 34, 61
Satisfied 92, 134, 142, 153
Satisfying 43
Saturday Evening Post xvii
Save 45, 57, 103
Scandalous 125
Scarcely 6, 15, 127, 138, 158
Scenery 60
Scheme 101
scheme (skEEm) n.
– a plan, design, or program of action; project.
– an underhand plot; intrigue.
– any system of correlated things, parts, etc., or the manner of its arrangement.
School 8, 69
Schoolmate 13
Science 31, 48, 49
Scientific xxvii
Scoffers 3
derived from: scoff (skôf) v.
– to speak derisively; mock; jeer.
– to mock at; deride.
– an expression of mockery, derision, doubt, or derisive scorn.
Scope xxx
Scotch 31
Scratched 19, 129
Screaming 107
Searches 22, 55, 96
Searching xxxi
Seasons 123
Secret 81
Secure 89
Security 65, 105, 123
Sedative 7, 22
Seek 16, 46
Seemed 26, 47, 51
Seemingly xiii, 47, 57
Seldom xxviii, 21, 73, 97, 132, 143
Selecting 155, 162
Self 35, 62, 64
Self-appraisal 72, 94
Self-centeredness 14, 61, 62, 64, 111*, 124
Self-confident 40, 68
Self-conscious 115
Self-control 26
Self-deception 31
Self-delusion 62
Self-destruction 56
Self-discipline 32
Self-esteem 64, 65
Self-evident 9
Self-imposed 53
Selfish 7, 21, 61, 67, 69, 82, 84, 86, 87
Selfishness 6, 62, 116
Self-justification 127
Self-knowledge 7, 39, 40, 42
Self-pity 8, 15, 61*, 62, 84, 86, 88, 104, 105, 116, 127
Self-propulsion 60
Self-reliance xxxi, 68
Self-revealing 29
Self-sacrificing 61, 93, 105
Self-searching 25
Self-seeker 61, 67
Self-seeking 84, 86
Self-sufficiency 52
Self-will 60, 62, 70, 71, 76, 87
Selves 30, 49, 59
Sensation xxviii, xxxi
Sense xiv, xxvii, xxix, 11, 12, 19, 22, 26, 46, 50, 72, 85
Senseless 21

Sensible 21, 68, 83, 148
Serenity 14, 68, 84
Service 77, 98, 133
Sex 58*, 65, 68, 69, 70, 81, 96*, 124*, 134*
Shortcuts 123
Significance 12, 69
Silkworth, Doctor xxxii
Simple 9, 14, 16, 25, 27, 28, 40, 46, 47, 50, 57, 58, 62, 88
Simple Rules xxix
Simply xiv, 9, 22, 48, 98
Sincere xxix, 18, 37, 63, 77, 95, 117
Sinful 135
Single 27, 37, 76
Sins 13, 61
Situations xxvi, xxx, 25, 69, 70, 79, 81, 84, 96, 104, 110, 114, 124, 141, 145, 155, 163
Sixth Sense 85
Skepticism 46
Skills 21
Skimped 75
Skip 72
Skipping 37
Slander 80
slander (slan'duhr) n.
– defamation; calumny.
– a malicious, false, and defamatory statement or report.
– Law. defamation by oral utterance rather than by writing, pictures, etc.
Sleep 21, 97
Sleeping xxviii
Slip 84, 100, 139
Slipped 110
Slow 51
Slowing 109
Slowly 109
Slyly 145
derived from: sly (slI) adj.
– cunning or wily.
– stealthy; surreptitious.
– mischievous or roguish: sly humor.
Small 5
Smashed 30
Smile 152
Smiled 55
Smilingly 9
Smoker 135
Smokers 135
Snags 117
Sneaked 105
Sober 4, 8, 33, 82, 99, 116, 127, 154, 156
Sobriety 32, 33, 101, 118, 119, 128, 129, 152
Social 19, 102, 115, 161
Society xiv, 11, 26, 53
Solemn 3, 105
solemn (sol'uhm) adj.
– grave; mirthless: solemn remarks.
– somberly sedate or profound: solemn music.
– serious; earnest: solemn assurances.
Solitary 72
Solution xxxi, xxvi, 17, 25, 43, 52, 91, 92, 95, 117, 141
Solutions 104, 145
Solve 42, 45, 52, 116, 117, 126
Solved 17, 25, 104
Solving xxviii, xxix, 32, 100
Someday 23, 30, 33
Somehow 23, 30, 53, 67
Something 9, 54, 60
Somewhat 46
Son 104
Sordid 102
sordid (sôr'did) adj.
– morally ignoble or base; vile.
– meanly selfish or mercenary.
– filthy; squalid.
Sore 65, 66
Sorry 70, 83, 118, 121
Sort 18, 35, 48, 54, 105, 158
Sots 8
Sought 59, 60, 106
Sound 10
Soundness xxvi
Source 109, 163
Speaks 43, 45, 47, 91, 136, 145
Special 1, 137
Specialized xxv
Specializing xxv
Spectres 123
derived from: spectre (spek'tuhr) n.
– a visible incorporeal spirit, esp. one of a terrifying nature; ghost; phantom; apparition.
– some object or source of terror or dread: the specter of disease.

Speed 49
Spell 27
Spheres 10
derived from: sphere (sfEEr) n.
– the environment within which a person or thing exists, acts, or operates.
– a field of something specified: a sphere of knowledge; a sphere of influence.
Spirit 46, 51, 84, 103, 152
Spirit of Nature 12
Spirit of Universe 10, 52, 75
Spiritual xxvi, 15, 25, 27, 29, 35, 39, 42-45, 47, 48, 50, 55, 56, 60, 63, 64, 66, 75, 76, 79, 83, 85, 93, 95, 97, 98, 100-102, 114, 116, 118, 120, 128, 130, 156, 160, 162
Spiritual activities 120, 129
Spiritual advisor 63
Spiritual approach 43, 95
Spiritual awakening 60
Spiritual basis 118, 135, 162
Spiritual convictions 130
Spiritual demonstration 98
Spiritual development 130
Spiritual experience 14*, 25*, 27, 29, 42*, 44*, 46*, 50, 56*, 66, 75, 79, 113*, 119, 124, 128, 130, 131, 155, 157, 158, 569
Spiritual growth 47, 129
Spiritual help 25, 27
Spiritual hilltop 95
Spiritual intoxication 128
Spiritual justification 129
Spiritual liberation 55
Spiritual life 15, 35, 83, 129
Spiritual living 133
Spiritual malady 64
Spiritual mode 133
Spiritual plane 116
Spiritual program 126, 130
Spiritual progress 60, 100, 127
Spiritual principles 42, 47, 83, 93, 97, 116, 156
Spiritual release 55
Spiritual remedy 112
Spiritual tangent 130
Spiritual tools 25, 95
Spiritual understanding 125, 127
Spiritual way 114, 159, 160
Spite 37
Splendid 40
Spoil 90, 91, 100
Spoiled 105
Sponsorship (no direct reference)
Spots 15, 42, 102
Spree xxix
Sprees 21, 32, 35, 37, 73, 92, 95, 143, 159
Spring 4, 26
Squander 66
Stability 49
Stable 39
Stages xxviii, 21, 73, 92, 107
Start xxx, 47, 58, 102, 117, 120
State xiii, 24, 35, 48, 61, 132
Statesman 50
Statesmen xxvi, 54
Status 135
Stayed 61, 109
Steal 101
Stealing 68
Steer 95
Step One 9*, 25*, 30*, 54*, 59, 92*, 157*
Step Two 12*, 46*, 55*, 59, 158*
Step Three 13*, 59, 60, 63, 100*
Step Four 25*, 59, 64-71, 73*, 75*, 76*, 94*
Step Five 25*, 59, 72-75, 94*, 156*
Step Six 59, 76
Step Seven 59, 76, 87*
Step Eight 59, 76, 87*
Step Nine 59, 69*, 76, 78*, 83*, 164*
Step Ten 59, 84, 86*, 99*
Step Eleven 59, 68*, 79, 85-87, 164*
Step Twelve xxv*, xxvii*, 19*, 20*, 60, 66*, 85*, 89-91, 94*, 158*, 159*, 160*, 163*
Stickler 48, 52
Stimulating 160
Stock 4, 64, 73
Stomach 36
Stop xiv, 20, 21, 23, 32-34, 39, 52, 82, 90, 92, 109, 113, 114, 141, 147, 148, 155, 164
Stopped 5
Stopped fighting 103, 134

Store 4
Story 36, 43, 50, 75, 80, 93, 112
Straight 37, 54, 69, 70, 143
Straighten 77, 94
Straining 126
Strange xxix, xxxi, 10, 13, 18, 38, 42, 128, 154
Stranger xxxi, 119, 157
Strapped 158
Streets 38, 77, 81
Strength 10, 13, 68, 70, 76, 98
Strenuous 64
Stress 93
Stricken 161
Strikes 43
Strivings 126
Strong 1, 21, 38, 75, 139
Stubbornness 140
Students 51
Stuff 20, 159
Struggle 86, 118
Struggles 16, 92, 108
Stumble 70, 113
Subject xxvii, 45, 76, 111, 112, 143
Subscribe 133
Subsequently 80
Substitute 152
Substituted 38
Subtle 8
subtle (sut'l) adj.
– thin, tenuous, or rarefied, as a fluid or an odor.
– fine or delicate in meaning or intent; difficult to perceive or understand: subtle irony.
– delicate or faint and mysterious: a subtle smile.
Succeeded 32, 101, 159
Success 3, 34, 60, 95, 98, 111, 127
Successfully 25, 27, 32, 39, 40, 42, 51, 63, 64, 100, 122
Succumbed xxx
derived from: succumb (suh kum') v.
– to give way to superior force; yield.
– to yield to disease, wounds, old age, etc.; die.
Sudden 57
Suddenly 6, 27
Suffer xxvi, 23, 58, 109, 114, 139, 159
Sufferings xxv, 22, 36, 44, 129
Suffices xxviii
derived from: suffice (suh fIs') v.
– to be enough or adequate, as for needs or purposes.
– to be enough or adequate for; satisfy.
Suggest xxx, 91, 92, 94, 113, 123, 142, 144
Suggested xxviii, xxx, 10, 12, 59, 86, 87, 94, 98, 111, 122, 130, 140, 164
Suicide 16, 56
Suitable 74
Sum 70, 80
Summa cum laude 172
summa cum laude
(soom'uh koom lou'duh) adv.
– with highest praise: used in diplomas to grant the highest of three special honors for grades above the average.
Summarize 20
Summer xvii, 90
Sumptuous 3
sumptuous (sump'chU uhs) adj.
– entailing great expense, as from choice materials, fine work, etc.; costly.
– luxuriously fine or large; lavish; splendid: a sumptuous feast.
Sunday 10, 52
Sunlight of the spirit 66
Superhuman 10
Superior 93, 129
Superstition 51
Supplanted 24
derived from: supplant (suh' plant) v.
– to take the place of (another), as through force, scheming, or strategy.
– to replace (one thing) by something else.
Support 53
Supreme xxx
Supreme Being 46
Sure xiii, 47
Surely xxv, 15
Surprisingly 28, 30, 86
Survive 15, 120, 125, 153
Suspect 23, 120
Suspend 9
Suspicion 69

Swearing 31
Sweets 133, 134
Swings 52
Switching 31
Sympathetic 115
Sympathy 105, 144
Symptoms 33, 38, 40, 106
Tact 77
tact (tacked) n.
– touch; a touching.
– the sense of touch.
– intuitive perception, especially a quick and fine perception of the proper thing to say or to do to avoid giving offense.
Tactful 83
Tangent 130
tangent (tan'juhnt) n.
– digressing suddenly from one course of action or thought and turning to another.
Tangible 99
tangible (tan'juh buhl) adj.
– capable of being touched; discernible by touch; material or substantial.
– real or actual, rather than imaginary or visionary.
– definite; not vague or elusive: no tangible grounds for suspicion.
Tedious 48
tedious (tEE'dEE uhs) adj.
– marked by tedium; long and tiresome.
– tiresomely wordy, as a speaker or writer.
Teetotaler 139
Telephone 8, 97
Temper 111
Temperament 108
temperament (tem'puhr uh muhnt) n.
– the combination of mental and emotional traits of a person; natural predisposition.
– unusual personal nature as manifested by peculiarities of feeling, temper, action, etc., often with a disinclination to submit to conventional rules or restraints: a display of temperament.
– (old physiology) the combination of the four cardinal humors, the relative proportions of which were supposed to determine physical and mental constitution.
Temperance 10
temperance (tem'per anse) n.
– self restraint in conduct.
– moderation in eating and drinking.
– total abstinence from alcoholic liquors.
Temporarily 111
Temptation 57, 85, 101, 120, 147, 181
Tendencies 24, 125, 134
Tension 73, 115
Terrible 23, 28, 141
Test 13
Testimony 55
Thanked 155
Theological 93
Theorizing 70
Theory 52
Think 24, 62, 68, 69, 126
Thinking 13, 24, 35, 37, 48, 50, 53, 70, 74, 86, 87, 114, 118, 158
Thorough 58, 62, 70
Thoroughly 58
Thoroughness 63
Thought 63
Thoughtful 123
Thought-Life 86
Threadbare 24
threadbare (thred'bâr) adj.
– having the nap worn off so as to lay bare the threads of the weave, as a fabric or garment.
– wearing threadbare clothes; shabby or poor.
– hackneyed; trite; ineffectively stale: threadbare arguments.
Threshold 41, 160
Thy will be done 88
Tight 21, 115
Tolerance 19, 67, 70, 83, 84, 118, 122, 125, 127, 138
Tomorrow 63
Tornado 82
Track 68, 100
Tragedies xxviii

Tragic 16, 21, 23, 24
Traits 92
Transcended 159
Transformation 133, 143
Traveling 49, 52, 104, 162
Treat 61, 67, 108, 129
Treatment xxv, xxxi, 13, 26, 30, 142, 143, 148, 157
Trembling 8, 73, 115
Tremendous 17
Tried 60, 66-68, 72
Trifle 126
trifle (trI'fuhl) n.
– something of very little value, importance, or consequence.
– a small, inconsiderable, or trifling amount of anything.
– a dessert of cake soaked in liqueur, then combined with custard, fruit, jam, etc., and topped with whipped cream.
Triumphant 62, 66
triumphant (trI um'fuhnt) adj.
– having achieved victory or success; victorious; successful.
– exulting over victory; rejoicing over success; exultant.
Trivial 37, 42, 120
Trouble 15, 20, 52, 56, 62, 69, 72, 79, 80, 85, 91, 95, 156
Troubles 68, 119, 131, 132
Troublesome 70
True 22, 23, 49
Truly xxvi
Trust 68, 80
Trust God 98
Truth 23, 26, 33, 64, 71, 73, 93, 98, 106, 144, 145*
Trying 60, 72, 77
Tumbler 5
Turn 59
Turning 59
Twenty-four hours 16, 86
Type xxx, 43, 109
Ugliness 50
Ugly 24, 90
Unabated 137
unabated (un'uh bAY'tid) adj.
– with undiminished force, power, or vigor.
Unable 34, 109
Unapproachable 18, 41, 111
Unconsciously 122
Underlying 51
Underneath 16
Understand 14, 38, 42, 74, 81, 94, 112, 121, 137, 140, 156, 164
Understanding xxvii, 17, 18, 63, 82, 112, 122
Understood xxx, 13, 14, 47, 59, 60, 63, 106
Undisciplined 88
Undoubtedly 81, 138, 149
Undue 99
Undying 144
Unearth 124
Unexpected 78
Unfavorably 128
Unfortunately 89
Unfortunates 58
Unhappiness 66, 104, 122, 123
Unhappy 3, 52, 74, 151
Uniquely 89
United States 3
Universal 11
Universe 10, 25, 49
Unjustifiably 69
Unknown 51
Unmanageable 59
Unmindful 9
Unpopular xxxi
Unreasonable 108
Unreasoning 48
Unsatisfactory 51
Unselfish 93, 105
Unselfishness xxvii, 127
Unthinking 82
Unwelcome 5
Unwilling xxx, 30
Uppermost 82
Upright 83, 141
Urge 34, 70, 83, 113, 148
Useful 19, 110, 158
Usefulness 8, 49, 76, 132
Useless 133
Uselessness 52
Usual 66, 155
Usually 26, 58, 65, 81
Utmost 13, 19, 147

Utopia 16, 61
Utopia (yU tO'pEE uh) n.
– an imaginary island described in Sir Thomas More's Utopia (1516) as enjoying perfection in law, politics, etc.
– any ideal place or state.
– any visionary system of political or social perfection.
Utter 34, 63
Utterly 26
Vacated 159
Vagaries 129
derived from: vagary (vuh gâr'EE) n.
– an unpredictable, capricious, or erratic action, occurrence, or course.
– a whimsical, wild, or unusual idea or notion.
Vague 23, 36, 86, 134
Vain 30, 49
Value 124, 129, 134
Vanished 5, 89, 133
Vanity 116
Variation 50
Varied 61
Varieties of religious experience xxx, 28, 54, 64, 109, 133
Various 16
Variously 105
Verdict 124
Veritable 17
veritable (ver'i tuh buhl) adj.
– being truly or very much so; genuine or real: a veritable triumph.
– true, as a statement or tale.
Vestiges 1
derived from: vestige(ves'tij) n.
– a mark, trace, or visible evidence of something that is no longer present or in existence.
– a very slight trace or amount of something: the last vestige of hope.
– a degenerate or imperfectly developed biological structure that performed a useful function at an earlier stage in the development of the individual or evolution of the species.
Veteran 1
Vicarious 101
vicarious (vI kâr'EE uhs) adj.
– performed, exercised, received, or suffered in place of another.
– taking the place of another person or thing.
– felt or enjoyed through imagined participation in the experience of others: a vicarious thrill.
Viciously 105
Vicissitude 56
vicissitude (vi sis'i tUd') n.
– regular change or succession of one state or thing to another.
– change or variation; mutation; mutability.
– "vicissitudes" successive or changing phases or conditions, as of life or fortune; ups and downs.
Victim 61, 140, 146
Victor 66
Victory 14, 63, 76, 125
View 52, 124
Viewpoints 20
Vigorous 63, 84
Violent 35, 110
Violently 5, 97
Virginia 137
Virtually 22
Virtuous 61
virtuous (vûr'chU uhs) adj.
– conforming to moral and ethical principles; morally excellent; upright.
– chaste: a virtuous young person.
Vision 85
Visited 13, 94, 160
Visiting 161
Visitors 157, 169
Visual 48
Vital 15, 27, 64, 72, 85, 93, 94
Vocation 19
Voice 8
Voicing 63
Volume 2, 18, 96, 144
Waiting 112
Walk 19, 53, 79, 154
Wall Street 2
Walter Hagen 3
Wandered 1, 123

War 1, 11
Warn 100
Warnings 1, 21, 37
Warped 18, 108, 142, 157
Warrant 79, 87, 133
Warranted 98
Warring 46
Washington 40, 42
Waste 75, 90, 148
Wastepipe 22
wastepipe (waste' pipe')n.
– a pipe for draining liquid waste or excess liquids.
– a pipe for draining away the wastes of a building other than those from water closets.
Watchwords 118
Water 22, 79
Wayward 130
Weak 20, 72, 115, 120, 154
Weakened 7
Weakest 48
Weakling 6
Wearily xxvii, 107
Weary 7, 110
Weather 122
Weddings 101
Week 24, 38, 105
Weight xxviii, 7
Welcomed xiv, 7, 53, 95, 96
Welfare 94, 161
Well-being 137, 149
Well-known xxv, 156
Well-to-do 4
West 162
Western 153, 162
Wet 112
Wherever 59
Whiskey 36, 37
Whisky 6
Whoopee 101
whoopee (woop'EE) Informal.
– (used as a shout of exuberant joy.)
– Idiom "make whoopee."
a. to engage in uproarious merrymaking.
b. to make love.
Wife 2, 5, 8, 15, 80-82, 97-100, 104, 107, 114, 116, 122, 127, 130, 135, 155, 160, 161
Will 7
Will Power xxxi, 11, 16*, 20, 22-24, 33, 34, 40, 42, 45*, 59*, 60*, 85, 87*, 92, 107, 116-117*, 155
William Silkworth xxxii
Willing 12, 26, 27, 47, 57-60, 69, 70, 77, 79, 92, 93, 97, 112, 118, 124, 141, 146, 153, 158, 159, 162
Willingness 12, 13, 26-28, 46, 47, 57, 60, 76, 118, 124, 163
Win 4, 33
Window 136
Wine 20, 31
Winters 61
Wise 123
Wished 26, 47, 61, 115, 145, 152
Withdrawing 102
Withholding nothing 75
Within 56
Witnessed xiii, 52, 63
Women xiii, 33, 50, 58, 106, 108, 111, 113, 118, 119, 159
Wonder 73
Wondered 9
Wonderful 17, 61, 100, 116, 152
Wonderfully 47
Wording 63
Work xiii, 4, 14, 19, 25, 26, 28, 76, 84, 87, 88, 93, 95, 98, 100, 108, 114, 117, 119, 122, 146, 153, 162-164
Workouts 117
World 2, 20, 46, 48, 51, 61, 62, 75, 100, 132
Worldliness 16
Worldly 13, 50, 128
Worry 86, 88, 112, 114, 116
Worse 30
Worship 54
Worships 55
Worst 132
Worth 18, 32
Worthwhile xxxi, 148
Wright Brothers 51
Write 2
Writing xiii
Written xxx, 5, 70, 157
Wrong 13, 56, 59, 66, 67, 83, 129, 135
Wrong-doing 66, 80
Wronged 67

Wrought 133
wrought (rôt) v.
– elaborated; embellished.
– not rough or crude.
– produced or shaped by beating with a hammer, as iron or silver articles.
Zeal 181
zeal (zEEl) n.
– fervor for a person, cause, or object; eager desire or endeavor; enthusiastic diligence; ardor.

*Subject reference

Note:
References to The Dr.'s Opinion are for the 4th Edition. In the 3rd Edition this chapter begins two pages beforehand, starting on xxiii rather than xxv. Pages 1-164 are the same in both editions.

This index is a "light" version of the reference material included in our Study Editions and our electronic reference guides.

See the back of this book or our website at http://anonpress.org for more information.

Translations of:

"How can I locate an Alcoholics Anonymous meeting?"

Afrikaans Waar is daar 'n Alkoholiste Anoniem (AA) vergadering?

Albanian Si mund te gjej një vendakim alkoolik anonime?

Armenian *Pronounced:* Vorteq em karogh ketnel AA`e-yee havakuyt-e?

Bahasa (Indonesia)
Tolong, dimana ada pertemuan Alcoholics Anonymous di kota ini?

Bisaya Asa nako makita ang alchohlics anonymous meeting?

Bulgarian Как мога да намеря среща на анонимните алкохолици?
Pronounced: Kak moga da nameria sreshta na anonimnite alkoholitzi?

Catalan A on puc trobar una reunio d' Alcholics Anonims?
Pronounced: Á Òn pÚk trÜbÁ una reunyÓ dalcÓlÌks ÁnÓnÌms?

Creole (Haiti) Ki koté réunion Alcohol Anonime?

Croatian Kako mogu pronaæi sastanak Anonimnih Alkoholièara?
Pronounced: Kaako mogoo pronachi sastanak Anoneemnih Alkocholeechara?

Czech Jak muzu najit setkani Annonymnich Alkoholiku?

Danish Hvordan finder jeg et AA-møde?

Dutch Hoe kan ik een Anonieme Alcoholisten bijeenkomst vinden?
Pronounced: Hu cann ik unn Aeknowniema Aelcollisten by eenkomst vin-done?

Esperanto Kiel mi povas trovi kunvenon de Alkoholuloj Anonimaj?

Estonian Kus asub lähim AA-rühm?

Farsi Jalseh-ye A.A. kojaa hast?

Flemish Waar kan ik een vergadering vinden van de Alkoholiekers Annoniem?

French Où trouver une réunion des Alcooliques Anonymes?

Finnish Kuinka voin löytää AA-kokouksen?

German Wie kann ich ein AA-Meeting finden?

Greek Πως μπορώ να βρώ μιά συγκέντρωση των Ανωνύμων Αλκοολικών?
Pronounced: Pos boro na vro mia singkentrosi ton Anonimon Alkoolikon?

Hebrew
Pronounced: aich eff-shar lim-zo p-gishot shell alkoholistim anonimim?

Hindi AA ki meeting kahan hoti hai kaise pata lag sakta hai?

Hungarian Hogyan találok egy Névtelen Alkoholisták gyűlését?
Pronounced: HOD-yan TAW-la-lok ed NAVE-tel-en AL-ko-ho-list-ak DYU-laish-ait?

Icelandic Hvar finn ég AA fundi?

Italian Come posso individuare una riunione di Alcolisti Anonimi?

Translations

Japanese *Pronounced:* AA-mitingu wa doko ni arimasuka?

Korean *Pronounced:* yoydieyaiseo yai yai yl chagyulsu ykseuo?

Latin Quo AA congressus est?

Latvian Kur deit varçtu atrast Anonîmu Alkoholiíu klubu sanâksmi?

Lithuanian Kaip aš galiu surasti Anoniminių Alkoholikų klubą?

Maltese Fejn nista' nsib laqgha tal Alkoholici Anonimi?

Marathi Mee AAchee sabha kashee shodhu?

Norwegian Hvor kan jeg finne et AA-møte?

Pidgin (West Africa)
Which place dey go find Alcoholics Anonymous meeting?

Polish Gdzie mogę znaleźć mityng Anonimowych Alkoholików?
Pronounced: Gdjieh mogae znaleshc mityng anonimowykh alkoholikuv?

Portuguese Como posso encontrar uma reunião de Alcoólicos Anónimos?

Romanian Unde pot sa gasesc un grup Alcoolicii Anonimi?

Russian Как можно найто собрание АА?
Pronounced: Kak moshno na-iti to sobraniye AA?

Serbian Kako mogu da pronađem sastanak Anonimnih Alkoholièara?

Slovak Kde najdem stretnutie Anonimových Alkoholikov?

Slovenian Kako lahko najdem sreèanje AA?

Spanish ¿Dónde puedo encontrar una reunión de Alcohólicos Anónimos?
Pronounced: DON-day PWAY-do en-con-TRAWR oo-na ray-oon-YON day al-KOH-lee-cose ah-NO-nee-mose?

Swahili Tafadhali, unaweza kuniambia vile naweza kuenda kwa mkutano wa Walevi ambao Hawajulikani?

Swedish Var kan jag hitta ett AA-möte någonstans?

Tagolog Saan ako makakatagpo ng Alcoholic Anonymous meeting?

Thai *Pronounced:* Kun ru wa gan brachum AA yu ti nai?

Turkish Adsýz Alkolikler Toplantýsý nerede yapýlýyor?

Ukranian Де можна знайти зібрання АА?
Pronounced: De mozhna znayty zibrannya AA?

Welsh Sut alla i ddod o hyd i gyfarfod Alcoholigion Anhysbys?

Yiddish Vi kon ikh gefinen du a meeting fun Alcoholics Anonymous?

Yup'ik Eskimo Nani-kiq AA-lrianek quyurtellrianek nalleksarcia maani?

Please see: http://anonpress.org/translate/ for updates.

Intergroup Phone Numbers

Additions and Corrections
For corrections and updated listings please visit: http://anonpress.org/phone/

ALABAMA

Auburn	334-663-1061
Baldwin County	800-477-1104
Birmingham	205-290-0060
Dothan	334-792-3422
Huntsville	256-885-0323
Mobile	251-479-9994
Montgomery	334-264-4122
Muscle Shoals	256-386-0663
Opelika	334-663-1061
Tuscaloosa	205-759-2497

ALASKA

Anchorage	907-272-2312
Fairbanks	907-456-7501
Homer	907-235-6822
Juneau	907-586-1161
Ketchikan	907-225-5154
Kodiak	907-942-0922
Sitka	907-747-8866
Wasilla	907-376-4777

ARIZONA

Bullhead City	928-763-4499
	800-864-1606
Casa Grande	520-426-9318
Cottonwood	928-646-9428
Flagstaff	928-779-3569
Glendale	623-937-7770
Kingman	800-864-1606
Lake Havasu	877-652-9005
Nogales	520-287-2585
Payson	928-474-3620
Phoenix	602-264-1341
Prescott	928-445-8691
Show Low	928-537-7800
Sierra Vista	866-780-9758
Tucson	520-624-4183
Yuma	928-782-2605

ARKANSAS

Batesville	870-793-3857
Fayetteville	479-443-6366
Fort Smith	479-783-0123
Hot Springs	501-623-6328
Little Rock	501-664-7303
Rogers	479-878-2730

CALIFORNIA

Anaheim	714-773-4357
Apple Valley	760-242-9292
Auburn	530-272-6287
Avalon	310-510-2545
Bakersfield	661-322-4025
Benicia	707-745-8822
Bishop	760-873-6700
Camarillo	805-389-1444
Campbell	408-374-8511
Cathedral City	760-324-4880
Chico	530-342-5756
Chino	909-628-4428
Claremont	626-914-1861
Clovis	559-221-6907
Colton	909-825-4700
Davis	800-970-9040
Dublin	925-829-0666
	888-859-3230
El Cajon	877-993-2422
El Centro	760-352-0807
Eureka	844-442-0711
Exeter	559-592-6999
Fort Bragg	877-546-9286
Fremont	510-431-2228
Fresno	559-221-6907
Fullerton	714-773-4357
Glendale	818-988-3001
Glendora	626-914-1861
Indio	760-324-4880
Jackson	209-223-4989
Joshua Tree	760-324-4880
Laguna Niguel	949-582-2697
Lake Isabella	760-379-4112
Lancaster	661-945-5757
Lodi	209-339-1201
Long Beach	562-989-7697
Los Angeles Central	323-936-4343
Westwood	310-474-7339
Lower Lake	707-995-3316
Mammoth Lakes	760-934-3434
Manteca	209-825-7541
Mariposa	209-966-3110
Modesto	209-572-2970
Monterey	831-646-4615
Napa	707-500-7001
Newark	510-791-9692
Oakhurst	559-683-1662
Oakland	510-839-8900
Palm Springs	760-324-4880
Pamona	626-914-1861
Paradise	530-342-5756
Placerville	530-622-3500
Pleasanton Valley	925-829-0666
Plumas County	530-283-4268
Redding	530-225-8955
Ridgecrest	760-375-5445
Sacramento	916-454-1100
Salinas	831-424-9874

Intergroup Phone Numbers

San Diego	619-265-8762
San Francisco	415-674-1821
San Jose	408-374-8511
San Luis Obispo	805-541-3211
San Mateo	650-577-1310
Santa Ana	714-556-4555
Santa Barbara	805-962-3332
Santa Clara	408-374-8511
Santa Clarita	661-250-9922
Santa Cruz	831-475-5782
Santa Maria	805-925-3782
Sonoma	707-544-1300
Soquel	831-475-5782
South Lake Tahoe	530-541-1243
Stockton	209-464-1594
Susanville	530-257-2880
Talmage	707-462-7123
Tehachapi	661-322-4025
Temecula	951-695-1535
Thousand Oaks	805-495-1111
Torrance	310-618-1180
Twain Harte	209-533-1134
Ukiah	707-462-7123
Vacaville	707-446-2244
Vallejo	707-745-8822
Van Nuys	818-988-3001
Visalia	559-592-6999
Vista	760-758-2514
Walnut Creek	925-939-5371
Yuba City	916-454-1100

COLORADO

Allenspark	303-747-2415
Arvada	303-420-6560
Aspen	970-245-9649
Aurora	303-695-7766
Boulder	303-447-8201
Breckenridge	970-453-2905
Colorado Springs	719-573-5020
Commerce City	303-287-9950
Denver	303-322-4440
Durango	970-247-1706
Eagle	970-328-3240
Fort Collins	970-224-3552
Fort Morgan	970-867-3461
Glenwood Springs	888-333-9649
Granby	970-887-2918
Grand Junction	970-245-9649
Greeley	970-224-3552
Pueblo	719-546-1173
Vail	970-476-0572

CONNECTICUT

Statewide	866-783-7712
Darien	203-855-0075
Greenwich	203-869-5221
Hartford	860-282-5924
Litchfield	860-482-1214
Manchester	860-646-2355
Middletown	860-267-5857
New Britain	860-674-6541
New Haven	203-624-6063
New London	860-885-6151
New Milford	860-354-9843
Norwalk	203-855-0075
Putnam	860-885-6151
Stratford	203-755-2124
Torrington	860-482-1214
Trumball	866-783-7712
Waterbury	203-755-2124
Westport	203-227-2496

DELAWARE

Dover	302-736-1567
Millsboro	302-856-6452
Wilmington	302-655-5999
	302-655-5113

FLORIDA

Casselberry	407-260-5408
Chiefland	352-949-2239
Cocoa	321-633-0052
Crystal River	352-621-0599
Daytona Beach	386-756-2930
Deland	888-756-2930
Delray Beach	561-276-4581
Fort Lauderdale	954-462-0265
Fort Myers	239-275-5111
Fort Pierce	772-873-9299
Fort Walton Beach	850-244-2421
Gainesville	352-372-8091
Inverness	352-621-0599
Jacksonville	904-399-8535
Key Largo	305-852-6186
Key West	305-296-8654
Kissimmee	407-870-8282
Lake City	386-758-4283
Lakeland	863-687-9275
Leesburg	352-360-0960
Melbourne	321-724-2247
Miami	305-461-2425
Naples	239-262-6535
New Port Richey	727-847-0777
North Port	941-426-7723
Ocala	352-867-0660
Okeechobee	863-763-1006
Orlando	407-260-5408
Palm Coast	386-445-4357
Panama City	850-784-7431
Pensacola	850-433-4191
Pinellas County	727-530-0415
Port St. Lucie	772-873-9299
Saint Augustine	904-829-1737
Saint Petersburg	727-530-0415
Sarasota	941-951-6810
Spring Hill	352-683-4597
Stuart	772-283-9337
Tallahassee	850-224-1818

Intergroup Phone Numbers

Tampa	813-933-9123
Venice	941-426-7723
Vero Beach	772-562-1114
West Palm Beach	561-655-5700

GEORGIA

Albany	229-435-2263
Athens	706-389-4164
Atlanta	404-525-3178
Augusta	706-860-8331
Brunswick	912-265-0892
Cairo	229-377-6174
Camilla	229-435-2263
Columbus	706-327-6078
Douglasville	770-489-1448
Jacksonville	904-399-8535
Macon	478-746-6652
Martinez	706-860-8331
Savannah	912-356-3688
Saint Simons Island	912-265-0892
Statesboro	912-764-4210
Tifton	912-764-4210

HAWAI'I

Hilo	808-961-6133
Honolulu	808-946-1438
Kailua Kona	808-329-1212
Kaua`i	808-245-6677
Maui	808-244-9673

IDAHO

Boise	208-344-6611
Coeur d'Alene	208-667-4633
Ketchum	208-721-0565
Lewiston	208-882-1597
Moscow	208-882-1597
Pocatello	208-235-1444
Twin Falls	208-733-8300

ILLINOIS

Alton	800-307-6600
Aurora	630-859-2444
Barrington	847-382-4455
Bartlett	630-830-6091
Bloomington	309-828-7092
Carbondale	800-307-6600
Champaign	217-373-4200
Chicago	312-346-1475
Crystal Lake	815-455-3311
Decatur	217-422-3766
Elgin	847-742-7870
Elk Grove	847-362-1811
Elmhurst	630-833-7897
Galesburg	309-343-1530
Glen Ellyn	630-653-6556
Harrisburg	800-307-6600
Hoffman Estates	847-240-2380
Joliet	815-741-6637
Kankakee	815-939-4996
Libertyville	847-362-1811
Macomb	309-837-5039
Moline	309-764-1016
Naperville	630-355-2622
Palatine	847-359-3311
Peoria	309-687-1329
Princeton	815-875-4279
Rockford	815-968-0333
Saint Charles	630-377-6610
South Roxana	618-251-4000
Springfield	217-525-5795
Waukegan	847-623-9660
West Frankfort	800-307-6600

INDIANA

Anderson	765-644-3212
Angola	866-608-3793
Bloomington	812-360-0040
Columbus	812-350-8949
Evansville	812-434-4952
Fort Wayne	260-471-6262
Hammond	219-844-6695
Indianapolis	317-632-7864
Kokomo	765-454-8799
Lafayette	765-742-1666
Marion	765-506-7801
Muncie	765-284-2515
Portage	219-763-6431
Richmond	765-935-9801
South Bend	574-234-7007
Terre Haute	812-235-7263
Vincennes	812-882-2800

IOWA

Ames	515-232-8642
Bettendorf	563-359-4152
Burlington	319-752-7409
Cedar Rapids	319-365-5955
Clinton	563-242-8136
Council Bluffs	712-328-9979
Davenport	309-764-1016
Decorah	563-387-0824
Des Moines	515-282-8550
Dubuque	563-557-9196
Iowa City	319-338-9111
Muscatine	563-263-4407
Sioux City	712-252-1333
Waterloo	319-291-3627
Waukon	563-568-4690

KANSAS

Arkansas City	620-442-5880
Gardner	913-884-8082
Hays	785-625-9860
Hutchinson	620-662-5166
Kansas City	816-471-7229
Lawrence	785-842-0110
Manhattan	785-537-8511
Salina	785-823-3338
Shawnee Mission	913-492-9697
Topeka	785-235-2226
Wichita	316-684-3661

Intergroup Phone Numbers

KENTUCKY

Bowling Green	270-782-5267
Covington	859-491-7181
Frankfort	502-227-4729
Georgetown	502-863-9086
Gilbertsville	800-606-6047
Lexington	859-225-1212
Louisville	502-582-1849
Newport	859-491-7181
Paducah	800-606-6047
Owensboro	270-683-0371

LOUISIANA

Baton Rouge	225-930-0026
Bossier City	318-865-2172
Lafayette	337-991-0830
Many	318-256-0367
Metairie	504-838-3399
Monroe	318-325-4414
Natchitoches	318-357-1331
New Orleans	504-838-3399
Ruston	318-513-9111
Shreveport	318-865-2172
Sulphur	337-475-0022

MAINE

Statewide	800-737-6237
Portland	207-774-4335

MARYLAND

Aberdeen	410-272-4150
Annapolis	410-268-5441
Baltimore	410-663-1922
Charlotte Hall	800-492-0209
Cumberland	301-722-6110
Easton	410-822-4226
Frederick	301-662-0544
Frostburg	301-722-6110
Hagerstown	301-733-1109
Hughesville	800-492-0209
Ocean City	410-600-5219
Salisbury	410-543-2266

MASSACHUSETTS

Boston	617-426-9444
Holyoke	413-532-2111
Hyannis	508-775-7060
Lowell	978-957-4690
Martha's Vineyard	508-627-7084
Methuen	978-957-4690
Nantucket	508-228-2334
Pittsfield	413-448-2382
Plymouth	508-746-5611
Worcester	508-752-9000

MICHIGAN

Adrian	517-265-3590
Alpena	989-354-2728
Ann Arbor	734-482-5700
Battle Creek	269-964-7577
Beaverton	866-227-0015
Detroit	877-337-0611
Durand	989-723-5711
Ferndale	248-541-6565
Flint	810-234-0815
Gaylord	866-336-9588
Grand Rapids	616-913-9216
Houghton Lake	866-227-0015
Iron Mountain	906-774-0900
Jackson County	517-789-8883
Kalamazoo	269-382-5244
Lansing	517-377-1444
Marquette	906-249-4430
Midland	989-698-2975
Newaygo	231-652-5574
Owosso	989-723-5711
Pigeon	989-670-4996
Pontiac	248-332-3521
Port Huron	810-987-8884
Riverdale	800-821-3014
Saginaw	989-776-1241
Stevensville	800-837-4247
Tecumseh	517-265-3590
Traverse City	231-946-8823
Ypsilanti	734-482-5700

MINNESOTA

Aitkin	218-927-6240
Arlington	507-357-4778
Austin	507-437-3797
Brainerd	218-829-3740
Duluth	218-727-8117
Ironton	218-232-4327
Mankato	507-388-8989
Maplewood	651-777-0405
Minneapolis	952-922-0880
Rochester	507-281-1747
Rosemount	651-423-3622
Saint Cloud	320-202-1895
St. Louis Park	612-922-0880
St. Paul	651-227-5502
Winona	507-452-2348

MISSISSIPPI

Cleveland	662-846-1132
Gulfport	228-575-9225
Hattiesburg	601-545-7109
Jackson	601-982-0081
Laurel	601-426-0108
Long Beach	228-575-9225
Oxford	662-533-9102
South Haven	662-280-3435
Tupelo	662-844-0374

MISSOURI

Blue Springs	816-228-7921
Branson	573-442-4424
Cape Girardeau	573-332-8339
Columbia	573-442-4424
Fulton	573-636-3618
Hazelwood	314-731-4854
Jefferson City	573-636-3618
Kansas City	816-471-7229

Intergroup Phone Numbers

St. Louis	314-647-3677
St. Peters	636-970-0013
Springfield	417-823-7125
Sunrise Beach	573-374-0618
West Plains	417-256-8988

MONTANA

Statewide	888-607-2000

NEBRASKA

Statewide	877-226-3632
Alliance	308-762-4824
Hastings	402-461-8732
Lincoln	402-438-5214
Minden	308-832-2267
Norfolk	402-371-9859
Omaha	402-556-1880

NEVADA

Elko	775-738-4747
Fallon	775-423-6009
Gardnerville	775-355-1151
Lake Tahoe North	530-546-1126
Lake Tahoe South	530-541-1243
Las Vegas	702-598-1888
Mammoth Lake	760-934-3434
Pahrump	775-513-7975
Reno-Sparks	775-355-1151
Winnemucca	775-623-9371

NEW HAMPSHIRE

Statewide	800-593-3330
Manchester	603-622-6967

NEW JERSEY

Statewide	908-687-8566
Southern New Jersey	856-486-4444
Trenton	609-298-7795
Union	908-687-8566

NEW MEXICO

Alamogordo	575-430-9502
Albuquerque	505-266-1900
Clovis	575-769-6052
Fairacres	575-527-1803
Farmington	505-327-0731
Gallup	505-722-4818
Hobbs	575-397-7009
Las Cruces	575-527-1803
Las Vegas	505-425-3577
Roswell	575-623-0166
Santa Fe	505-982-8932
Silver City	575-388-1802
Taos	575-758-3318
Truth or Consequences	575-527-1803

NEW YORK

Albany	518-463-0906
Batavia	888-854-8322
Binghamton	607-722-5983
Brooklyn	718-339-4777
Buffalo	716-853-0388
Canton	315-268-0120
Catskill	518-625-2002
Corning	607-962-8161
Cornwall	845-534-8525
Cortland	607-753-1344
Elmira	607-737-6733
Geneseo	585-245-4440
Geneva	315-789-5955
Glens Falls	518-793-1113
Gloversville	518-736-2644
Goshen	845-534-8525
Hudson	518-625-2002
Ithaca	607-273-1541
Kingston	845-331-6360
Lakewood	716-488-2233
Nassau County	516-292-3040
New York	212-647-1680
GSO	212-870-3400
Niagara Falls	716-286-1717
Old Forge	315-369-2281
Oneida	315-533-1227
Owego	800-307-4285
Patchogue	631-669-1124
Plattsburgh	518-561-8444
Potsdam	315-268-0120
Poughkeepsie	845-452-1111
Queens	718-520-5021
Queensbury	518-793-1113
Rochester	585-232-6720
Rockland County	845-352-1112
Saranac Lake	518-561-8444
Saratoga Springs	518-587-0407
Spring Valley	845-352-1112
Stafford	888-854-8322
Suffolk County	631-669-1124
Sullivan County	866-490-5686
Syracuse	315-463-5011
Utica	315-732-6880
Watertown	315-788-2280
Waverly	800-233-3840
West Nyack	845-352-1112
White Plains	914-949-1200
Woodstock	845-331-6360

NORTH CAROLINA

Albemarle	704-983-1600
Asheville	828-254-8539
Benson	919-894-7070
Boone	828-264-1212
Brevard	828-885-2788
Burlington	336-228-7611
Cary	919-286-9499
Chapel Hill	888-237-3235
Charlotte	704-377-0244
Durham County	919-286-9499
Fayetteville	910-678-8733
Franklin	828-349-4357
Gastonia	704-865-1561
Greensboro	336-854-4278
Greenville	252-758-0787

Intergroup Phone Numbers

High Point	336-885-8520
Jacksonville	910-455-3666
Jefferson	336-982-2641
Kitty Hawk	252-256-0850
Lexington	336-249-6636
Lowell	704-865-1561
Morehead City	252-726-8540
Morganton	828-433-4440
Murphy	828-837-4440
New Bern	252-633-3716
Raleigh	919-783-8214
Rocky Mount	252-977-7744
Sanford	919-776-5522
SouthernPines	800-496-1742
Statesville	704-878-6404
Whiteville	910-646-1228
Wilmington	910-794-1840
Winston-Salem	336-725-6031

NORTH DAKOTA

Fargo	701-235-7335
Langdon	701-256-2256
Minot	701-857-0529
Williston	701-572-9882

OHIO

Akron	330-253-8181
Ashtabula	440-992-8383
Bowling Green	419-352-1545
Canton	330-491-1989
Cincinnati	513-351-0422
Cleveland	216-241-7387
Columbus	614-253-8501
Dayton	937-222-2211
Findlay	419-423-6273
Fremont	419-625-5995
Lancaster	740-653-4869
Lima	419-234-3800
Lorain	440-246-1800
Mansfield	419-522-4800
Marion	740-387-5546
Middletown	513-423-0102
Newark	740-345-7060
Sandusky	419-625-5995
Toledo	419-380-9862
Youngstown	330-270-3000

OKLAHOMA

Bartlesville	918-336-7900
Enid	580-242-9000
Oklahoma City	405-949-0910
Shawnee	405-878-6012
Tulsa	918-627-2224

OREGON

Albany	541-967-4252
Astoria	503-861-5526
Baker City	541-519-2640
Bend	541-548-0440
Brookings	541-469-2440
Coos Bay	541-347-1720
Corvallis	541-967-4252
Depoe Bay	541-265-1953
Eugene	541-342-4113
Florence	541-902-0152
Grants Pass	541-474-0782
Hermiston	877-770-1670
Klamath Falls	541-883-4970
Lincoln City	541-265-1953
McMinnville	503-472-1172
Medford	541-773-4848
Newport	541-265-1953
Pendleton	877-770-1670
Portland	503-223-8569
Redmond	541-923-8199
Roseburg	541-673-7552
Salem	503-399-0599
Tillamook	503-842-8958
The Dalles	800-999-9210
Umatilla	877-770-1670
Warrenton	503-861-5526

PENNSYLVANIA

Allentown	610-882-0558
Altoona	814-946-9002
Bedford	888-202-9042
Bethlehem	610-882-0558
Bristol	215-923-7900
Bryn Mawr	610-527-9711
Carlisle	717-422-4888
Charleroi	724-489-0740
Dingmans Ferry	570-654-0488
Dubois	800-400-2346
Erie	814-452-2675
Greensburg	724-836-1404
Hanover	800-296-9289
Harrisburg	717-234-5390
Huntingdon	814-643-0623
Indiana	724-349-4061
Irwin	724-836-1404
Johnstown	814-533-5907
Lancaster	717-394-3238
Lebanon	717-279-4989
Lehighton	800-640-7545
Lewisburg	570-286-7436
Lewistown	717-242-1517
Lyndora	724-679-5647
Malvern	610-644-9675
Mars	724-935-7238
Meadville	814-337-4019
Milford	570-296-5344
Monesson	724-489-0740
Oil City	800-227-2421
Philadelphia	215-923-7900
Pittsburgh	412-471-7472
Pittston	570-654-0488
Pottstown	610-323-3450
Pottsville	610-373-6500
Reading	717-279-4989
Scranton	570-654-0488

Intergroup Phone Numbers

Sellersville	215-721-3656
Sharon	866-309-1090
State College	814-237-3757
Stroudsburg	570-424-8532
Sunbury	570-286-7436
Tamaqua	800-640-7545
Warren	866-839-3401
Wellsboro	800-316-2636
Williamsport	570-327-2860
York	717-854-4617

RHODE ISLAND

East Providence	401-438-8860
Newport	401-846-2622
Warwick	401-739-8777

SOUTH CAROLINA

Aiken	803-648-1509
Bluffton	888-534-0192
Camden	803-432-9511
Charleston	843-723-9633
Columbia	803-254-5301
Florence	843-669-6345
Greenville	864-233-6446
Hilton Head	888-534-0192
Lugoff	803-438-5575
Myrtle Beach	843-445-7119
North Augusta	803-279-1060
Spartanburg	864-585-1930
Sumter	803-775-1852

SOUTH DAKOTA

Aberdeen	605-225-1292
Rapid City	605-343-1091
Sioux Falls	605-334-5419
Sturgis	605-584-2350
Watertown	605-886-9070

TENNESSEE

Bristol	423-968-2020
Chattanooga	423-499-6003
Columbia	931-381-1048
Crossville	931-484-6467
Greenville	423-928-0871
Jackson	877-426-8330
Johnson City	423-928-0871
Knoxville	865-974-9888
Lewisburg	570-286-7436
Memphis	901-726-6750
Murfreesboro	615-893-0854
Nashville	615-831-1050
Oak Ridge	865-482-5200
Pulaski	931-363-1854

TEXAS

Abilene	325-673-2711
Alpine	432-837-5590
Amarillo	806-373-4600
Arlington	817-861-8100
Austin	512-444-0071
Ballinger	325-657-6645
Bandera	888-816-8800
Baytown	281-427-2500
Beaumont	409-832-1107
Brownsville	800-930-3215
Bryan	979-823-6391
Corpus Christi	866-672-7029
Dallas	214-887-6699
Del Rio	830-775-7008
Denison	903-465-4430
El Paso	915-562-4081
Fort Worth	817-332-3533
Fredericksburg	888-816-8800
Galveston	713-686-6300
Georgetown	512-863-9938
Grand Prairie	972-660-5278
Greenville	903-455-8648
Harlingen	956-421-4823
Henderson	903-657-8144
Houston	713-686-6300
Huntsville	936-291-3376
Irving	972-579-9676
Jacksonville	903-586-0713
Katy	713-686-6300
Kerrville	888-816-8800
Kingsville	361-592-5385
Longview	800-979-4191
Lubbock	806-741-8780
Marble Falls	888-299-3590
McAllen	800-930-3215
McKinney	972-548-9161
Mercedes	956-421-4823
Midland	432-682-8162
Palestine	903-729-1887
Paris	903-785-1951
Plano	972-424-1812
San Antonio	210-821-6325
San Benito	956-421-4823
San Marcos	512-396-2060
Sanford	806-373-4600
Seabrook	281-474-9066
Seguin	830-379-4773
Sherman	903-868-2734
Sulphur Springs	903-885-0295
Temple	254-770-4629
Texarkana	903-798-1024
Tyler	903-597-1796
Waco	254-754-3336
Weatherford	817-598-9021

UTAH

Ogden	801-393-4728
Orem	801-375-8620
Park City	435-649-0022
Provo	801-375-8620
Salt Lake	801-484-7871
St. George	435-674-4791

VERMONT

Barre	802-229-5100
Bennington	802-447-1285
Brattleboro	802-257-5801

Intergroup Phone Numbers

Burlington	802-864-1212
Dorset	802-447-1285
Manchester	802-447-1285
Middlebury	802-388-9284
Montpelier	802-229-5100
Newport	877-334-1213
Rutland	802-775-0402
Springfield	802-885-8281
St. Albans	802-741-7100
Waterbury	802-229-5100

VIRGINIA

Charlotesville	434-293-6565
Covington	540-969-4222
Danville	434-799-4111
Fairfax	703-293-9753
Hampton	757-595-1212
Harrisonburg	540-434-8870
Hopewell	804-452-1959
Lynchburg	434-847-4733
Newport News	757-595-1212
Onancock	757-710-8821
Richmond	804-355-1212
Roanoke	540-343-6857
Staunton	540-885-6912
Virginia Beach	757-490-3980
Waynesboro	540-949-7777
Williamsburg	757-253-1234
Winchester	540-667-0322

WASHINGTON

Aberdeen	360-532-2691
Bellevue	425-454-9192
Bellingham	360-734-1688
Bothell	425-672-0987
Centralia	360-807-0902
Colville	509-684-3000
Edmonds	425-672-0987
Ellensburg	509-925-1771
Everett	425-252-2525
Friday Harbor	888-360-1564
Ilwaco	360-642-2902
Kitsap County	360-830-6283
Long Beach	360-642-2902
Longview	360-423-2520
Moses Lake	888-755-4614
North Beach	360-642-2902
Oak Harbor	888-360-1564
Okanogan	509-826-6299
Olympia	360-352-7344
Orcas Island	360-376-4522
Port Angeles	360-452-4212
Pullman	208-882-1597
Republic	509-826-6299
Seattle	206-587-2838
Snohomish	425-672-0987
Spanaway	253-474-8897
Spokane	509-624-1442
Tacoma	253-474-8897
Tri-Cities	509-735-4086
Tumwater	360-352-7344
Vancouver	360-694-3870
Walla Walla	509-522-5059
Yakima	509-453-7680

WASHINGTON, D.C.

Washington	202-966-9115

WEST VIRGINIA

Statewide	800-333-5051
Bradley	304-252-9444
Charleston	800-333-5051
Morgantown	304-291-7918

WISCONSIN

Appleton	920-997-0221
Eau Claire	715-835-5543
Fond Du Lac	920-922-7512
Green Bay	920-432-2600
Janesville	608-774-2812
Kenosha	262-654-8246
La Crosse	608-784-7560
Madison	608-222-8989
Milwaukee	414-771-9119
Oshkosh	920-410-4620
Racine	262-554-6611
Rhinelander	715-367-7920
Stevens Point	888-292-6677
Sturgeon Bay	920-746-0900
Superior	715-394-1189
West Bend	262-338-1111

WYOMING

Casper	307-266-9578
Cheyenne	307-632-7706
Cody	307-587-3024
Evanston	307-288-5762
Genesee	888-854-8322
Gillette	307-686-6107
Jackson Hole	307-733-5322
Lander	307-332-0394
Laramie	307-745-3322
Rock Springs	307-362-8421
Sheridan	307-672-6257

Intergroup Phone Numbers

Outside The USA - English Speaking

ANTIGUA

St. John's 268-463-3155

AUSTRALIA

National Helpline 61-3-00222222
Alice Springs 61-8-89530802
Armidale 61-2-67714445
Ballina 61-2-66868599
Brisbane 61-7-32559962
Brompton 61-8-83464004
Cairns 61-7-40512872
Canberra 61-2-62873020
Croydon 61-2-97991199
Darwin 61-8-89485202
Dubbo 61-2-68826429
Geelong 61-3-52291710
Gosford 61-2-43233890
Hamilton 61-2-49623844
Hawksbury 61-2-45886172
Hobart 61-3-62348711
Jesmond 61-2-49641555
Katoomba 61-2-47822412
Launceston 61-3-63347060
Nambour 61-7-54762166
Southport 61-7-55912062
Saint Ives 61-2-94889820
Sydney 61-2-93896333
GSO 61-2-95998866
Townsville 61-7-47715411
Victoria 61-3-94291833
Wallsend 61-2-49246111
Wollongong 61-2-42856788

BAHAMAS

Nassau 242-322-1685

BAHRAIN

Manama 973 394 342 00

BARBADOS

Bridgetown 246-426-1600

BELIZE

Belize 501-25-3363

BERMUDA

Hamilton 441-297-0965

BOTSWANA

Gabarone 267-7444-7112
Maun 267-7696-7124

CANADA

Abbotsford 604-850-0811
Amherst 902-667-7098
Barrie 705-725-8682
Belleville 877-961-2134
Brockville 613-342-8452
Calgary 403-777-1212
Campbell River 250-287-4313
Cambridge 519-658-8222
Castlegar 250-368-5651
Chatham 866-242-8811
Chilliwack 604-819-2644
Comax 250-338-8042
Cornwall 613-938-1984
Cobourg 866-951-3711
Cumberland 902-667-7098
Drummondville 819-478-7030
Edmonton 780-424-5900
Elliot Lake 705-461-3150
Fernie 250-423-2131
Fort Assinivoine 403-584-2000
Fort Mcleod 403-444-6789
Fort Saint John 250-785-8866
Gander 709-651-2001
Gibsons 877-373-8255
Goderich 800-706-9833
Grande Prairie 780-532-1772
Grand Falls 709-489-5443
Guelph 519-836-1522
Gulf Islands 250-537-2135
Halifax 902-461-1119
Hamilton 905-522-8392
Kamloops 250-374-2456
Kelowna 250-763-5555
Kingston 613-549-9380
Kitchener 519-742-6183
Langley 604-533-2600
Leamington 519-999-1234
Lethbridge 403-327-8049
Lloydminister 780-875-3571
London 519-438-9006
Medicine Hat 403-527-2065
Moncton 506-382-5087
Montreal 514-376-9230
Nanaimo 250-753-7513
North Bay 705-474-7940
Oakville 905-845-5900
Oshawa 905-728-1020
Ottawa 613-237-6000
Owen Sound 519-376-4193
Pembroke 613-735-9928
Penticton 250-490-9216
Peterborough 705-745-6111
Prince George 250-564-7550
Quebec 418-523-9993
Rankin Inlet 867-645-2939
Red Deer 403-347-8650
Regina 306-545-9300
Revelstoke 250-837-9400
Saint Catharines 905-682-2140
Saint John's 709-579-6091
Saint Jerome 450-560-3902
Saint Thomas 519-633-0430
Saskatoon 306-665-6727
Sault Ste. Marie 705-254-1312
Stratford 519-271-7755
Sudbury 705-674-6217
Summerside 902-436-7721
Swift Current 306-773-7494
Thetford Mines 418-338-2724
Thunder Bay 807-623-1712
Timmins 705-360-8650
Toronto 416-487-5591
Trail 250-368-5651
Trenton 866-951-3711

Intergroup Phone Numbers

Vancouver	604-434-3933
Vernon	250-545-4933
Victoria	250-383-7744
Walkerton	519-396-2233
Windsor	519-256-9975
Winnipeg	204-942-0126
Whitehorse	867-668-5878
Yellowknife	867-444-4230

CHANNEL ISLANDS

Guernsey	44-1481-713480
Jersey	44-1534-26681

CAYMAN ISLANDS

Grand Cayman	345-949-9044

CHILE

Santiago	56-98-951-0172

CHINA

Beijing	86-139-11389075
Shanghai	86-137-01715848

COSTA RICA

San Jose	506-291-3831

CUBA

Havana	53-732-0004
Holguin	53-54-22182

ENGLAND

Bedford	44-11582-484948
Birmingham	44-1212-120111
Blackpool	44-1253-792632
Bournemouth	44-1202-296000
Brighton	44-1273-203343
Bristol	44-117-9265520
Cambridge	44-1603-621128
Cheshire	44-151-709-2900
Chester	44-1244-659759
Chiltern/Thames	44-1628-530055
Cornwall	44-1752-791111
Coventry	44-2920-612211
Derbyshire	44-1159-417100
Devon	44-1752-791111
Dorset	44-1202-296000
Durham	44-1915-214400
East Yorkshire	44-1482-830083
Essex	44-11245-256147
Exeter	44-1392-221444
Gloucester	44-1452-418515
Great Yarmouth	44-1493-440396
Hertfordshire	44-1438-747475
High Wycombe	44-1628-530055
Ipswich	44-1473-212224
Isle of Man	44-11624663676
Kent east	44-1227-455557
Kent west	44-1622-751842
Kings Lynn	44-1603-621128
Leicestershire	44-1159-417100
Lincolnshire	44-1472-362058
Liverpool	44-1151-7092900
London	44-20-78330022
GSO	44-1904-644026
Mid Surrey	44-1252-521133
Manchester	44-161-839-2881
Middlesex	44-2078-330022
Newcastle	44-191-5214400
Norfolk	44-1603-621128
Northampton	44-1604-37788
Norwich	44-1603-621128
Nottingham	44-1115-9417100
Northdown	44-23-80223198
Oxford	44-1865-242373
Reading	44-1189-597494
Redditch	44-1527-64715
Scarborough	44-1132-454567
Sheffield	44-1114-2701984
Shrewsbury	44-1792-301907
Southdown	44-2392-580776
Southampton	44-2380-223198
South Bedfordshire	44-1582-484948
South Humberside	44-1472362058
Stevenage	44-1438747475
Stoke on Trent	44-1782266366
Suffolk	44-1473-212224
Sunderland	44-1915-214400
Surry	44-1883-330720
Sussex	44-1622-751842
Watford	44-1923-211122
West Midlands	44-1384-482929
Wiltshire	44-1380-729064
Worcester	44-1792-301907
York	44-1904-644026
Yorkshire	44-113-2454567

FRANCE

Paris	33-1-46345965
Nice	33-8-20200257

GERMANY

Berlin	49-30-7875188
Frankfurt	49-69-5974265
Gelsenkirchen	49-157-54721069
Mannheim	49-621-291441
Zürich	49-1-2413043

GREECE

Athens	30-10-522041

GREENLAND

Nuuk	299-24858

GUAM

Barrigada	671-646-7233

HONDURAS

Roatan	3342-6607

HONG KONG

Hong Kong	852 25225665

IRELAND

Belfast	44-28-90434848
Connaught	353-91-767777
Cork	352-87-6657105
Dublin	353-1-4538998
GSO	353-1-8420700
Galway	353-91-567807
Kerry	353-66-7128720
Leinster	353-1-890412412
Limerick	353-61-311222
Waterford	353-51-373173
West Cork	353-87-6114969

Intergroup Phone Numbers

ISRAEL

Jerusalem	972-2-5630524
Tel Aviv	972-3-5786663

ITALY

Rome	39 06-4742913

JAMAICA

Kingston	876-605-5248

JAPAN

Kyoto	81-75-7121703
Misawa	81-176-570703
Okinawa	81 98-933-2414
Tokyo	81-3-39711471
GSO	81 3-35905377

KENYA

Nairobi	254-2-784654

KIRIBATI

Tarawa	28114

KOREA

Seoul	82-2-319-5861
GSO	82-2-774-3797

KUWAIT

Kuwait	965-99641389

LITHUANIA

Vilnius	370-5-2160017

MALTA

Bugibba	356-21-579613
Valletta GSO	356 - 21-239264

MARIANA ISLANDS

Saipan	670-235-4437

MARSHALL ISLANDS

Kwajalein	692-238-7994

MEXICO

Cozumel	52-987-21007
Guadalajara	52-33-3121-2306
Islamajeras	52-2-1177
Mexico City	52-5511-1213
Playa de Carmen	52-984-876-0882

MOZAMBIQUE

Maputo	258- 82-895-9610

NETHERLANDS

Amsterdam	31-20-6256057

NEW ZEALAND

Auckland	64-9-366 6688
Carterton	64-6-379 7822
Christchurch	64-3-379 0860
Dunedin	64-800-229 6757
Gisborne	64-6-867 5831
Golden Bay	64-3-525 9047
Hamilton	64-7-855 8544
Invercargill	64-3-218 2227
Kawerau	64-7-323 7367
Levin	64-6-367 2079
Motueka	64-3-526 8001
Napier	64-6-844 1151
Nelson	64-800-229 6757
New Plymouth	64-6-753 4909
Paeroa	64-7-862 8340
Palmerston North	64-6-356 3215
Picton	64-3-578 8856
Queenstown	64-3-442 3181
Richmond	64-3-544 8744
Rotorua	64-800-229 6757
Taupo	64-7-378 5922
Tauranga	64-7-544 4465
Te Puke	64-7-573 7071
Temuka	64-3-615 7877
Thames	64-7-868 3287
Timaru	64-3-684 9855
Waipawa	64-6-857 8957
Wanganui	64-6-348 8286
Wellington	64-800-229 6757
Whangarei	64-9-430 1051

NORFOLK ISLAND

Kingston	672 (3) 2 3150

PAPUA NEW GUINEA

Port Moresby	675-213401

THE PHILIPPINES

Angeles City	63 45-892-4258
Manila	63 2-896-5707

PUERTO RICO

San Juan	787-704-1634

SCOTLAND

Nationwide	44-345-697555
Aberdeen	44-1224-582184
Dumbarton	44-1389-30700
Dundee	44-1382-818850
Edinburgh	44-131-2252727
Glasgow	44-141-2262214
	44-845-7697555
Perth	44-1738-639999
Stornoway	44-1851-702221

SINGAPORE

Singapore	65-64750890

SLOVENIA

Ljubljana	386-1-2832402

SOUTH AFRICA

National	27 86-143-5722
Benoni	27 11-421-1748
Cape Town	27 21-418-0908
Durban	27 31-301-4959
East London	27 43-12-4033
East Rand	27 11-421-1748
Goodwood	27 21-592-5047
Johannesburg	21 11-683-9101
GSO	27 11-452-9907
Pietermaritzburg	27 33-345-6795
Port Elizabeth	27 41-452-7328
Pretoria	27 12-331-2446
Vereeniging	27 16-455-2986

SPAIN

Barcelona	34-65-534-9617
Benidorm	34-96-6495345
Madrid	34-1-3091947

SRI LANKA

Colombo	94-11-2365794

Intergroup Phone Numbers

SWITZERLAND

Geneva	41 022 328 9286
Zurich	41 01 241 043

TANZANIA

Dar Es Salaam	255658553553

THAILAND

Bangkok	66-2-231-8300

TRINIDAD & TOBAGO

Couva	868-679-0066
Montrose	868-664-5854
Port of Spain	868-628-2288
Southern	868-754-3816

TURKEY

Ankara	90-312-4334607
Istanbul	90-212-2503470

UNITED ARAB EMIRATES

Dubai	971-4-3949198
Abu Dhabi	971-4-4143042

VIRGIN ISLANDS- US

St. Thomas	340-776-5283

WALES

Aberystwyth	44-1970-625574
Cardiff	44-0292-0373939
Carmarthen	44-1267-238888
Milford Haven	44-8457-697555
Pontypridd	44-1685-875070
Swansea	44-1792-301907
Telford	44-1952-256370

ZIMBABWE

Bulawayo	263-0771 288760
Harare	263-7-12212424

Outside The USA - Non English Speaking

ARGENTINA

Avellaneda	54-1-2017943
Buenos Aires	54-1-49316666
GSO	54-1-143251813
Lanus Este	54-1-2416774
Mar Del Plata	54-223-4910787
Rio Cuarto	54-5-8622957
San Isidro	54-1-7439584
Villa Maria	54-353-154087873

ARUBA

Noord	297-586-7295

AUSTRIA

Graz	43-316-574740
Innsbruck	43-663-054761
Salzburg	43-662-435218
Vienna	43-1-7995599

BANGLADESH

Dhaka	0175 104 510

BELARUS

Minsk	375-17-2067914

BELGIUM

Aywaille	32-4-3847498
Antwerp	
Flemish GSO	32-3-2391415
Brussels	32-2-5132336
French GSO	32-2-5114030
Charleroi	32-71-324668
Liege	32-4-2402424
Jemappes	32-65-825999
Ottignies	32-10-242888
Seraing	32-4-2341718

BOLIVIA

Santa Cruz	591-3-3329720
GSO	591-7-0046275

BRAZIL

Aracaju	55-79-2112027
Belem	55-91-2242965
Belo Horizonte	55-31-224774
Brasili	55-61-2260091
Campo Grande	55-67-3831854
Cuiaba	55-65-3211020
Curitiba	55-41-2222422
Florianopolis	55-48-2226713
Fortaleza	55-85-2312437
Goiania	55-62-2230445
Ipatinga	55-31-8213758
Joao Pessoa	55-83-2222256
Juazeiro	55-85-5112466
Juiz de fora	55-32-2158503
Macapa	55-96-2225154
Macae	55-22-99197528
Manaus	55-92-6333232
Maringa	55-44-2632875
Montes Claros	55-38-32214199
Natal	55-84-2212777
Niteroi	55-21-7184956
Palmares	55-81-36621555
Patos	55-83-4213414
Pelotas	55-532-250373
Piracicaba	55-19-4349879
Porto Alegre	55-51-2240140
Recife	55-81-2213592
Rio de Janeiro	55-21-22334813
Sao Luis	55-98-2224050
Sao Paulo	55-11-33159333
Taubate	55-12-2213611
Terezina	55-86-2235919
Ubaitaba	55-73-2301442
Vitoria	55-27-2237268

CHILE

Copiapo	56-52-237320
Santiago	56-27-354470
Santiago Norte	56-2-7354470
Temuco	56-45-210785
Valdivia	56-63-298997
Vallparaiso	56-32-220202

COLOMBIA

Barranquilla	57-953-440317
Bogota	57-1-7843428
Bucaramanga	57-976-340643
Cartagena	57-956-641619
Cucuta	57-0975-5718726
Manizales	57-6-8808011
Medellin GSO	57-4-2517887
Popayan	57-928-242493

Intergroup Phone Numbers

Rionegro	57-94-5617542
Sogamoso	57-312-3482948
Villavicencio	57-986-623030

COSTA RICA

Alajuela	506-441-5891
Desamparados	506-259-4685
Golfito	506-253-9684
Liberia	506-666-2195
San Jose	506-222-1906
GSO	506-222-5224

CROATIA

Zagreb	38 5915360635

CYPRUS

Nicosia	357 4 333063

CUBA

Havana	53 7 32-0004
Holguin	53-53977083

CZECH REPUBLIC

Prague	420-224-818247

DENMARK

Copenhagen	45-70-101224
Jutland	45-86-841200

DOMINICAN REPUBLIC

Santo Domingo	809-241-2622

ECUADOR

Azogues	593-7-242206
Babahoyo	593-4-753340
Cuenca	593-7-864695
De Los Colorados	593-9-4352042
Guayaquil	593-4-2693293
Manta	593-4-612405
Quito	593-2-580545
Riobamba	593-3-968304
Santo Domingo	593-2-2753145

EL SALVADOR

Delgado	503-2512-8981
Mejicanos	503-2268-1162
San Miguel	503-2661-0837
San Salvador	503-3-2162279
GSO	503-2-259526
Santa Ana	503-2447-1764
Soyapango	503-2-773579

ESTONIA

Tallinn	372-529-9955

FAROE ISLANDS

Tórshavn	298-310555

FINLAND

Helsinki	358-9-712058
Jyvaskyla	358-14-3100522
Kolmio	358-09-712058
Tampere	358-3-9315514
Turku	358-2-2501125
Vantaa	358-9-8387040

FRANCE

Angers	33-241-484948
Auray	33-2-97460874
Auxerre	33-386-529473
Brest	33-2-98464454
Cannes	33-4-93063209
Calvados	33-2-31948909
Coubron	33-1-43301852
Eure	33-2-35077300
Eure Et Loir	33-2-37347302
Forbach	33-3-87842388
Franconville	33-3-4442368
La Roche-sur-Yon	33-2-51052673
Limoges	33-555-384322
Melun	33-1-64094002
Mulhouse	33-389-460317
Paris	33-1-43257500
Quimper	33-2-98537504
Rennes	33-2-99870120
St. Brieuc	33-296-623106
St. Etienne	33-477-797411
St. Genis Pouilly	33-450-422628
St. Malo	33-2-99825100
St. Tropez	33-4-94491840
Strasbourg	33-388-441666
Thuir	33-4-68536085
Versailles	33-139-507262

GERMANY

Aachen	49-241-19295
Ansbach	49-981-19295
Aschaffenburg	49-6021-74255
Augsburg	49-821-19295
Berlin	49-30-4537199
Bonn	49-228-19295
Bremen	49-421-19295
Bremerhaven	49-471-19295
Delmenhorst	49-4221-53355
Erlangen	49-9131-19295
Flensburg	49-461-582626
Frankfurt	49-69-19295
Freiburg	49-761-19295
Giessen	49-641-19295
Hamburg	49-40-19295
Kaiserslautern	49-631-19295
Karlsruhe	49-721-19295
Koblenz	49-261-36830
Koln	49-221-19295
Lahr	49-7821-37977
Mannheim	49-621-19295
Minden	49-571-21962
Munich	49-89-19295
GSO	49-8731-325730
Nuernberg	49-911-19295
Osnabruck	49-541-23912
Saarbrueken	49-681-19295
Stuttgart	49-711-19295
Wurzburg	49-931-883131

GREECE

Athens	30-210-5220416

GUATEMALA

Guatemala	502-2-2546565

HONDURAS

Comayaguela	504-238-7930
Tegucigalpa	504-22-6674

HUNGARY

Budapest	36-1-2510051

ICELAND

Akranes	354-4312540
Akureyri	354-4622373
Egilsstadir	354-4711972
Hafnarfjordur	354-5658353
Keflavik	354-4211800
Reykjavik	354-8951050

Intergroup Phone Numbers

GSO	354-5512010
Selfoss	354-4821787
Vestmannaeyjar	354-4811140

INDIA

Bangalore	91-80-2215253
Chandigarh	91-94-17037358
Chandrapur	91-7172-251443
Chennai	91-44-6441941
Goa	91-832-6570221
Kerala	91-495-9249994350
Kharagpur	91-94-34414121
Kolkatta	91-33-2841202
Mangalore	91-824-211573
Mumbai	91-24-122203
Mumbai West	91-22-26844400
Nagpur	91-5533765
New Delhi	91-11-55684980
Pune	91-20-4468087
Vasai	91-932-6477682
Vijaywada	91-944-1119954
Wayanad	91-4936-255255

INDONESIA

Jakarta	081-813-4556
Bali	0361-756-652

ITALY

Bologna	39-51-6414436
Firenze	39-55-6503254
Genova	39-10-6513346
Milano	39-2-876664
Palermo	39-91-6889788
Rome	39-06-6636629
	39-06-6628334
Torino	39-11-4364978
Venezia	39-41-720312
Verona	39-45-8343444

JAPAN

Hiroshima	81-82-2468608
Kagoshima	81-992-480057
Nagoya	81-52-9151602
Okinawa	81-98-9893154
Osaka	81-66-5360828
Sendai	81-22-2765210
Tokyo	81-3-39711471
GSO	81-3-35905377
Toyohira-Ku	81-11-8113770

LATVIA

Riga	371-2-7333523

LITHUANIA

Vilnius	370-685-05191

LUXEMBOURG

Luxembourg	352-480322

MALAYSIA

Kuala Lumpur	60-3-2380564

MALTA

Valletta	356-21-239264

MEXICO

Acapulco	52-74-37382
Aguascalientes	52-491-57497
Campeche	52-981-60950
Cancun	52-98-841271
Chiapas	52-962-59276
Colima	52-331-33730
Corodoba	52-271-28444
Cuautla	52-735-29116
Cuernavaca	52 73-122824
Durango	52-181-20799
Fresnillo	52-493-23461
Gomez Palacio	52-17-147523
Guadalajara	52-333798-1270
Guaymas	52-622-28555
Hidalgo	52-962-1439039
Huatusco	52-273-41555
Iguala	52-733-23940
Irapuato	52-462-64422
Jalapaa	52-28-179464
Jalisco	52-33-36331839
Jojutla	52-734-23125
Juarez	52-932-143669
La Peidad	52-352-25179
Lagos de Moreno	52-474-21199
Lazaro Cardenas	52-961-21910
Leon	52-47-634560
Los Reyes	52-5-21151
Merida	52-99-230165
Mexico City	52-5-3683943
	52-5-946384
Mexico D.F.	52-55-5264-2588
Monterrey	52-83-426660
Morelia	52-451-24488
Navojoa	52-642-25953
Oaxaca	52-514-6627
Obregon	52-64-241886
Ocotlan	52-372-21235
Orizaba	52-27-256977
Pachuca	52-771-51971
Poza Rica	52-782-27602
Puerto Vallarta	52-322-21878
Queretaro	52-42-2158493
Quintana	52-98-841271
Salamanca	52-464-83599
Saltillo	52-841-29556
San Cristobal	52-967-84450
Tampico	52-121-25634
Tapachula	52-1962-59276
Taxco	52-762-22936
Tepic	52-321-26130
Tijuana	52-664-6384450
Toluca	52-72-25824
Torreon	52-17-120790
Tuxtla Gutierrez	52-961-23586
Uruapan	52-452-32502
Veracruz	52-272-7256977
Villahermosa	52-931-40318
Zacapu	52-456-30831
Zapopan	52-63-31839

MONGOLIA

Ulaanbaatar	976-11-351-056

NETHERLANDS

Amsterdam	31-20-6256057
	31-20-6817431
Driebergen	31-34-3813102
The Hague	31 70-3886268
Hertogenbosch	31-7-3417553
Hilversum	31-35-5381467
Rotterdam	31-10-2430175

NEVIS

Charlestown	869-469-5776

Intergroup Phone Numbers

NICARAGUA

Managua	505-7250-8368
Matagalpa	505-61-22865

NORWAY

Oslo GSO	47-22-468965
Bergen	47-5-94680597
Drammen	47-32-90921593
Kristiansand	47-42-70737
Mjondalen	47-94-77168
Ridabu	47-30-60528
Sadnes	47 51629780
Stavanger	47-4-536895

PANAMA

Panama City	507-264-8962
GSO	507-225-3585

PARAGUAY

Asuncion	595-21-907805

PERU

Cusco	51-84-226260
Palermo	51-44-234140
Trujillo	51-44-291985

POLAND

Boleslawiec	48-757-343693
Bydgoszcz	48-52-3721682
Gdansk	48-58-329163
Katowicz	48-32-2537983
Krakow	48-12-564680
Legnica	48-609-732729
Olsztyn	48-89-5260136
Opole	48-77-4745574
Ostrow Wielkopolski	48-62-5918989
Poznan	48-61-8531616
Siedlce	48-25-435843
Szczawno Zdrój	48-74-8438792
Szczecin	48-91-4500176
Warszawa	48-22-6160568
GSO	48-22-8280494
Zielona Gora	48-68-271863

PORTUGAL

Barreiro	351-212-160399
Lisboa GSO	351-21-7162969
Lisbon	351-21-9264203
Porto	351-22-2088126
Povoa D' Varzim	351-252-682926

ROMANIA

Bucharest	40-216-534100
Timisoara GSO	40-256-430835

RUSSIA

Magadan	7-413-2294404
Moscow	7-495-1854000
Omsk	7-381-2560692
St. Petersburg	7-812-9241224
Samara	7-846-2666484
Tomsk	7-382-2621416
Yekaterinburg	7-343-2610901

SAINT MAARTEN

Simpson Bay	599-552-2120

SLOVAKIA

Nitra	412-37-651-6235

SLOVENIA

Ljubljana	386-1-4338225

SOUTH KOREA

Kwangju	82-119-785-4667

SPAIN

Alicante	34-96-5219471
Aviles	34-649-235531
GSO	34-985-566345
Barcelona	34-93-3177777
Cadiz	34-606-210001
Las Palmas	34-928-202638
Logrono	34-941-251339
Madrid	34-1-3418282
Palma de Mallorca	34-616-088883
Santander	34-942-212155
Sevilla	34-686-863997
Zaragoza	34-976-293835

SWEDEN

Gottenburg	46-31-418182
Kalix	46-923-21450
Malmoe	46-40-305544
Malung	46-26-91050
Mora	46-250-15152
Norrköping	46-11-164893
Ostersund	46-63-103828
Sandoverken	46-612-33503
Sandviken	46-26-255130
Skelleftea	46-910-778026
Stockholm	46-8-7203842
GSO	46-8-6422609
Uppsala	46-18-158888

SWITZERLAND

Bern	41-26-6731430
Geneva	41-22-3443322
Zurich	41-1-2413043
GSO	41-44-3701383

TAIWAN

Kaohsiung	886-7-2265218
Taipei	886-2-29714620
GSO	886-2-23777791

TURKEY

Ankara	90-312-4341223
Izmir	90-232-4651132

UKRAINE

Kiev	380-44-2786174
Lviv	380-677-489158

URUGUAY

Montevideo	598-2-9022822
GSO	598-4-104592

VENEZUELA

Caracas	58-212-6331061
GSO	58-212-5432286
Maracaibo	58-261-9311734
San Cristobal	58-276-3444172

Up-to-date listings are online at http://anonpress.org/phone

Prayers

The Third Step Prayer

Many of us said to our Maker, *as we understood Him*: "God, I offer myself to Thee-to build with me and to do with me as Thou wilt. Relieve me of the bondage of self, that I may better do Thy will. Take away my difficulties, that victory over them may bear witness to those I would help of Thy Power, Thy Love, and Thy Way of life. May I do Thy will always!" Page 63

The Seventh Step Prayer

When ready, we say something like this:
"My Creator, I am now willing that you should have all of me, good and bad. I pray that you now remove from me every single defect of character which stands in the way of my usefulness to you and my fellows. Grant me strength, as I go out from here, to do your bidding. Amen." Page 76

Serenity Prayer

God grant me the serenity to
Accept the things I cannot change;
Courage to change the things I can;
And the Wisdom to know the difference.

Living one day at a time;
Accepting hardships as the pathway to peace;
Taking as He did, this World as it is,
Not as I would have it.

Trusting that He will make all things right if I surrender to His will;
That I may be reasonably happy in this life
And Supremely happy with Him,
Forever in the next.

Reinhold Niebuhr — 1932

Price List

Mini Edition

1-9 **$2.60** 10-19 **$2.50** 20-49 **$2.30** 50-99 **$2.00**
100-499 **$1.60** 500-999 **99¢** 1000+ **89¢**

Study Edition - Hardcover

- Hardbound leather cover with heavy paper and two place keeping ribbons
- Lined pages opposite the text for taking notes
- Extensive subject index, word index and dictionary
- Special "lay-flat" binding in burgundy or black leather

1-9 **$19.50** 10-19 **$18.50** 20-49 **$17.50**
50-99 **$16.00** 100+ **$15.00**

Study Edition - Softcover

The Study Edition with lighter paper and no place keeping ribbons.

1-9 **$6.25** 10-19 **$6.00** 20-49 **$5.70** 50-99 **$5.40** 100+ **$5.15**

First Edition Reprint - Softcover

An inexpensive reprint of the first edition of Alcoholics Anonymous. Includes an appendix detailing many of the differences between this original text and the modern text. Cover is designed to look like the original dustjacket.

1-9 **$4.00** 10-19 **$3.80** 20-49 **$3.65** 50-99 **$3.50**
100-499 **$3.30** 500+ **$3.10**

Index

The same index found in this book. Sized to fit inside a standard Big Book.

1-9 **$1.10** 10-19 **$1.00** 20-49 **85¢** 50-99 **76¢** 100+ **65¢**

Concordance

Practically every word shown highlighted within the sentence it occurs.

1-9 **$24** 10+ **$19**

Extra Large Print

Uses huge type that is much bigger than even a typical "large print" book.

1-9 **$19** 10+ **$17**

Electronic Editions

Windows, Mac, Android, iPhone, iPad, Kindle and more. **$6-$15**

Prices current as of October 2021 and subject to change.
Please check our website for current pricing & shipping options.

To order please visit:
http://anonpress.org

Also Available From The Anonymous Press

Study Edition of *Alcoholics Anonymous*

-576 full-size pages on fine heavy weight paper
-Leather bound in burgundy or black
-Special "lay-flat" binding for easy study
-Two ribbons to keep your place
-Opposite each text page is a ruled page for notetaking
-Text paragraphs numbered for easy reference
-The changes to the 1st Edition Big Book are noted
-Footnotes explaining the more obscure references
-Very comprehensive word and subject indexes - indexed by paragraph
-Word dictionary with definitions from 1937

Includes the entire 1938 "Original Manuscript" with stories.

Softcover Study Edition

The same content as the hardbound Study Edition in a more affordable paperback cover. Also includes a "lay flat" binding for easy study. Does *not* include the heavy paper, place keeping ribbons or the gilding option.

The Anonymous Press Index

We have put this book's index into pamphlet form so that all groups can use this invaluable guide. Fits inside a regular Big Book.

More than 8000 references & 200 word definitions.

First Edition Reprint - Softcover

Reprint of the first printing of the first edition of *Alcoholics Anonymous*. Includes a **comparison section** showing many of the places where the first printing text differs from the modern text.

Concordance to *Alcoholics Anonymous*

Practically every word shown highlighted within the sentence it occurs.

Extra Large Print Edition of *Alcoholics Anonymous*

Uses huge type that is much bigger than even a "large print" book.

Electronic Editions at http://anonpress.org

The text and extensive reference material for almost any type of computer. Windows, Macintosh, Android, iPhone, iPad, Kindle, etc.

The main text is available for nearly any device for free.

See opposite side for prices and ordering information